California Uncovered

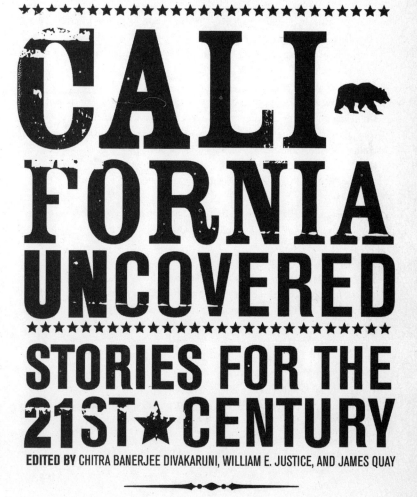

CALI-FORNIA UNCOVERED

STORIES FOR THE 21ST ★ CENTURY

EDITED BY CHITRA BANERJEE DIVAKARUNI, WILLIAM E. JUSTICE, AND JAMES QUAY

California Council for the Humanities, San Francisco, California

Heyday Books, Berkeley, California

This project is supported in part by a generous grant from The James Irvine Foundation, as well as through funds provided by the National Endowment for the Humanities and the California Council for the Humanities as part of the Council's multiyear California Stories Initiative.

Library of Congress Cataloging-in-Publication Data

California uncovered : stories for the 21st century / edited by Chitra Banerjee Divakaruni, William E. Justice, and James Quay.
   p. cm.
 ISBN 1-890771-97-X (pbk. : alk. paper)
  1. California--Literary collections. 2. American literature--California. 3. American literature--21st century. I. Divakaruni, Chitra Banerjee, 1956- II. Quay, James. III. Justice, William E.
  PS571.C2C25 2004
  810.8'09794'090511--dc22

                 2004018365

Cover Design: Lee Queza of Stoller Design Group
Interior Design/Typesetting: Rebecca LeGates and Lorraine Rath
Printing and Binding: Delta Printing Solutions, Valencia, California

Orders, inquiries, and correspondence should be addressed to:
    Heyday Books
    P.O. Box 9145, Berkeley, CA 94709
    (510) 549-3564, Fax (510) 549-1889
    www.heydaybooks.com

Printed in the United States of America

10 9 8 7 6 5 4 3 2 1

Contents

Preface

No other region in the modern world has undergone the population change California has experienced in recent decades. Only half of the people now living in California were born here. Of the rest, half came here from another state, half from another country. As a result of this immigration, California is the most populous and most ethnically diverse state in the nation.

Those are the demographic facts, but what is the human reality that lies beneath them? How are natives and newcomers living together? What kind of literature is being created here and what does it reflect? What are we learning about the ways people of different cultures clash and connect here?

The book in your hands was created to generate some discussion of these questions and offer some answers. It contains great stories from authors of a dozen different ethnic backgrounds about life in today's California. The stories collected here present characters who both love the idea of California and struggle with its realities. They display courage and confusion, encounter hostility and kindness. Their stories show us many different Californias and the many ways Californians have of embracing and resisting the place we call home.

Through the magic of imaginative literature, the stories give us access to the feelings and thoughts of people we might otherwise never meet. They invite us to consider how their experience is like or unlike our own, or that of our family members, or that of our neighbors. They invite us to imagine the lives of others.

This book also comes with a second invitation. In April 2005, it will be the centerpiece of a statewide campaign called "California Stories Uncovered." Thousands of Californians will gather in libraries, schools, community centers, and living rooms to talk about the stories presented here and to share their own California stories. On behalf of the California Council for the Humanities, I invite you to be one of them. The discussion guide in the back of the book is meant to provide some questions to ponder, whether you're in a room filled with people or alone with the book. You can learn more about the campaign and its activities at our website: www.californiastories.org.

This anthology and the California Stories Uncovered campaign offer Californians the opportunity to come together about who we are and who we are becoming. Like the characters in these stories, like the other thirty-five million people who now live in California, we are learning how it changes us to live here, whether we are natives or newcomers. And though it seems that no one person can really say what it means to *be* a Californian, we know that *becoming* a Californian means making a common life here with people from all over the world.

That's something worth imagining. We hope you enjoy the stories.

James Quay

Acknowledgments

The editors have many to thank. The creation of this anthology was a collaborative process between two cultural institutions: the California Council for the Humanities and Heyday Books. It was an enriching and lively exchange. We're deeply indebted to Ralph Lewin, Alden Mudge, Julie Levak, Maura Hurley, and all the staff members at CCH who were among the first readers of this anthology. Malcolm Margolin, publisher of Heyday Books, and Jeannine Gendar provided indispensable literary advice and great personal warmth during the selection process. Thanks also to Sara Bernard, Rebecca LeGates, Lorraine Rath, and the rest of the staff at Heyday Books for doing the dirty work that made this book possible.

Chitra Banerjee Divakaruni

Introduction

California Uncovered arises out of two premises that set it apart from other California anthologies. The first is that all Californians have their own uniquely flavored stories about how they fit into this beautiful and complex state of ours, which is as much a mythic space as a geographical location. The second premise is that sharing these stories is of great importance, especially at this fraught and fractured time in post–9/11 America. For it is the nature of good stories to reach into the heart and foster understanding and compassion on a level that is deeper than that of other kinds of discourse. It is with the intention of introducing the multiplicity of Californian experiences to readers across the state, and hopefully beyond its borders, that the editors—William E. Justice, James Quay, and I—have carefully gathered the works that form this book.

Putting together this anthology was a challenging task, especially because we were confronted by an embarrassment of riches. Lack of space forced us to leave out many fine pieces we wanted to include. I am sure some of our readers will regret these omissions. But then, as Dana Gioia astutely states in his introduction to *California Poetry*, "Almost by definition, an anthology is a book that omits one's favorite [writer]...and canonizes [pieces] one abhors." It is my hope, though, that our selections will meet with favor—not only because of their literary excellence, but also because they help to make *California Uncovered* a special and unusual collection. One of our aims was to mix well-known voices—such as those of Maxine Hong Kingston and John Steinbeck (whose classic *Travels with Charley* we have excerpted here)—with many brave new ones that have rarely, if ever, been anthologized. I believe the result gives our collection a special freshness while preserving a sense of literary history.

As its subtitle indicates, *California Uncovered* looks into the future, into the California that is to come. But any meaningful vision of the future depends on an understanding of the past and the present, and so the book presents many different experiences from different times. From white settlers coming over the Sierra Nevada in the 1840s to the building of the first suburb with a mall, outside of Los Angeles, in the 1940s, to Afghanis trying vainly to feel at home in Fremont in the 2000s, *California Uncovered* traces an ongoing California experience.

An early editorial decision was that we would focus on prose—mainly because there are several excellent poetry anthologies covering this region. We have, however, included five poems—by Rubén Martínez, Gary Soto, Robert Hass, Shirley Geok-Lin Lim, and Robinson Jeffers—that articulate the California story eloquently. Central to the book is a group of interviews by James Quay with people of various backgrounds— a Hmong refugee, a Jesuit priest, a justice of the California Supreme Court, a farmworker. They discuss, among other things, what being Californian means to them, to what degree they feel a sense of belonging, and how they envision the future of California. The unstudied spontaneity of their responses, juxtaposed with the more structured literary pieces, adds texture to the book.

While aiming to present a totality of Californian experience that is larger than the sum of its parts, the editors wanted also to ensure that different regions of the state were included in the dialogue presented in this anthology. Thus, we have chosen stories from north and south, coast, inland, and elsewhere, taking care to preserve the authenticity of neighborhoods and towns. Luis J. Rodriguez's "My Ride, My Revolution" invites us into the life of a limousine driver who doubles as a singer in a rock band in inner-city Los Angeles. Maxine Hong Kingston's "The Grandfather of the Sierra Nevada Mountains" documents the travails of Chinese railroad workers in the rugged northern landscape in the mid-nineteenth century. Greg Sarris's "The Magic Pony" takes us into the Native American community of Santa Rosa, where young people must navigate carefully between tradition and the lure of modernity. And my story, "Mrs. Dutta Writes a Letter," focuses on the difficulties faced by an old Indian woman who has exchanged the world she knows and loves for her son's house in suburban San Jose.

To further capture the multiplicity of voices that tell the California story, we made it a point to include the unique inflections of urban, small-town, suburban, and rural voices, as well as voices from different ethnic backgrounds. For example, in the excerpt from *The Gangster We Are All Looking For*, lê thi diem thúy follows a Vietnamese child's journey through San Diego in search of a place she can call home. In "Pruning Generations," David Mas Masumoto reflects on ancestral figures, Japanese traditions, and the care of grapevines on his family's farm in the Central Valley. In "The Light Takes Its Color from the Sea," James D. Houston generously shares with readers his intimate musings on what it means to make a home in Santa Cruz. In "Melvin in the Sixth Grade," a story with a very different tone, Dana Johnson's African American protagonist suddenly finds herself in a cruel white suburban school. And Paul Beatty, detailing with irreverent humor one family's move into the 'hood, demonstrates in an excerpt from *The White Boy Shuffle* that cruelty need not come from outside one's own community.

While we have presented the harsh reality of what life means for many Californians, we have also made an attempt to break stereotypes. The protagonist of Yxta Maya Murray's *The Conquest* is a Latina book restorer who works in the Getty Museum, while Khaled Hosseini's young hero is an aspiring fiction writer.

The Californian adventure is a marvelous one—with manifold outcomes. In this collection we have tried to balance the hope and the disappointment of this complex experience. On one hand there are great and unexpected victories, as in Laila Halaby's "The American Dream," where an impoverished nursing aide beats the system—at least for the moment. On the other hand lurks violence, as in the excerpt from Dao Strom's *Grass Roof, Tin Roof*, in which a part-Danish, part-Vietnamese family transplanted into the bewilderingly beautiful northern California countryside is threatened by a hostile neighbor who wants no part of them. Sometimes what happens is hilarious and sad and ironic all at once, as when Brian Ascalon Roley's protagonists in *American Son* abandon their Filipino identity for a Latino one. Sometimes pain and joy are mixed into the same experience. As Shirley Geok-Lin Lim writes in her poem "Riding into California":

> The good thing about being Chinese on Amtrak
> is no one sits next to you. The bad thing is
> you sit alone all the way to Irvine.

Three major themes dominate *California Uncovered;* we found ourselves classifying selections under the headings "Loss and Discovery," "Encounters," and "Becoming Californian"—or choosing not to. But after much discussion, the editors decided not to break the book into three parts. We chose instead to allow each selection to flow into another, to speak to the pieces before and behind it. This, we felt, created a greater sense of unity in diversity, something often lacking in such anthologies. Our decision was also influenced by the fact that many of our selections, such as Richard Rodriguez's "Where the Poppies Grow," touch on more than one theme. However, for readers who are interested in thematic groupings and would like to read the book in such a way, we have provided an alternate thematic table of contents in the back of the book, listing each selection according to its major focus.

Apart from providing pleasure to the discerning reader who enjoys the book in the privacy of his or her home, we hope this collection will, as part of the California Council for the Humanities' statewide California Stories Uncovered campaign, become part of many group reading and discussion experiences. We hope it will inspire Californians to realize the value and validity of their own stories. We hope it will lead them to reflect on these stories and share them with others—in homes, in communities, and in classrooms—and through such sharing, begin weaving the stories of the future.

In presenting, through this collection, the many ways of being Californian, we have attempted to get at the reality of lives, the reality that is often buried beneath statistics and stereotypes. We hope this anthology will change, for the better, the way we look at friends, neighbors, and strangers. How can we not, once their stories have enchanted us? The result, we hope, will engender trust, understanding, and fellowship—and create a stronger community of Californians. Such a community is essential for our survival—for, as Rubén Martínez writes in "Manifesto,"

everyone is everywhere now
so careful how you shoot.

Rubén Martínez

"Manifesto"

Rubén Martínez was born in 1962. He is an award-winning journalist and the author of four major works, most recently the nonfiction collection *The New Americans*. He has also contributed essays, opinions, and reportage to a number of magazines and newspapers, including the *New York Times*, *Washington Post*, *Los Angeles Times*, *Village Voice*, and *The Nation*. His awards include a Loeb Fellowship from Harvard University, a Lannan Foundation Fellowship, a Freedom of Information Award from the ACLU, and an Emmy Award for hosting PBS-affiliate KCET-TV's *Life and Times* series. Martínez is currently both an associate editor for Pacific News Service and a musician. He divides his time between California, New Mexico, and Texas.

> *Can anyone tell me what time it is?*
> *¿O es que nadie lo sabe?*
> *Doesn't anyone know?*
> *¡Vamos, across the continent, North y Sur!*
> *What time is it in downtown L.A.*

when the LAPD raids the sanctuary at La Placita?
And in the city that bans santería sacrifices,
a thousand Pollo Loco stands notwithstanding?
What time is it where little Saigon meets little Havana
    meets little Tokyo meets little Armenia and we all meet
    the sea speaking in tongues?

Can you feel the earth shudder?
This generation's shaky, bro',
dancing a San Andreas cumbia!
It is 1991 and I live and die
in Guatemala, San Salvador, Mexico City
Tijuana and L.A.
This is not 1969 and Marx
has a bad rap on the international scene,
but there's the FMLN in downtown San Salvador,
(and the death squads are in L.A.)
and
¡Híjole! There goes the Berlin mauer down!

Can anyone tell me what time it is
in the great cities of the States
where Third World kids etch the walls
with a message clear
as civil war:
wildstyle, a violent
rainbow, a pistol pointed at your head!

And what time is it in L.A. when
a guatemalteco wears an Africa Now T-shirt
and a black kid munches carnitas and all
together now dance to Easy-E. and B.D.P.,
crossing every border ever held sacred?

But it's live ammunition
on the streets of Southcentral L.A.
and in Westwood and San Salvador
and East L.A.;
as real as video.

This is war, and the battle
will be block to block wherever
the Wes and Theys face off.
Third World in the First:
that's what time it is.

History is on fast forwad
it's the age of synthesis
which is not to say
that the Rainbow Coalition is
heaven on earth and let's party.
This be neither a rehash of
the Summer of Love or
Fidel and Che.
All kinds of battles are yet to come
(race and class rage bullets and blood);
choose your weapons…
just know that everyone is everywhere now
so careful how you shoot.

Los Angeles, 1989

Maxine Hong Kingston

"The Grandfather of the Sierra Nevada Mountains"
from *China Men*

Maxine Hong Kingston was born in 1940 in Stockton, California. Her father was a scholar and the manager of an illegal gambling house, while her mother was a practitioner of medicine and midwifery as well as a field hand. Her undergraduate years at the University of California, Berkeley, coincided with the free speech movement, and Kingston has long advocated nonviolent means to achieve social change. Her novels include *The Woman Warrior: Memoirs of a Girlhood Among Ghosts, China Men,* and *Tripmaster Monkey: His Fake Book.* She recently published *The Fifth Book of Peace,* a work of memoir and reflection. Kingston lives in Oakland with her husband, Earll, and has been a senior lecturer in the English department of UC Berkeley since 1990.

"The Grandfather of the Sierra Nevada Mountains" is taken from *China Men,* first published in 1980. The novel chronicles three generations of Chinese men in America through an expert mixing of myth, folklore, and history. *China Men* is a follow-up to Kingston's first book, *The Woman Warrior*, both of which have won the National Book Critics Circle Award.

The trains used to cross the sky. The house jumped and dust shook down from the attic. Sometimes two trains ran parallel going in opposite directions; the railroad men walked on top of the leaning cars, stepped off one train onto the back of the other, and traveled the opposite way. They headed for the caboose while the train moved against their walk, or they walked toward the engine while the train moved out from under their feet. Hoboes ran alongside, caught the ladders, and swung aboard. I would have to learn to ride like that, choose my boxcar, grab a ladder at a run, and fling myself up and sideways into an open door. Elsewhere I would step smoothly off. Bad runaway boys lost their legs trying for such rides. The train craunched past—pistons stroking like elbows and knees, the coal cars dropping coal, cows looking out between the slats of the cattlecars, the boxcars almost stringing together sentences—Hydro-Cushion, Georgia Flyer, Route of the Eagle—and suddenly sunlight filled the windows again, the slough wide again and waving with tules, for which the city was once named; red-winged blackbirds and squirrels settled. We children ran to the tracks and found the nails we'd placed on them; the wheels had flattened them into knives that sparked.

Once in a while an adult said, "Your grandfather built the railroad." (Or "Your grandfathers built the railroad." Plural and singular are by context.) We children believed that it was that very railroad, those trains, those tracks running past our house; our own giant grandfather had set those very logs into the ground, poured the iron for those very spikes with the big heads and pounded them until the heads spread like that, mere nails to him. He had built the railroad so that trains would thunder over us, on a street that inclined toward us. We lived on a special spot of the earth, Stockton, the only city on the Pacific coast with three railroads—the Santa Fe, Southern Pacific, and Western Pacific. The three railroads intersecting accounted for the flocks of hoboes. The few times that the train stopped, the cows moaned all night, their hooves stumbling crowdedly and banging against the wood.

Grandfather left a railroad for his message: We had to go somewhere difficult. Ride a train. Go somewhere important. In case of danger, the train was to be ready for us.

The railroad men disconnected the rails and took the steel away. They did not come back. Our family dug up the square logs and rolled them downhill home. We collected the spikes too. We used the logs for benches, edged the yard with them, made bases for fences, embedded them in the ground for walkways. The spikes came in handy too, good for paperweights, levers, wedges, chisels. I am glad to know exactly the weight of ties and the size of nails.

Grandfather's picture hangs in the dining room next to an equally large one of Grandmother, and another one of Guan Goong, God of War and Literature. My grandparents' similarity is in the set of their mouths; they seem to have hauled with their mouths. My mouth also feels the tug and strain of weights in its corners. In the family album, Grandfather wears a greatcoat and Western shoes, but his ankles show. He hasn't shaved either. Maybe he became sloppy after the Japanese soldier bayoneted his head for not giving directions. Or he was born slow and without a sense of direction.

The photographer came to the village regularly and set up a spinet, potted trees, an ornate table stacked with hardbound books of matching size, and a backdrop with a picture of paths curving through gardens into panoramas; he lent his subjects dressy ancient mandarin clothes, Western suits, and hats. An aunt tied the fingers of the lame cousin to a book, the string leading down his sleeve; he looks like he's carrying it. The family hurried from clothes chests to mirrors without explaining to Grandfather, hiding Grandfather. In the family album are group pictures with Grandmother in the middle, the family arranged on either side of her and behind her, second wives at the ends, no Grandfather. Grandmother's earrings, bracelets, and rings are tinted jade green, everything and everybody else black and white, her little feet together neatly, two knobs at the bottom of her gown. My mother, indignant that nobody had readied Grandfather, threw his greatcoat over his nightclothes, shouted, "Wait! Wait!" and encouraged him into the sunlight. "Hurry," she said, and he ran, coat flapping, to be in the picture. She would have slipped him into the group and had the camera catch him like a peeping ghost, but Grandmother chased him away. "What a waste of film," she said. Grandfather always appears alone with white stubble on his chin. He was a thin man with big eyes that looked straight ahead. When we children talked about overcoat men, exhibitionists, we meant Grandfather, Ah Goong, who must have yanked open that greatcoat—no pants.

MaMa was the only person to listen to him, and so he followed her everywhere, and talked and talked. What he liked telling was his journeys to the Gold Mountain. He wasn't smart, yet he traveled there three times. Left to himself, he would have stayed in China to play with babies or stayed in the United States once he got there, but Grandmother forced him to leave both places. "Make money," she said. "Don't stay here eating." "Come home," she said.

Ah Goong sat outside her open door when MaMa worked. (In those days a man did not visit a good woman alone unless married to her.) He saw her at her loom and came running with his chair. He told her that he had found a wondrous country, really gold, and he himself had gotten two bags of it, one of which he had had made into a ring. His wife had given that ring to their son for his wedding ring. "That ring on your finger," he told Mother, "proves that the Gold Mountain exists and that I went there."

Another of his peculiarities was that he heard the crackles, bangs, gunshots that go off when the world lurches; the gears on its axis snap. Listening to a faraway New Year, he had followed the noise and come upon the blasting in the Sierras. (There is a Buddhist instruction that that which is most elusive must, of course, be the very thing to be pursued; listen to the farthest sound.) The Central Pacific hired him on sight; chinamen had a natural talent for explosions. Also there were not enough workingmen to do all the labor of building a new country. Some of the banging came from the war to decide whether or not black people would continue to work for nothing.

Slow as usual, Ah Goong arrived in the spring; the work had begun in January 1863. The demon that hired him pointed up and up, east above the hills of poppies. His first job was to fell a redwood, which was thick enough to divide into three or four beams. His tree's many branches spread out, each limb like a little tree. He circled the tree. How to attack it? No side looked like the side made to be cut, nor did any ground seem the place for it to fall. He axed for almost a day the side he'd decided would hit the ground. Halfway through, imitating the other lumberjacks, he struck the other side of the tree, above the cut, until he had to run away. The tree swayed and slowly dived to earth, creaking and screeching like a green animal. He was so awed, he forgot what he was supposed to yell. Hardly any branches broke; the tree sprang, bounced, pushed at the ground with its arms. The limbs did not wilt and fold; they were a small forest, which he chopped. The trunk lay like a long red torso; sap ran from its cuts like crying blind eyes. At last it stopped fighting. He set the log across sawhorses to be cured over smoke and in the sun.

He joined a team of men who did not ax one another as they took alternate hits. They blew up the stumps with gunpowder. "It was like uprooting a tooth," Ah Goong said. They also packed gunpowder at the roots of a whole tree. Not at the same time as the bang but before that, the tree rose from the ground. It stood, then plunged with a tearing of veins and muscles. It was big enough to carve a house into. The men measured themselves against the upturned white roots, which looked like claws, a sun with claws. A hundred men stood or sat on the trunk. They lifted a wagon on it and took a photograph. The demons also had their photograph taken.

Because these mountains were made out of gold, Ah Goong rushed over to the root hole to look for gold veins and ore. He selected the shiniest rocks to be assayed later in San Francisco. When he drank from the streams and saw a flash, he dived in like a duck; only sometimes did it turn out to be the sun or the water. The very dirt winked with specks.

He made a dollar a day salary. The lucky men gambled, but he was not good at remembering game rules. The work so far was endurable. "I could take it," he said.

The days were sunny and blue, the wind exhilarating, the heights godlike. At night the stars were diamonds, crystals, silver, snow, ice. He had never seen diamonds. He had never seen snow and ice. As spring turned into summer, and he lay under that sky, he saw the order in the stars. He recognized constellations from China. There—not a cloud but the Silver River, and there, on either side of it—Altair and Vega, the Spinning Girl and the Cowboy, far, far apart. He felt his heart breaking of loneliness at so much blue-black space between star and star. The railroad he was building would not lead him to his family. He jumped out of his bedroll. "Look! Look!" Other China Men jumped awake. An accident? An avalanche? Injun demons? "The stars," he said. "The stars are here." "Another China Man gone out of his mind," men grumbled. "A sleepwalker." "Go to sleep, sleepwalker." "There. And there," said Ah Goong, two hands pointing. "The Spinning Girl and the Cowboy. Don't you see them?" "Homesick China Man," said the China Men and pulled their blankets over their heads. "Didn't you know they were here? I could have told you they were here. Same as in China. Same Moon. Why not same stars?" "Nah. Those are American stars."

Pretending that a little girl was listening, he told himself the story about the Spinning Girl and the Cowboy: A long time ago they had visited earth, where they met, fell in love, and married. Instead of growing used to each other, they remained enchanted their entire lifetimes and beyond. They were too happy. They wanted to be doves or two branches of the same tree. When they returned to live in the sky, they were so engrossed in each other that they neglected their work. The Queen of the Sky scratched a river between them with one stroke of her silver hairpin—the river a galaxy in width. The lovers suffered, but she did devote her time to spinning now, and he herded his cow. The King of the Sky took pity on them and ordered that once each year, they be allowed to meet. On the seventh day of the seventh month (which is not the same as July 7), magpies form a bridge for them to cross to each other. The lovers are together for one night of the year. On their parting, the Spinner cries the heavy summer rains.

Ah Goong's discovery of the two stars gave him something to look forward to besides meals and tea breaks. Every night he located Altair and Vega and gauged how much closer they had come since the night before. During the day he watched the magpies, big black and white birds with round bodies like balls with wings; they were a welcome sight, a promise of meetings. He had found two familiars in the wilderness: magpies and stars. On the meeting day, he did not see any magpies nor hear their chattering jaybird cries. Some black and white birds flew overhead, but they may have been American crows or late magpies on their way. Some men laughed at him, but he was not the only China Man to collect water in pots, bottles, and canteens that day. The water would stay fresh forever and cure anything. In ancient days the tutelary gods of the mountains sprinkled corpses with this water and brought them to life. That night, no women to light candles, burn incense, cook special food, Grandfather watched for the convergence and bowed. He saw the two little stars next to Vega—the couple's children. And bridging the Silver River, surely those were black flapping wings of magpies and translucent-winged angels and faeries. Toward morning, he was awakened by rain, and pulled his blankets into his tent.

The next day, the fantailed orange-beaked magpies returned. Altair and Vega were beginning their journeys apart, another year of spinning and herding. Ah Goong had to find something else to look forward to. The Spinning Girl and the Cowboy met and parted six times before the railroad was finished.

When cliffs, sheer drops under impossible overhangs, ended the road, the workers filled the ravines or built bridges over them. They climbed above the site for tunnel or bridge and lowered one another down in wicker baskets made stronger by the lucky words they had painted on four sides. Ah Goong got to be a basketman because he was thin and light. Some basketmen were fifteen-year-old boys. He rode the basket barefoot, so his boots, the kind to stomp snakes with, would not break through the bottom. The basket swung and twirled, and he saw the world sweep underneath him; it was fun in a way, a cold new feeling of doing what had never been done before. Suspended in the quiet sky, he thought all kinds of crazy thoughts, that if a man didn't want to live any more, he could just cut the ropes or, easier, tilt the basket, dip, and never have to worry again. He could spread his arms and the air would momentarily hold him before he fell past the buzzards, hawks, and eagles, and landed impaled on the tip of a sequoia. This high and he didn't see any gods, no Cowboy, no Spinner. He knelt in the basket though he was not bumping his head against the sky. Through the wickerwork, slivers of depths darted like needles, nothing between him and air but thin rattan. Gusts of wind spun the light basket.

"Aiya," said Ah Goong. Winds came up under the basket, bouncing it. Neighboring baskets swung together and parted. He and the man next to him looked at each other's faces. They laughed. They might as well have gone to Malaysia to collect bird nests. Those who had done high work there said it had been worse; the birds screamed and scratched at them. Swinging near the cliff, Ah Goong stood up and grabbed it by a twig. He dug holes, then inserted gunpowder and fuses. He worked neither too fast nor too slow, keeping even with the others. The basketmen signaled one another to light the fuses. He struck match after match and dropped the burnt matches over the sides. At last his fuse caught; he waved, and the men above pulled hand over hand hauling him up, pulleys creaking. The scaffolds stood like a row of gibbets. Gallows trees along a ridge. "Hurry, hurry," he said. Some impatient men clambered up their ropes. Ah Goong ran up the ledge road they'd cleared and watched the explosions, which banged almost synchronously, echoes booming like war. He moved his scaffold to the next section of cliff and went down in the basket again, with bags of dirt, and set the next charge.

This time two men were blown up. One knocked out or killed by the explosion fell silently, the other screaming, his arms and legs struggling. A desire shot out of Ah Goong for an arm long enough to reach down and catch them. Much time passed as they fell like plummets. The shreds of baskets and a cowboy hat skimmed and tacked. The winds that pushed birds off course and against mountains did not carry men. Ah Goong also wished that the conscious man would fall faster and get it over with. His hands gripped the ropes, and it was difficult to let go and get on with the work. "It can't happen twice in a row," the basketmen said the next trip down. "Our chances are very good. The trip after an accident is probably the safest one." They raced to their favorite basket, checked and double-checked the four ropes, yanked the strands, tested the pulleys, oiled them, reminded the pulleymen about the signals, and entered the sky again.

Another time, Ah Goong had been lowered to the bottom of a ravine, which had to be cleared for the base of a trestle, when a man fell, and he saw his face. He had not died of shock before hitting bottom. His hands were grabbing at air. His stomach and groin must have felt the fall all the way down. At night Ah Goong woke up falling, though he slept on the ground, and heard other men call out in their sleep. No warm women tweaked their ears and hugged them. "It was only a falling dream," he reassured himself.

Across a valley, a chain of men working on the next mountain, men like ants changing the face of the world, fell, but it was very far away. Godlike, he watched men whose faces he could not see and whose screams he did not hear roll and bounce and slide like a handful of sprinkled gravel.

After a fall, the buzzards circled the spot and reminded the workers for days that a man was dead down there. The men threw piles of rocks and branches to cover bodies from sight.

The mountainface reshaped, they drove supports for a bridge. Since hammering was less dangerous than the blowing up, the men played a little; they rode the baskets swooping in wide arcs; they twisted the ropes and let them unwind like tops. "Look at me," said Ah Goong, pulled open his pants, and pissed overboard, the wind scattering the drops. "I'm a waterfall," he said. He had sent a part of himself hurtling. On rare windless days he watched his piss fall in a continuous stream from himself almost to the bottom of the valley.

One beautiful day, dangling in the sun above a new valley, not the desire to urinate but sexual desire clutched him so hard he bent over in the basket. He curled up, overcome by beauty and fear, which shot to his penis. He tried to rub himself calm. Suddenly he stood up tall and squirted out into space. "I am fucking the world," he said. The world's vagina was big, big as the sky, big as a valley. He grew a habit: whenever he was lowered in the basket, his blood rushed to his penis, and he fucked the world.

Then it was autumn, and the wind blew so fiercely, the men had to postpone the basketwork. Clouds moved in several directions at once. Men pointed at dust devils, which turned their mouths crooked. There was ceaseless motion; clothes kept moving; hair moved; sleeves puffed out. Nothing stayed still long enough for Ah Goong to figure it out. The wind sucked the breath out of his mouth and blew thoughts from his brains. The food convoys from San Francisco brought tents to replace the ones that whipped away. The baskets from China, which the men saved for high work, carried cowboy jackets, long underwear, Levi pants, boots, earmuffs, leather gloves, flannel shirts, coats. They sewed rabbit fur and deerskin into the linings. They tied the wide brims of their cowboy hats over their ears with mufflers. And still the wind made confusing howls into ears, and it was hard to think.

The days became nights when the crews tunneled inside the mountain, which sheltered them from the wind, but also hid the light and sky. Ah Goong pickaxed the mountain, the dirt filling his nostrils through a cowboy bandanna. He shoveled the dirt into a cart and pushed it to a place that was tall enough for the mule, which hauled it the rest of the way out. He looked forward to cart duty to edge closer to the entrance. Eyes darkened, nose plugged, his windy cough worse, he was to mole a thousand feet and meet others digging from the other side. How much he'd pay now to go swinging in a basket. He might as well have gone to work in a tin mine. Coming out of the tunnel at the end of a shift, he forgot whether it was supposed to be day or night. He blew his nose fifteen times before the mucus cleared again.

The dirt was the easiest part of tunneling. Beneath the soil, they hit granite. Ah Goong struck it with his pickax, and it jarred his bones, chattered his teeth. He swung his sledgehammer against it, and the impact rang in the dome of his skull. The mountain that was millions of years old was locked against them and was not to be broken into. The men teased him, "Let's see you fuck the world now." "Let's see you fuck the Gold Mountain now." But he no longer felt like it. "A man ought to be made of tougher material than flesh," he said. "Skin is too soft. Our bones ought to be filled with iron." He lifted the hammer high, careful that it not pull him backward, and let it fall forward of its own weight against the rock. Nothing happened to that gray wall; he had to slam with strength and will. He hit at the same spot over and over again, the same rock. Some chips and flakes broke off. The granite looked everywhere the same. It had no softer or weaker spots anywhere, the same hard gray. He learned to slide his hand up the handle, lift, slide and swing, a circular motion, hammering, hammering, hammering. He would bite like a rat through that mountain. His eyes couldn't see; his nose couldn't smell; and now his ears were filled with the noise of hammering. This rock is what is real, he thought. This rock is what real is, not clouds or mist, which make mysterious promises, and when you go through them are nothing. When the foreman measured at the end of twenty-four hours of pounding, the rock had given a foot. The hammering went on day and night. The men worked eight hours on and eight hours off. They worked on all eighteen tunnels at once. While Ah Goong slept, he could hear the sledgehammers of other men working in the earth. The steady banging reminded him of holidays and harvests; falling asleep, he heard the women chopping mincemeat and the millstones striking.

The demons in boss suits came into the tunnel occasionally, measured with a yardstick, and shook their heads. "Faster," they said. "Faster. Chinamen too slow. Too slow." "Tell us we're slow," the China Men grumbled. The ones in top tiers of scaffolding let rocks drop, a hammer drop. Ropes tangled around the demons' heads and feet. The cave China Men muttered and flexed, glared out of the corners of their eyes. But usually there was no diversion—one day the same as the next, one hour no different from another—the beating against the same granite.

After tunneling into granite for about three years, Ah Goong understood the immovability of the earth. Men change, men die, weather changes, but a mountain is the same as permanence and time. This mountain would have taken no new shape for centuries, ten thousand centuries, the world a still, still place, time unmoving. He worked in the tunnel so long, he learned to see many colors in black. When he stumbled out, he tried to talk about time. "I felt time," he said. "I saw time. I saw world." He tried again, "I saw what's real. I saw time, and it doesn't move. If we break through the mountain, hollow it, time won't have moved anyway. You translators ought to tell the foreigners that."

Summer came again, but after the first summer, he felt less nostalgia at the meeting of the Spinning Girl and the Cowboy. He now knew men who had been in this country for twenty years and thirty years, and the Cowboy's one year away from his lady was no time at all. His own patience was longer. The stars were meeting and would meet again next year, but he would not have seen his family. He joined the others celebrating Souls' Day, the holiday a week later, the fourteenth day of the seventh month. The supply wagons from San Francisco and Sacramento brought watermelon, meat, fish, crab, pressed duck. "There, ghosts, there you are. Come and get it." They displayed the feast complete for a moment before falling to, eating on the dead's behalf.

In the third year of pounding granite by hand, a demon invented dynamite. The railroad workers were to test it. They had stopped using gunpowder in the tunnels after avalanches, but the demons said that dynamite was more precise. They watched a scientist demon mix nitrate, sulphate, and glycerine, then flick the yellow oil, which exploded off his fingertips. Sitting in a meadow to watch the dynamite detonated in the open, Ah Goong saw the men in front of him leap impossibly high into the air; then he felt a shove as if from a giant's unseen hand—and he fell backward. The boom broke the mountain silence like fear breaking inside stomach and chest and groin. No one had gotten hurt; they stood up laughing and amazed, looking around at how they had fallen, the pattern of the explosion. Dynamite was much more powerful than gunpowder. Ah Goong had felt a nudge, as if something kind were moving him out of harm's way. "All of a sudden I was sitting next to you." "Aiya. If we had been nearer, it would have killed us." "If we were stiff, it would have gone through us." "A fist." "A hand." "We leapt like acrobats." Next time Ah Goong flattened himself on the ground, and the explosion rolled over him.

He never got used to the blasting; a blast always surprised him. Even when he himself set the fuse and watched it burn, anticipated the explosion, the bang—*bahng* in Chinese—when it came, always startled. It cleaned the crazy words, the crackling, and bingbangs out of his brain. It was like New Year's, when every problem and thought was knocked clean out of him by firecrackers, and he could begin fresh. He couldn't worry during an explosion, which jerked every head to attention. Hills flew up in rocks and dirt. Boulders turned over and over. Sparks, fires, debris, rocks, smoke burst up, not at the same time as the boom *(bum)* but before that—the sound a separate occurrence, not useful as a signal.

The terrain changed immediately. Streams were diverted, rockscapes exposed. Ah Goong found it difficult to remember what land had looked like before an explosion. It was a good thing the dynamite was invented after the Civil War to the east was over.

The dynamite added more accidents and ways of dying, but if it were not used, the railroad would take fifty more years to finish. Nitroglycerine exploded when it was jounced on a horse or dropped. A man who fell with it in his pocket blew himself up into red pieces. Sometimes it combusted merely standing. Human bodies skipped through the air like puppets and made Ah Goong laugh crazily as if the arms and legs would come together again. The smell of burned flesh remained in rocks.

In the tunnels, the men bored holes fifteen to eighteen inches deep with a power drill, stuffed them with hay and dynamite, and imbedded the fuse in sand. Once, for extra pay, Ah Goong ran back in to see why some dynamite had not gone off and hurried back out again; it was just a slow fuse. When the explosion settled, he helped carry two-hundred-, three-hundred-, five-hundred-pound boulders out of the tunnel.

As a boy he had visited a Taoist monastery where there were nine rooms, each a replica of one of the nine hells. Lifesize sculptures of men and women were spitted on turning wheels. Eerie candles under the suffering faces emphasized eyes poked out, tongues pulled, red mouths and eyes, and real hair, eyelashes, and eyebrows. Women were split apart and men dismembered. He could have reached out and touched the sufferers and the implements. He had dug and dynamited his way into one of these hells. "Only here there are eighteen tunnels, not nine, plus all the tracks between them," he said.

One day he came out of the tunnel to find the mountains white, the evergreens and bare trees decorated, white tree sculptures and lace bushes everywhere. The men from snow country called the icicles "ice chopsticks." He sat in his basket and slid down the slopes. The snow covered the gouged land, the broken trees, the tracks, the mud, the campfire ashes, the unburied dead. Streams were stilled in mid-run, the water petrified. That winter he thought it was the task of the human race to quicken the world, blast the freeze, fire it, redden it with blood. He had to change the stupid slowness of one sunrise and one sunset per day. He had to enliven the silent world with sound. "The rock," he tried to tell the others. "The ice." "Time."

The dynamiting loosed blizzards on the men. Ears and toes fell off. Fingers stuck to the cold silver rails. Snowblind men stumbled about with bandannas over their eyes. Ah Goong helped build wood tunnels roofing the track route. Falling ice scrabbled on the roofs. The men stayed under the snow for weeks at a time. Snowslides covered the entrances to the tunnels, which they had to dig out to enter and exit, white tunnels and black tunnels. Ah Goong looked at his gang and thought, If there is an avalanche, these are the people I'll be trapped with, and wondered which ones would share food. A party of snowbound barbarians had eaten the dead. Cannibals, thought Ah Goong, and looked around. Food was not scarce; the tea man brought whiskey barrels of hot tea, and he warmed his hands and feet, held the teacup to his nose and ears. Someday, he planned, he would buy a chair with metal doors for putting hot coal inside it. The magpies did not abandon him but stayed all winter and searched the snow for food.

The men who died slowly enough to say last words said, "Don't leave me frozen under the snow. Send my body home. Burn it and put the ashes in a tin can. Take the bone jar when you come down the mountain." "When you ride the fire car back to China, tell my descendants to come for me." "Shut up," scolded the hearty men. "We don't want to hear about bone jars and dying." "You're lucky to have a body to bury, not blown to smithereens." "Stupid man to hurt yourself," they bawled out the sick and wounded. How their wives would scold if they brought back deadmen's bones. "Aiya. To be buried here, nowhere." "But this is somewhere," Ah Goong promised. "This is the Gold Mountain. We're marking the land now. The track sections are numbered, and your family will know where we leave you." But he was a crazy man, and they didn't listen to him.

Spring did come, and when the snow melted, it revealed the past year, what had happened, what they had done, where they had worked, the lost tools, the thawing bodies, some standing with tools in hand, the bright rails. "Remember Uncle Long Winded Leong?" "Remember Strong Back Wong?" "Remember Lee Brother?" "And Fong Uncle?" They lost count of the number dead; there is no record of how many died building the railroad. Or maybe it was demons doing the counting and chinamen not worth counting. Whether it was good luck or bad luck, the dead were buried or cairned next to the last section of track they had worked on. "May his ghost not have to toil," they said over graves. (In China a woodcutter ghost chops eternally; people have heard chopping in the snow and in the heat.) "Maybe his ghost will ride the train home." The scientific demons said the transcontinental railroad would connect the West to Cathay. "What if he rides back and forth from Sacramento to New York forever?" "That wouldn't be so bad. I hear the cars will be like houses on wheels." The funerals were short. "No time. No time," said both China Men and demons. The railroad was as straight as they could build it, but no ghosts sat on the tracks; no strange presences haunted the tunnels. The blasts scared ghosts away.

When the Big Dipper pointed east and the China Men detonated nitroglycerine and shot off guns for the New Year, which comes with the spring, these special bangs were not as loud as the daily bangs, not as numerous as the bangs all year. Shouldn't the New Year be the loudest day of all to obliterate the noises of the old year? But to make a bang of that magnitude, they would have to blow up at least a year's supply of dynamite in one blast. They arranged strings of chain reactions in circles and long lines, banging faster and louder to culminate in a big bang. And most importantly, there were random explosions—surprise. Surprise. SURPRISE. They had no dragon, the railroad their dragon.

The demons invented games for working faster, gold coins for miles of track laid, for the heaviest rock, a grand prize for the first team to break through a tunnel. Day shifts raced against night shifts, China Men against Welshmen, China Men against Irishmen, China Men against Injuns and black demons. The fastest races were China Men against China Men, who bet on their own teams. China Men always won because of good teamwork, smart thinking, and the need for the money. Also, they had the most workers to choose teams from. Whenever his team won anything, Ah Goong added to his gold stash. The Central Pacific or Union Pacific won the land on either side of the tracks it built.

One summer day, demon officials and China Man translators went from group to group and announced, "We're raising the pay—thirty-five dollars a month. Because of your excellent work, the Central Pacific Railroad is giving you a four-dollar raise per month." The workers who didn't know better cheered. "What's the catch?" said the smarter men. "You'll have the opportunity to put in more time," said the railroad demons. "Two more hours per shift." Ten-hour shifts inside the tunnels. "It's not ten hours straight," said the demons. "You have time off for tea and meals. Now that you have dynamite, the work isn't so hard." They had been working for three and a half years already, and the track through the Donner Summit was still not done.

The workers discussed the ten-hour shift, swearing their China Man obscenities. "Two extra hours a day—sixty hours a month for four dollars." "Pig catcher demons." "Snakes." "Turtles." "Dead demons." "A human body can't work like that." "The demons don't believe this is a human body. This is a chinaman's body." To bargain, they sent a delegation of English speakers, who were summarily noted as troublemakers, turned away, docked.

The China Men, then, decided to go on strike and demand forty-five dollars a month and the eight-hour shift. They risked going to jail and the Central Pacific keeping the pay it was banking for them. Ah Goong memorized the English, "Forty-five dollars a month—eight-hour shift." He practiced the strike slogan: "Eight hours a day good for white man, all the same good for China Man."

The men wrapped barley and beans in ti leaves, which came from Hawai'i via San Francisco, for celebrating the fifth day of the fifth month (not May but mid-June, the summer solstice). Usually the way the red string is wound and knotted tells what flavors are inside—the salty barley with pickled egg, or beans and pork, or the gelatin pudding. Ah Goong folded ti leaves into a cup and packed it with food. One of the literate men slipped in a piece of paper with the strike plan, and Ah Goong tied the bundle with a special pattern of red string. The time and place for the revolution against Kublai Khan had been hidden inside autumn mooncakes. Ah Goong looked from one face to another in admiration. Of course, of course. No China Men, no railroad. They were indispensable labor. Throughout these mountains were brothers and uncles with a common idea, free men, not coolies, calling for fair working conditions. The demons were not suspicious as the China Men went gandying up and down the tracks delivering the bundles tied together like lines of fish. They had exchanged these gifts every year. When the summer solstice cakes came from other camps, the recipients cut them into neat slices by drawing the string through them. The orange jellies, which had a red dye stick inside soaked in lye, fell into a series of sunrises and sunsets. The aged yolks and the barley also looked like suns. The notes gave a Yes strike vote. The yellow flags to ward off the five evils—centipedes, scorpions, snakes, poisonous lizards, and toads—now flew as banners.

The strike began on Tuesday morning, June 25, 1867. The men who were working at that hour walked out of the tunnels and away from the tracks. The ones who were sleeping slept on and rose as late as they pleased. They bathed in streams and shaved their moustaches and wild beards. Some went fishing and hunting. The violinists tuned and played their instruments. The drummers beat theirs at the punchlines of jokes. The gamblers shuffled and played their cards and tiles. The smokers passed their pipes, and the drinkers bet for drinks by making figures with their hands. The cooks made party food. The opera singers' falsettos almost perforated the mountains. The men sang new songs about the railroad. They made up verses and shouted Ho at the good ones, and laughed at the rhymes. Oh, they were madly singing in the mountains. The storytellers told about the rise of new kings. The opium smokers when they roused themselves told their florid images. Ah Goong sifted for gold. All the while the English-speaking China Men, who were being advised by the shrewdest bargainers, were at the demons' headquarters repeating the demand: "Eight hours a day good for white man, all the same good for China Man." They had probably negotiated the demons down to nine-hour shifts by now.

The sounds of hammering continued along the tracks and occasionally there were blasts from the tunnels. The scabby white demons had refused to join the strike. "Eight hours a day good for white man, all the same good for China Man," the China Men explained to them. "Cheap John Chinaman," said the demons, many of whom had red hair. The China Men scowled out of the corners of their eyes.

On the second day, artist demons climbed the mountains to draw the China Men for the newspapers. The men posed bare-chested, their fists clenched, showing off their arms and backs. The artists sketched them as perfect young gods reclining against rocks, wise expressions on their handsome noble-nosed faces, long torsos with lean stomachs, a strong arm extended over a bent knee, long fingers holding a pipe, a rope of hair over a wide shoulder. Other artists drew faeries with antennae for eyebrows and brownies with elvish pigtails; they danced in white socks and black slippers among mushroom rings by moonlight.

Ah Goong acquired another idea that added to his reputation for craziness: The pale, thin Chinese scholars and the rich men fat like Buddhas were less beautiful, less manly than these brown muscular railroad men, of whom he was one. One of ten thousand heroes.

On the third day, in a woods—he would be looking at a deer or a rabbit or an Injun watching him before he knew what he was seeing—a demon dressed in a white suit and tall hat beckoned him. They talked privately in the wilderness. The demon said, "I Citizenship Judge invite you to be U. S. citizen. Only one bag gold." Ah Goong was thrilled. What an honor. He would accept this invitation. Also what advantages, he calculated shrewdly; if he were going to be jailed for this strike, an American would have a trial. The Citizenship Judge unfurled a parchment sealed with gold and ribbon. Ah Goong bought it with one bag of gold. "You vote," said the Citizenship Judge. "You talk in court, buy land, no more chinaman tax." Ah Goong hid the paper on his person so that it would protect him from arrest and lynching. He was already a part of this new country, but now he had it in writing.

The fourth day, the strikers heard that the U.S. Cavalry was riding single file up the tracks to shoot them. They argued whether to engage the Army with dynamite. But the troops did not come. Instead the cowardly demons blockaded the food wagons. No food. Ah Goong listened to the optimistic China Men, who said, "Don't panic. We'll hold out forever. We can hunt. We can last fifty days on water." The complainers said, "Aiya. Only saints can do that. Only magic men and monks who've practiced." The China Men refused to declare a last day for the strike.

The foresighted China Men had cured jerky, fermented wine, dried and strung orange and grapefruit peels, pickled and preserved leftovers. Ah Goong, one of the best hoarders, had set aside extra helpings from each meal. This same quandary, whether to give away food or to appear selfish, had occurred during each of the six famines he had lived through. The foodless men identified themselves. Sure enough, they were the shiftless, piggy, arrogant type who didn't worry enough. The donors scolded them and shamed them the whole while they were handing them food: "So you lived like a grasshopper at our expense." "Fleaman." "You'll be the cause of our not holding out long enough." "Rich man's kid. Too good to hoard." Ah Goong contributed some rice crusts from the bottoms of pans. He kept how much more food he owned a secret, as he kept the secret of his gold. In apology for not contributing richer food, he repeated a Mohist saying that had guided him in China: "'The superior man does not push humaneness to the point of stupidity.'" He could hear his wife scolding him for feeding strangers. The opium men offered shit and said that it calmed the appetite.

On the fifth and sixth days, Ah Goong organized his possessions and patched his clothes and tent. He forbore repairing carts, picks, ropes, baskets. His work-habituated hands arranged rocks and twigs in designs. He asked a reader to read again his family's letters. His wife sounded like herself except for the polite phrases added professionally at the beginnings and the ends. "Idiot," she said, "why are you taking so long? Are you wasting the money? Are you spending it on girls and gambling and whiskey? Here's my advice to you: Be a little more frugal. Remember how it felt to go hungry. Work hard." He had been an idle man for almost a week. "I need a new dress to wear to weddings. I refuse to go to another banquet in the same old dress. If you weren't such a spendthrift, we could be building the new courtyard where we'll drink wine among the flowers and sit about in silk gowns all day. We'll hire peasants to till the fields. Or lease them to tenants, and buy all our food at market. We'll have clean fingernails and toenails." Other relatives said, "I need a gold watch. Send me the money. Your wife gambles it away and throws parties and doesn't disburse it fairly among us. You might as well come home." It was after one of these letters that he had made a bonus checking on some dud dynamite.

Ah Goong did not spend his money on women. The strikers passed the word that a woman was traveling up the railroad and would be at his camp on the seventh and eighth day of the strike. Some said she was a demoness and some that she was a Chinese and her master a China Man. He pictured a nurse coming to bandage wounds and touch foreheads or a princess surveying her subjects; or perhaps she was a merciful Jesus demoness. But she was a pitiful woman, led on a leash around her waist, not entirely alive. Her owner sold lottery tickets for the use of her. Ah Goong did not buy one. He took out his penis under his blanket or bared it in the woods and thought about nurses and princesses. He also just looked at it, wondering what it was that it was for, what a man was for, what he had to have a penis for.

There was rumor also of an Injun woman called Woman Chief, who led a nomadic fighting tribe from the eastern plains as far as these mountains. She was so powerful that she had four wives and many horses. He never saw her though.

The strike ended on the ninth day. The Central Pacific announced that in its benevolence it was giving the workers a four-dollar raise, not the fourteen dollars they had asked for. And that the shifts in the tunnels would remain eight hours long. "We were planning to give you the four-dollar raise all along," the demons said to diminish the victory. So they got thirty-five dollars a month and the eight-hour shift. They would have won forty-five dollars if the thousand demon workers had joined the strike. Demons would have listened to demons. The China Men went back to work quietly. No use singing and shouting over a compromise and losing nine days' work.

There were two days that Ah Goong did cheer and throw his hat in the air, jumping up and down and screaming Yippee like a cowboy. One: the day his team broke through the tunnel at last. Toward the end they did not dynamite but again used picks and sledgehammers. Through the granite, they heard answering poundings, and answers to their shouts. It was not a mountain before them any more but only a wall with people breaking through from the other side. They worked faster. Forward. Into day. They stuck their arms through the holes and shook hands with men on the other side. Ah Goong saw dirty faces as wondrous as if he were seeing Nu Wo, the creator goddess who repairs cracks in the sky with stone slabs; sometimes she peeks through and human beings see her face. The wall broke. Each team gave the other a gift of half a tunnel, dug. They stepped back and forth where the wall had been. Ah Goong ran and ran, his boots thudding to the very end of the tunnel, looked at the other side of the mountain, and ran back, clear through the entire tunnel. All the way through.

He spent the rest of his time on the railroad laying and bending and hammering the ties and rails. The second day the China Men cheered was when the engine from the West and the one from the East rolled toward one another and touched. The transcontinental railroad was finished. They Yippee'd like madmen. The white demon officials gave speeches. "The Greatest Feat of the Nineteenth Century," they said. "The Greatest Feat in the History of Mankind," they said. "Only Americans could have done it," they said, which is true. Even if Ah Goong had not spent half his gold on Citizenship Papers, he was an American for having built the railroad. A white demon in top hat tap-tapped on the gold spike, and pulled it back out. Then one China Man held the real spike, the steel one, and another hammered it in.

While the demons posed for photographs, the China Men dispersed. It was dangerous to stay. The Driving Out had begun. Ah Goong does not appear in railroad photographs. Scattering, some China Men followed the north star in the constellation Tortoise the Black Warrior to Canada, or they kept the constellation Phoenix ahead of them to South America or the White Tiger west or the Wolf east. Seventy lucky men rode the Union Pacific to Massachusetts for jobs at a shoe factory. Fifteen hundred went to Fou Loy Company in New Orleans and San Francisco, several hundred to plantations in Mississippi, Georgia, and Arkansas, and sugarcane plantations in Louisiana and Cuba. (From the South, they sent word that it was a custom to step off the sidewalk along with the black demons when a white demon walked by.) Seventy went to New Orleans to grade a route for a railroad, then to Pennsylvania to work in a knife factory. The Colorado State Legislature passed a resolution welcoming the railroad China Men to come build the new state. They built railroads in every part of the country—the Alabama and Chattanooga Railroad, the Houston and Texas Railroad, the Southern Pacific, the railroads in Louisiana and Boston, the Pacific Northwest, and Alaska. After the Civil War, China Men banded the nation North and South, East and West, with crisscrossing steel. They were the binding and building ancestors of this place.

Ah Goong would have liked a leisurely walk along the tracks to review his finished handiwork, or to walk east to see the rest of his new country. But instead, Driven Out, he slid down mountains, leapt across valleys and streams, crossed plains, hid sometimes with companions and often alone, and eluded bandits who would hold him up for his railroad pay and shoot him for practice as they shot Injuns and jackrabbits. Detouring and backtracking, his path wound back and forth to his railroad, a familiar silver road in the wilderness. When a train came, he hid against the shaking ground in case a demon with a shotgun was hunting from it. He picked over camps where he had once lived. He was careful to find hidden places to sleep. In China bandits did not normally kill people, the booty the main thing, but here the demons killed for fun and hate. They tied pigtails to horses and dragged chinamen. He decided that he had better head for San Francisco, where he would catch a ship to China.

Perched on hillsides, he watched many sunsets, the place it was setting, the direction he was going. There were fields of grass that he tunneled through, hid in, rolled in, dived and swam in, suddenly jumped up laughing, suddenly stopped. He needed to find a town and human company. The spooky tumbleweeds caught in barbed wire were peering at him, waiting for him; he had to find a town. Towns grew along the tracks as they did along rivers. He sat looking at a town all day, then ducked into it by night.

At the familiar sight of a garden laid out in a Chinese scheme—vegetables in beds, white cabbages, red plants, chives, and coriander for immortality, herbs boxed with boards—he knocked on the back door. The China Man who answered gave him food, the appropriate food for the nearest holiday, talked story, exclaimed at how close their ancestral villages were to each other. They exchanged information on how many others lived how near, which towns had Chinatowns, what size, two or three stores or a block, which towns to avoid. "Do you have a wife?" they asked one another. "Yes. She lives in China. I have been sending money for twenty years now." They exchanged vegetable seeds, slips, and cuttings, and Ah Goong carried letters to another town or China.

Some demons who had never seen the likes of him gave him things and touched him. He also came across lone China Men who were alarmed to have him appear, and, unwelcome, he left quickly; they must have wanted to be the only China Man of that area, the special China Man.

He met miraculous China Men who had produced families out of nowhere—a wife and children, both boys and girls. "Uncle," the children called him, and he wanted to stay to be the uncle of the family. The wife washed his clothes, and he went on his way when they were dry.

On a farm road, he came across an imp child playing in the dirt. It looked at him, and he looked at it. He held out a piece of sugar; he cupped a grassblade between his thumbs and whistled. He sat on the ground with his legs crossed, and the child climbed into the hollow of his arms and legs. "I wish you were my baby," he told it. "My baby." He was very satisfied sitting there under the humming sun with the baby, who was satisfied too, no squirming. "My daughter," he said. "My son." He couldn't tell whether it was a boy or a girl. He touched the baby's fat arm and cheeks, its gold hair, and looked into its blue eyes. He made a wish that it not have to carry a sledgehammer and crawl into the dark. But he would not feel sorry for it; other people must not suffer any more than he did, and he could endure anything. Its mother came walking out into the road. She had her hands above her like a salute. She walked tentatively toward them, held out her hand, smiled, spoke. He did not understand what she said except "Bye-bye." The child waved and said, "Bye-bye," crawled over his legs, and toddled to her. Ah Goong continued on his way in a direction she could not point out to a posse looking for a kidnapper chinaman.

Explosions followed him. He heard screams and went on, saw flames outlining black windows and doors, and went on. He ran in the opposite direction from gunshots and the yell—*eeha awha*—the cowboys made when they herded cattle and sang their savage songs.

Good at hiding, disappearing—decades unaccounted for—he was not working in a mine when forty thousand chinamen were Driven Out of mining. He was not killed or kidnapped in the Los Angeles Massacre, though he gave money toward ransoming those whose toes and fingers, a digit per week, and ears grotesquely rotting or pickled, and scalped queues, were displayed in Chinatowns. Demons believed that the poorer a chinaman looked, the more gold he had buried somewhere, that chinamen stuck together and would always ransom one another. If he got kidnapped, Ah Goong planned, he would whip out his Citizenship Paper and show that he was an American. He was lucky not to be in Colorado when the Denver demons burned all chinamen homes and businesses, nor in Rock Springs, Wyoming, when the miner demons killed twenty-eight or fifty chinamen. The Rock Springs Massacre began in a large coal mine owned by the Union Pacific; the outnumbered chinamen were shot in the back as they ran to Chinatown, which the demons burned. They forced chinamen out into the open and shot them; demon women and children threw the wounded back in the flames. (There was a rumor of a good white lady in Green Springs who hid China Men in the Pacific Hotel and shamed the demons away.) The hunt went on for a month before federal troops came. The count of the dead was inexact because bodies were mutilated and pieces scattered all over the Wyoming Territory. No white miners were indicted, but the government paid $150,000 in reparations to victims' families. There were many family men, then. There were settlers—abiding China Men. And China Women. Ah Goong was running elsewhere during the Drivings Out of Tacoma, Seattle, Oregon City, Albania, and Marysville. The demons of Tacoma packed all its chinamen into boxcars and sent them to Portland, where they were run out of town. China Men returned to Seattle, though, and refused to sell their land and stores but fought until the army came; the demon rioters were tried and acquitted. And when the Boston police imprisoned and beat 234 chinamen, it was 1902, and Ah Goong had already reached San Francisco or China, and perhaps San Francisco again.

In Second City (Sacramento), he spent some of his railroad money at the theater. The main actor's face was painted red with thick black eyebrows and long black beard, and when he strode onto the stage, Ah Goong recognized the hero, Guan Goong; his puppet horse had red nostrils and rolling eyes. Ah Goong's heart leapt to recognize hero and horse in the wilds of America. Guan Goong murdered his enemy—crash! bang! of cymbals and drum—and left his home village—sad, sad flute music. But to the glad clamor of cymbals entered his friends—Liu Pei (pronounced the same as Running Nose) and Chang Fei. In a joyful burst of pink flowers, the three men swore the Peach Garden Oath. Each friend sang an aria to friendship; together they would fight side by side and live and die one for all and all for one. Ah Goong felt as warm as if he were with friends at a party. Then Guan Goong's archenemy, the sly Ts'ao Ts'ao, captured him and two of Liu Pei's wives, the Lady Kan and the Lady Mi. Though Ah Goong knew they were boy actors, he basked in the presence of Chinese ladies. The prisoners traveled to the capital, the soldiers waving horsehair whisks, signifying horses, the ladies walking between horizontal banners, signifying palanquins. All the prisoners were put in one bedroom, but Guan Goong stood all night outside the door with a lighted candle in his hand, singing an aria about faithfulness. When the capital was attacked by a common enemy, Guan Goong fought the biggest man in one-to-one combat, a twirling, jumping sword dance that strengthened the China Men who watched it. From afar Guan Goong's two partners heard about the feats of the man with the red face and intelligent horse. The three friends were reunited and fought until they secured their rightful kingdom.

Ah Goong felt refreshed and inspired. He called out Bravo like the demons in the audience, who had not seen theater before. Guan Goong, the God of War, also God of War and Literature, had come to America—Guan Goong, Grandfather Guan, our own ancestor of writers and fighters, of actors and gamblers, and avenging executioners who mete out justice. Our own kin. Not a distant ancestor but Grandfather.

In the Big City (San Francisco), a goldsmith convinced Ah Goong to have his gold made into jewelry, which would organize it into one piece and also delight his wife. So he handed over a second bag of gold. He got it back as a small ring in a design he thought up himself, two hands clasping in a handshake. "So small?" he said, but the goldsmith said that only some of the ore had been true gold.

He got a ship out of San Francisco without being captured near the docks, where there was a stockade full of jailed chinamen; the demonesses came down from Nob Hill and took them home to be servants, cooks, and baby-sitters.

Grandmother liked the gold ring very much. The gold was so pure, it squished to fit her finger. She never washed dishes, so the gold did not wear away. She quickly spent the railroad money, and Ah Goong said he would go to America again. He had a Certificate of Return and his Citizenship Paper.

But this time, there was no railroad to sell his strength to. He lived in a basement that was rumored to connect with tunnels beneath Chinatown. In an underground arsenal, he held a pistol and said, "I feel the death in it." "The holes for the bullets were like chambers in a beehive or wasp nest," he said. He was inside the earth when the San Francisco Earthquake and Fire began. Thunder rumbled from the ground. Some say he died falling into the cracking earth. It was a miraculous earthquake and fire. The Hall of Records burned completely. Citizenship Papers burned, Certificates of Return, Birth Certificates, Residency Certificates, passenger lists, Marriage Certificates—every paper a China Man wanted for citizenship and legality burned in that fire. An authentic citizen, then, had no more papers than an alien. Any paper a China Man could not produce had been "burned up in the Fire of 1906." Every China Man was reborn out of that fire a citizen.

Some say the family went into debt and sent for Ah Goong, who was not making money; he was a homeless wanderer, a shiftless, dirty, jobless man with matted hair, ragged clothes, and fleas all over his body. He ate out of garbage cans. He was a louse eaten by lice. A fleaman. It cost two thousand dollars to bring him back to China, his oldest sons signing promissory notes for one thousand, his youngest to repay four hundred to one neighbor and six hundred to another. Maybe he hadn't died in San

Francisco, it was just his papers that burned; it was just that his existence was outlawed by Chinese Exclusion Acts. The family called him Fleaman. They did not understand his accomplishments as an American ancestor, a holding, homing ancestor of this place. He'd gotten the legal or illegal papers burned in the San Francisco Earthquake and Fire; he appeared in America in time to be a citizen and to father citizens. He had also been seen carrying a child out of the fire, a child of his own in spite of the laws against marrying. He had built a railroad out of sweat, why not have an American child out of longing?

Yxta Maya Murray

from *The Conquest*

Yxta Maya Murray was born in 1970 in California. She is the author of three novels—*Locas, What It Takes to Get to Vegas,* and *The Conquest*—and in 1999 she received a Whiting Writers' Award for fiction. She has taught at Loyola Law School in Los Angeles since 1995.

This excerpt is from Murray's most recent book, *The Conquest,* published in 2002. It is a literary detective novel linking two Latina women across four centuries and spanning settings as distant as the basement of the Getty Museum and the ships of Cortés.

Standing in the Getty's courtyard the morning after seeing Karl, I warm my hands against a paper cup of coffee and look out at the ocean miles away. No one is here but the birds and the guards, it's so early. The cold weather glazes the magnificent buildings and sage grass. Steam from the coffee cup makes shapes in the air. Charcoal figures wearing stiff-brimmed hats move behind the windows.

Stunned from too little sleep and blinking at the dawn, I am still waking up. My imagination is the most supple at times like this, during the early hours when I can still feel connected to my dreams. Memories and trifles float and bump through my mind like dark leaves in water.

I sip my coffee, thinking of Karl, and the way he looked on the bed the day before. The thought makes me feel a little raw. I let myself drift into other fantasies, recollections.

It is not hard to do in a place like this.

Standing here, I could believe myself the queen of a deserted Greek kingdom in the far, far future. Modern battlements of travertine rise out of the sea mist, and the polished stone floor spreads like a perfect Sahara beneath my feet; here are the yarwoods, birds of paradise, the oaks and lavender; here is the heroic ocean, like another piece in this vast collection.

Getty, our benefactor, would have hated it. His biographers note that he preferred the look of old Italian villas or English mansions, as they helped maintain his hallucination that he was a British lord and no ordinary son of Minneapolis. All of his resources were devoted to this fiction—as they certainly were not invested in his family (he was married five times) or his friends (a notorious miser, he installed pay phones for guests at his Surrey estate). The only thing that mattered to him was cold and glittering rarities. He wanted to be remembered as a Medici. He wanted to live forever.

What a terrific failure. We remember not just his philanthropy but also his personal delinquencies and strange death (he passed, fully dressed in a Savile Row suit, ignoring his cancer pangs as he attempted to do paperwork at his desk). Sometimes I imagine Getty's shade floating through the museum's piazza and frightening the patrons by howling at the Schindler references, the feminist interpretations and Spanish translations. Instead of a simulacrum of the British Museum's hushed, gloved propriety, this poor shade sees hordes of minorities thronging through the halls of contemporary architecture.

Minorities like me. I've worked here for over six years and can think of few things better than spending my days in this cloister. At the moment the watery light spills over the galleries' faces of pale stone, a fossil-studded Tivoli travertine from the same quarry used to build St. Peter's Basilica. The rock glows shell-pale, with spots of light glinting off embedded crystals and the bone prints left by sea creatures that used to swim with Neptune. I am leaning up against the west pavilion's rotunda, and in a nearby stone I notice the skeleton of a leaf, each delicate vein perfectly preserved. A similar fossil will probably be found in Peter's Basilica, as identical rock was installed by Michelangelo's men during that great period of its construction, though the gold that floods its halls and lit the altar where Urban VIII prayed hailed from a different source—the melted American gods and glittering streambeds that once ran scarlet from murders committed in that same saint's name.

I love the museum because it is a garden of such secret histories. For the past few years, I've made a home in this place, surrounded by these relics of lost empires and the breath of the great dead. It's in the Getty that I've learned I have a knack for resurrecting and protecting a history that not everyone else can see, and it is one of the greatest passions in my life. I spend all my days, all my weekends, all my evenings at it, unless I'm with Karl. He has trouble understanding why I work as hard as I do, but I'm still looking for proof of my own past in these pages that I mend—maybe a foreign name obscured under a false title, the dusky blood in the provenance, an unexpected tint in the skin of a genius—any afterimage of the dark continents burned by the *lumen gratiae* of these brilliant civilizations protected by the Getty, and, more generally, anything that might rattle the cage of this perfect collection I feel so many things about. I suppose you could say I'm an eccentric looking for something that doesn't exist, like that famous cracked knight who saw a princess Dulcinea in the big-hipped girl busy slopping pigs. But though some of my esteemed colleagues do levy such slanders my way, they don't ruffle my whiskers even a little bit. When I do find these arcana—that is, now, when I do *establish* them—I know I'll have started to realize the aspiration that used to grip me when I'd dream my afternoons away in the university library, and when I'd think of my mother, as she's the one who first planted in me this hunger for our own burned and buried past.

Though she didn't imagine that I would ever wind up here.

She trained me from an early age to distrust this kind of zoo. And working as a conservator at the Getty does have a whiff of collaboration to it—I catalogue the gods plucked from dead temples; I store soldiers' stories in gilded rooms, even as those same soldiers burned other, strange libraries. A Mexican, she taught me, and a woman, can only have an uneasy rapport with these menageries. My mother died two decades ago, but I know that if she were still here she would tell me to quit this job that I love. She would want me to be an *enemy* of museums, donning a black cowl and stealing into archives to filch mummies, medals, idols, amphorae, in order to send them back to their homes.

But those are not my methods. I admire Mr. Getty's jewels with a Mexican eye. Sometimes I feel like a happy spy who lives in the emperor's castle.

If my mother were alive today, I'd tell her that I'm working toward her ends from the opposite angle.

All of us can identify accidents and inspirations experienced in early years that have guided us through our lives. My accident, my inspiration for all my work, has been my mother, Beatrice, though this may sound strange, as she was a magnificent criminal. And I mean that literally! She was a dazzling felon, cardamom-dark and black-eyed like her family in Jalisco, Mexico, and predisposed to poetry and illegality on account of a worldview that regarded everything around her as hijacked. After she and her mother immigrated here in 1944, my grandmother fell ill, and the impoverished young Beatrice thereafter suffered an adventure that I do not know too many details of, except that it involved being the consort of a wealthy Anglo man who expected liberal compensation for his patronage. As a consequence of this bargain, she developed a high-strung pessimism: She became a person who no longer could "believe everything she read"; she did not "judge books by their covers." And her incredulity did not soften after she met my father, Reynaldo, or experienced motherhood. She never forgot to look at the world with a sub-altern's eyes, and her skepticism flourished, perhaps too much, as, bit by bit, she eventually rejected a quantity of the premises that underwrite much social intercourse, which is the classic strategy of neurotics, novelists, and thieves.

To witness this development was also, as it turns out, a perfect education for a future custodian of incunabula.

When I was nine years old Mother took me to a show of pre-Hispanic artifacts at a Long Beach museum, a retrospective so provocatively exotic that it stunned the tongues of our town's art circle. I still remember the docents whispering among the ithyphallic sculptures, cagily pointing to the nonpornographic motifs, and pressing their faces up to the glass traps holding naked warriors wielding knives, nubile servant girls bearing grain.

Beatrice stopped in front of one display of a scrap of very large, old, thick paper upon which faded drawings of singing men could be seen. When I looked down at the sign I saw that the paper was a rare remnant of an *amoxtli*, or a sixteenth-century Mesoamerican book, made of the amate tree's crushed bark and inscribed in red and black ink by Nahuatl sages.

My mother remained in front of the bolted glass box that held the relic. She stayed there and stared at it for a very long time.

"All of this is stolen," she told me finally. "Did you know that?"

I only looked at her. She took a breath; her lips wavered.

"I am so homesick," she said.

She stared at the fragment for another moment then reached up and jiggled the bolt that locked the box. By virtue of a lucky negligence, the curator had forgotten to fasten it. It sprang open without any effort and the front glass panel slid open. She reached inside and fingered the page. No bells rang; the guard had turned the other way; docents chattered in another room. She lifted it from its plinth and rolled it into a scroll that she tucked into her bag. One patron, over by the Mayan stelae, gaped.

And then we left.

At home, we unrolled the soft and flaking page onto my parents' bed and looked at it. It was printed with spare drawings of an old man sitting before an assembled group of youths. Scrolls emanated from the elder's mouth—symbols that I would learn later are the pictographic signs for the speech of a *tlamatini*, or master of flower and song.

I finally got up the nerve to ask "Why'd you take it?" after about half an hour. Several people had already called us (we hadn't answered the phone), and some of them had been pounding on our door.

My mother smiled at me and let out her braids, shook her hair.

At this point the doorbell rang, and the knocking started up again.

I was terrified. I asked her again, why she had taken it.

"Why'd I take it? Because it didn't belong to them, that's why. It made me mad, *hija*. These museums are just like a big lie, you know? And those people, their eyes have no idea what they're looking at when they see the pretty pictures. To them it's invisible! They are looking at *me*, and they don't know it. They are looking at *you*. They might as well put us in one of those glass boxes. You get me?"

Now the knocking was louder. I heard the words, Museum Security.

"Oh, *sssssh,* don't get nervous," she continued. I can see it is hard to understand. And later, your father will say, *Oh, your mother, what a crazy-brain! What a nut case! Forget all that business she told you.* And it will be even more confusing. But between you and me, Sara, if you want to be a smart girl, my advice is for you to remember everything."

"Mom, you *stole* something from the museum."

"Yes, okay. I guess so. You could call it that. Your dad, he will call it that. This guy outside the door with the thumping will call it that. But *to steal, to lie*—these things are all upside down and sideways for me. Other people say those words, and I hear *blah blah blah.* And in this case—sure, those words have zero meaning. This book, what used to be this book, it was ripped off a long time ago before I ever saw it. But I already told you about that, didn't I? About the libraries?"

I shook my head, shrugged.

"I have told you so many stories, but not that one?" She traced the drawing with her fingers. The beads around her neck and wrists clicked. "Oh, you should know it, you'll run through life with the brains of an iguana if you don't. So, okay: *Years* back, a very hardheaded kid, a soldier named Bernal, followed General Cortés into the heart of Mexico, looking for gold. They wandered through the hot jungle, always moving to the right, so that this Spanish boy thought he was circling down to the center of the Earth or even Hell itself, but of course it would not be an *infierno* until he got there. When they finally arrived at the great city, filled with the temples and the gardens and the beautiful strangers who looked something like you and me, this soldier, he could not believe his eyes. Were these people animals? he wondered. Were they devils? So wild they looked with their black skin—they were pagans, surely. And more important, such creatures could not have any use for gold.

"And this idea, this gold, that is what kept him moving, though he was skinny as a chicken, and he was so tired. These dark girls, he thought, they will pour hot water into a gold bath and clean me with their soft hands when I am through with them. He planned to drink from cups of gold and bring a hundred perfect emeralds back to his wife. He gripped at his sword, dragging himself through the town, until he came upon a temple. At last, he said to himself, I will make my fortune here! This must be the place where they hide the treasure! And he was right. When he entered it, he saw that it was filled with *nothing but these books*. Worthless! the idiot shouted. I am tricked! he yelled. Or maybe, *just maybe* he looked at one of these books. Maybe he saw how perfect it was, and he put it into his pocket because be knew that *here* was the real gold. Maybe this paper here comes from the book he stole. But even if he was so smart that he could see he had found the true treasure, it did not matter. For now he could already smell smoke. He saw the flames eating the books. As he had stood there, trying to read these pages, the other soldiers had already set this magnificent library on fire."

My mother stopped talking. The phone now rang. There were voices behind the front door and another loud series of knocks.

She winced, but fixed her eyes on me, and touched me with her cold hand.

"Do you see what I'm trying to tell you?"

She looked lovely and strange, and I knew then that she wasn't like other people in some very important ways. I could smell her perfume—tuberose. I pressed my palm to the dark paper and the image of the man with the scroll on his tongue. And I didn't have the heart to tell her that I didn't see, I didn't understand her, at all.

My mother was arrested that evening for grand theft (the *amoxtli* remnant, even then, was worth almost one hundred and fifty thousand dollars), although my father, Reynaldo,

was able to get the charges dropped by encouraging the view
that she was experiencing a tragic but temporary klepto distress.
"Why you want to break my heart like this, *corazón?*" I heard him
asking her that night, through my bedroom wall. "*Mi* little
flower, *mi preciosa loca con la cabeza quebrada,* all I want is for *you*
to be happy. I give my *life* for this happiness, you know that. But
my baby, my birdbrain, you can't go stealing that shit from the
museum!" Mother didn't answer his arguments or inquiries, and
instead cried all night. I know that he couldn't decipher her
motives any more than I; she never explained them to him,
either. She died sixteen months later of a undiagnosed and con-
genital heart condition known as atrial septal defect, which is
nothing more complicated than a hole in the heart, and after she
was gone, subjects like this became off-limits because it hurt like
hell to talk about them out loud.

But I was afraid to forget her, and collected everything that I
could and stored her inside of me—every eyelash, the tones her
voice could take, the clicking of the beads around her wrists and
throat. When I got older, those memories did help me. I finally
figured out that on that afternoon she had, within the limitations
of her opportunities and era, tried to redress a nearly five
hundred-year-old theft—though this was a revelation that eventually tutored me to see the world, like her, "upside down and
sideways." By the time I reached college, I had already begun to
look inside books, museums, sculpture gardens, and not to
observe what lay on the surface of the images assembled there,
but to detect some secret that might lie beneath them—some
evidence of that crime she'd tried to redress, some other history
that escaped the bonfires—and that's been forgotten for centuries. It is a method of seeing that I have retained. This odd
habit of always peering under the skin of things has also kept my
mother alive for me, and so bright in my mind that lately I've
begun to think it is not always so good. I hope that when I
disrupt something in this *beautiful* museum I will feel better

about her death and her obsessions, which is why I work so hard. It is the reason I left Camp LeJeune and came to this temple built in Jean Paul Getty's memory. It is the reason I have not always been as available to Karl as I should.

It is also why I have now devoted myself to this old, contested book I call *The Conquest*.

This book is a charm. When I hold it I imagine all the dead men who once read it, the monks and the soldiers gasping at its racy sections. I can see financiers thumbing it like a shilling shocker and young girls sneaking peeks at the accounts of battle behind governesses' backs.

This book is a mystery.

Although the folio's plain morocco binding and Rotunda script dates it to sixteenth-century Spain, there is no record of its origin or early history. For over two hundred years it might have lain under glass in a palace or moldered in a barn—although it was most certainly stolen, perhaps several times. Nevertheless, we have no way of knowing, and so possess no obligations concerning its rightful owners, as it survives these eras without a trace until the year 1813, when it emerges in Madrid during the Peninsular Wars.

After Napoleon gave Spain to his fumbling brother as a gift, King Joseph did little more with his rule than aggravate the natives and the tough, tough British. He did, however, have the foresight to hire a highly efficient majordomo who catalogued each of the Crown's treasures. From these records we learn that included in the temporary sovereign's cache were a stable of jet Andalusians, Charles V's own gold tableware, a giant carved emerald from the Americas, and this modestly bound folio.

Maybe the King read it on the throne to take his mind off his losses, as the mountain guerrillas descended in the dark. Commander Jourdan assembled his staggering troops while

Arthur Wellesley's men stormed the countryside now black with musket smoke and cannon scars. Joseph ignored the sound of fire by losing himself in a scandalous passage of the book while irregulars approached his doors with daggers in hand.

Joseph fled with his treasures to Paris, and after that to Bordentown, New Jersey, where he would live for the following twenty years. The folio was sold there, and lingered in rich paneled libraries for the next century and a half, remaining largely unhandled because of translation difficulties—although I like to imagine some curious, bilingual debutante reading it, and becoming corrupted by its blasphemous and erotic content.

An anonymous seller put it up for sale last year, at a famous auction house in New York. Despite the folio's bad repair, the word had already spread that it was a recovered work of the insane novelist Padre de Pasamonte and so the lot spurred lively bidding. Still, there is no purse like the Getty's and we purchased it for an astonishing sum.

And so now, in a way, it's mine.

I am examining the folio at my desk, as blue light ripples in from the windows. The lab where I work sits on the bottom floor of the library, and is a large, white, open space housing several paper conservationists. The color in the room comes from the objects scattered casually on tables and windowsills: a seventeenth-century gilded Bible someone pulled down from storage; a Murano glass horse; oxblood pottery vases filled with blue bearded irises extending pollen tongues; rosewood lettering pens. There is also the oak book press, and a Benedictine book of hours from the fifteenth century. This last item sits on the table across from mine, at which my boss Teresa Shaughnessey sits and appears to labor over the book's fading illuminations. She bends her yellow-kerchiefed head over the pages; from under the paisley cotton tight gold scrolls of hair reflect the morning light—this is the first growth since her chemotherapy ended eight months before. Her fine pale face, with its wedges of cheekbone and the gray eyes with their small fringe of bronze lashes, hovers over a picture of Bathsheba posing near a fountain in a transparent dress as David admires her from a window in a tower. Age and oxygen distress the portrait; when Teresa touches the fountain with her finger the page tints her flesh with crumbled blue, though this does not make her snatch her hand away.

"I can go get you a pair of gloves if you want me to," I say.

"No thanks." She smiles up at me. "Don't look so nervous, I'm not *hurting* it, sweetheart."

"The paint's coming off."

She looks at her finger and smiles. "So it is!" Closing the book, she props her elbows on it and cups her chin in her hands. "You'll never guess where I went last night. I had the most naughty and *delicious* evening!"

"I don't know. Let's see—a strip club?"

"No, I gorged on those months ago. And all that flapping about does get on the nerves, I have to say. I went to this fantastic club in Hollywood where these pretty little girls played some sort of feminist acid rock until four in the morning. Amazing! They wore tiny dresses made of…some kind of electric tape, I believe, strategically placed, and they had the most wonderfully filthy mouths. All very fuck this and fuck that, phallus this, prick that, while they flung their pink hair about like Medusas. It was not as vulgar as it must sound. It was almost beautiful, like one of those fabulous car crashes by Carlos Almaraz."

I shake my head at her.

"Aren't you quite too young to be a prude, Sara? I wish you could have come, but then you would have had to stay up until two o'clock in the morning, and I know that *you* like to be asleep by eight."

"That's not true."

"It is unless you're having another one of your flings with that paramour of yours. Karl, the dashing sailor."

"The dashing marine—whom I did see yesterday, I'll have you know."

"Well, bravo. At least there's that. But you should come out with me some evening—there are the most absurd things to see in this town after dark. Not that I would have known it a year ago. Sweetie, I was just like you, so angelic and responsible and, excuse me, boring. And after the hospital...you know, I realized— What have I been doing all these years? Spending it here, alone? Watching the damned television? Now, of course, I go to clubs, I go out dancing, and then there are my lovely parties,"—here, her voice lowered into a whisper—"In fact, I think I will invite a few friends to the museum next month for another soirée. What do you think? Canapés? Champagne, foie gras? A giant tiramisu?"

"No foie gras," I say.

Teresa continues ticking off her menu for the next of her secret parties (secret, at least from the Getty's trustees) that are a kind of museum geek's equivalent of the goings-on in the basement of Studio 54 during the early 70s. They are scandalous extravaganzas, which only a select few are invited to, as they are constructed around the premise of gallivanting around the museum as if it were your own home, where you can prop your feet up on the eighteenth-century silk divan once owned by Napoleon and sip gimlets from gold goblets that littered the tables of Rudolf II.

I've told her a million times that her fêtes are unethical, and probably even felonious, even if they're events at which the most mousy curators, antiquities experts, historians, restorers, and archaeologists go positively bananas with fun. But she ignores me. Before each party, Teresa pays off the guards, and after the museum has closed she turns off the alarms in one or two galleries, then removes the silk ropes from the antique settles and fauteuils and hauls out the Louis XIV silver from Decorative Arts. By midnight, the place is jumping. Scholars french-kiss and sip Cosmopolitans on neoclassical chaise longues, or attempt to dance to the low jazz bubbling from a boom box, taking time-outs to peer up at the Rembrandts, Turners, Titians, getting as close to the work as they like. No whoop whoop sounds when they get within sixteen inches of the French canvas or Aztec calendar; no warning bells shriek when they drink from an Etruscan chalice or slip on the pure gold armband made by sixth-century Mayans. A month ago a squib of duck liver did flop onto the peach satin of a rococo sofa, and last winter a drunk Egyptologist left a light lipstick imprint on a Vermeer when she tried to kiss it—disasters that I spent frantic weeks remedying. I play a kind of cop at these parties, armed with Q-Tips and foaming soap, terrified of red wine, and go especially crackers when anybody gets close to the pre-Columbian artifacts, but even I have to admit that our inventory doesn't show one theft and no one has blown the whistle on Teresa. As she points out, she's only satisfying an innocent fetish: The experts who have committed themselves to preserving precious artifacts also have a mania for touching and using them—many say they've felt closer to the eras of their obsession when they can handle their relics like ordinary things.

If you'd asked any of them a year ago, though, not one would have guessed that Teresa Shaughnessey, Ph.D., winner of a Guggenheim, a MacArthur "genius" grant, onetime lecturer at Harvard in book arts, author of three monographs on Padeloup bindings and two on fore-edge paintings, should be the one to give them the opportunity.

For twenty long years she was the undisputed queen of incunabula restoration, having devoted her life energies to the problems of faded watered-silk endpapers, disintegrating German Girdle books, the three best ways to restore the delicate miniatures of Domenico Ghirlandaio. She was respected, yes, but not well-liked. She was not known by anyone well enough to be liked. Dr. Shaughnessey, as we called her, wore her hair in a tight little bun and bulky snowflake-patterned sweaters that could not drown her huge breasts; she shuffled down the hallways with her head tilted in a strange birdlike angle toward the ground and made eye contact with no one. Occasionally, she would peer up from her work and give a colleague a shy smile, but then snap her eyes right back down to work. And there were rumors that Dr. Shaughnessey held eccentric conversations either with herself or with her books—rumors that I started, actually, since we shared an office and I'd occasionally catch her in the midst of some comic observations, or even laughing at one of her own jokes, but as soon as she saw me she turned as quiet as a cat.

Then she became sick. This, again, was rumor, as she simply vanished for six months, and the disappearance was shrouded in an eerie silence. When she returned, though, we knew from the different shape of her sweater and her sleek head that the stories were true. And it was not just the cosmetics that had changed. During her first week back, when I referred to her by the title I always used, she placed her hand on my shoulder, then asked me to call her by her first name. I obliged; she took me to lunch, and our intimacy dates from that afternoon. She was confiding, though exhausted from her treatment. She told me that despite her fatigue she had started meeting people, going dancing, and in general trying to "gobble up the gorgeous world." She also said she was going to quit.

"I have discovered that I've made the terrible error of substituting *objects* for people in my life," she said, chewing on her sandwich. "Quite depressing, really. Dashes of paint on a canvas take the place of lovers. Leather and paper replace a child. History?! My hallowed passion! It is nothing more than a phantom, which though entertaining cannot be *kissed*. It simply does not exist—try to touch it in a hospital, Sara, while you are imprisoned in all that gleaming progress. It disappears like ether! There is no *real* life in a *Morte d'Arthur*, is there? No matter how gorgeous the binding? Happiness does not reside in Gutenberg's ink. Not even in your precious Mexican calendars, I think, dear. Everything should be used up, swallowed up! *Not* saved. Not hoarded like the bones of saints. And I *do* see this place as a kind of fantastic tomb. What I am saying to you is, this is a long-delayed offer of friendship. I was *such* an idiot for keeping to myself for so long. It is also, however, a good-bye. I am quitting the museum to become...I don't know. A travel agent, perhaps. A dog groomer. Something a bit more substantial, I hope."

But she wouldn't get her wish. The Getty would not let her go—not its most gifted restorer, not the woman who had resurrected Joachim of Fiore's *Vaticinia Pontificum* from a few scraps of dirty vellum into a glowing scripture! Not the magician who had conjured Francesco Alvarotti's glittering *Consilia et allegationes* out of a heap of filthy leather! They offered her money, then more money, then so much she had to stay. On her own terms, though—which are, I have to say, essentially dangerous to the historical project. She is a kind of saboteur. Most of her efforts to restore books have ceased, since she doesn't see the effort as worthwhile any longer, and believes even the greatest, most beautiful works should be allowed to molder gracefully into the ground or, better yet, be worn down to smooth nubs after being handled, touched, experienced directly, and not in the white-gloved way we currently interact with the great relics. And so she will filch a precious folio from storage and bring it to a local middle school, where she'll let the students leaf through the vivid pages (after washing their hands, at least). And so she'll let the moldering folios' pages bloom with perilous green gardens (I am trying to fix these in my spare time). And so the parties, where all the laws of preservation-observation are suspended—which she continues talking about now.

"You *are* coming?" she asks. "It's going to be an amazing time. I'm holding it in the south pavilion, with all the rococo.

And I think I'll drag out some of the gowns from storage, like the ones we bought last year, supposedly worn by Veronica Franco?"

"I don't think I can make it. I have a lot of work to do."

"Not on *that?*" She points at *The Conquest.* "You could finish it during work hours, shouldn't take you more than six months. *If* you want to do it, that is."

"I want to do it."

"I certainly don't see what all your fuss is about. Like I've said before, I think this whole business is ludicrous."

"What we do is not ludicrous, Teresa."

"Well, I think you're particularly consumed with this one, in any event. And have you catalogued it yet? Under *de Pasamonte?*"

"I'm still working on my theory."

"Yes, my sweet, I have noticed that you seem to be in the thrall of another one of your bat-brained hypotheses. File it under *Peter Pan* for all I care, but for Christ's sake don't get fixated."

"Unlike some people I care if the cataloguing's accurate."

Teresa closes her book of hours and looks at me. "If you *insist*—I will go over this with you. *Again.* Unfortunately for you, I am nearly an expert on our old padre. In 1560, '66, '68, de Pasamonte writes *Las Tres Furias, La Noche Triste,* and *El Santo de España*—books with the same simple morocco, what looks to be the same handwriting. Am I wrong? No. And they have the same themes, the same narrative style."

"But those books were signed. And I don't think a man wrote this. I don't think a *Spaniard* could have written this book."

"Well, Mr. Joyce made old Molly Bloom up, didn't he?"

"This is different."

"And how is this so very different?"

I can feel my face flush. I look down and flip the book's pages. "I don't know. I just think it is."

"Well, I'm not going to press you on it anymore. I can see you're getting upset."

"I'm not upset."

"Of course you are! You're a sensitive one! And I used to be just like you, worrying and bollixing over every little thing. But that's not what I wanted to talk to you about today. I only want you to come to my party. *Do* come. It will be such a blast!"

I tilt my head up at her, and smile. "Actually, I may not be able to for another reason."

"Which is?"

"Karl. I hope I'll be seeing him that night."

"Oh dear, there's no competing with a naked man, even I know that. So, in that case, I will let you off. But just this once."

Grinning, she reopens her book of hours, and turns away from me. On the page in front of her, Bathsheba continues shimmering half-naked by the fountain; David gawks from his tower.

I return to *The Conquest*.

I open the front board to the first flyleaf. Immediately, a scent of dust and age reaches me, and after that the faded words.

Reading has always been like dreaming for me, and I have to settle into a story much as the mind slowly rises from sleep into the night's strange forest. If I'm reading a love story, let's say a tragedy, some feature of the beloved's comes into focus first— Anna Karenina's eyes, dark as wine, then the glimmer of a gold thread in her dress. Sensations overlap from page to page like lines of music, for on top of the dress and eyes is Karl's face, or my mother's. Next comes the thread of a mazurka, pale breath in the train station, then the face of Tolstoy, white-bearded and dying in Astapovo. Last, there's the feel of the book under my hand.

The book is a body and your mind will mold to its individual curves much in the way it will to any other lover—at least, until it buckles beyond use.

That's where I come in.

The folio's text block has almost completely loosened from the case; the spine has broken. The morocco peels back from the boards and there is a canker of mold on the last twenty pages, which, besides damaging the vellum, also obscures the script. I spent several months studying the best approach to its restoration, and then cleaned the leather and sized and washed the leaves. Now I am onto the next stage, which is repairing the ulcered sections of the book's skin with the Japanese paper, dyed the same old-blood color as the morocco. The leaves will be mended with this same, undyed paper. For the text, I'll mix an ink of my own recipe—a silky, mink-colored ink, an ink like the one Cervantes once used—and repaint the Rotunda characters with one of Teresa's beautiful rosewood lettering pens.

But not *too* well. Out of respect for all of the dead, some sign of the centuries should stay. And besides, the book is a different thing now than when it was first written. The author's hands were once here (delicate, I'm sure, a small brown woman's hands, and not a pale monk's), but also thieves', and a thieving king's, and eons of New Jersey scions. To remind readers of this history I won't repair this scar on the back board, or even repaint the less faded letters.

I now lift the book off the desk, and flakes of vellum come off on my palms. Every time I pick up this volume, microscopic bits must erode onto my skin or travel from my fingers up to my lips, and in this way my cells absorb them like a poison or an oral vaccine.

A few years ago, while perusing a volume on extreme cases of philobiblism for my own amusement, I read about a psychotic who loved books so much he ate them julienned and pan-roasted with potatoes, bell peppers, and a little garlic. Bibliophagia, I think was the diagnosis. I wondered what effect the works of Dickens would have on such a gourmand, as opposed to, say, those of Balzac or Schopenhauer.

I wonder what effect this book might be having on me.

Something is loosening inside of me; I feel a new transparency, a susceptibility. At night I have difficulty getting to sleep, as I'm plagued by fantasies. I imagine myself outside of Karl's apartment, looking up at his window from the shadows. I'd like to serenade him as the Italians did; I would sing an aria from *Don Giovanni* before scaling his balcony and kissing his mouth so that I am perched, thrilled, in thin air.

Maybe the girl who wrote these pages is running through me like a drug borne on a scrap of paper. A girl Teresa thinks was a wayward monk. A love affair no one but me thinks really existed. I think this mysterious narrator is affecting me somehow. She makes me want to go to extremes. After feasting on her story, I feel brave enough to scale a tower for Karl. I would ignore the limitations of my era and sex and win him in sword battle like a sixteenth-century *magnifico*. I would embrace him in the long, wet grass until he remembered no other name but my own.

I turn the flyleaf. I read.

D. J. Waldie

from *Holy Land*

D. J. Waldie was born in 1948 in Lakewood, California. His books include *Holy Land: A Suburban Memoir, Where We Are Now: Notes from Los Angeles,* and, most recently, *Close to Home: An American Album.* In 1994 he received a National Endowment for the Arts fellowship and *Holy Land* received the California Book Award for nonfiction from the Commonwealth Club of California. He still lives in Lakewood, where he is the public relations officer.

This excerpt is from the opening pages of *Holy Land,* published in 1996. Waldie combines a minute biography of Lakewood, the first suburb built around a shopping mall, with a lyrical and restrained personal memoir.

1

That evening he thought he was becoming his habits, or— even more—he thought he was becoming the grid he knew.

He knew his suburb's first 17,500 houses had been built in less than three years. He knew what this must have cost, but he did not care.

The houses still worked.

He thought of them as middle class even though 1,100-square-foot tract houses on streets meeting at right angles are not middle class at all.

Middle-class houses are the homes of people who would not live here.

2

In a suburb that is not exactly middle class, the necessary illusion is predictability.

3

When he thinks of his parents, he remembers them as they were in their early middle age—energetic, strong, and more capable than any other adult he knew.

He is older now than his parents had been then, and he is less competent than his father and mother seemed to him, even less competent than they were in fact.

This thought rarely troubles him.

4

Whether liked or disliked, it is for himself, and not for what he has done, that others judge him. He has generally done nothing at all.

5

It rained once for an entire week in 1953, when I was five. The flat streets flooded. Schools closed. Only the rain happened, while I waited at the window.

Waiting was one of the first things I understood fully. Rain and the hydrogen bomb were two aspects of the same loss.

6

Moral choice does not enter his thinking.

He believes, however, that each of us is crucified. His own crucifixion is the humiliation of living the life he has made for himself.

7

You and I grew up in these neighborhoods when they were an interleaving of houses and fields that were soon to be filled with more houses.

A particular sound marked the boundary of the neighborhood. It was the barking of dogs near full dark in summer. Do you remember it?

The flat barking skipped from block to block, unhinged from causes, not necessarily your neighbors' dog, but their dog too.

That sound became the whole neighborhood clearing its throat before going to bed and sleep.

8

At some point in your story grief presents itself.

Now, for the first time, your room is empty, not merely unoccupied.

9

Before they put a grid over it, and restrained the ground from indifference, any place was as good as any other.

10

There were only a few trees here, eighty years ago. They were eucalyptus trees near some farm buildings, deliberately planted for shade. Men waited under them before their work began.

The men's faces were brown on the jaw and chin, and pale above.

In the fields, only the upper part of a man's face is shaded by his hat, salt-stained along the base of the crown.

Work began for the men when each man pulled himself to a high wooden seat above a harvester's moving rack of teeth.

This contraption was pulled by twenty mules, straining as the men joked.

11

The grid is the plan above the earth. It is a compass of possibilities.

12

In 1949, three developers bought 3,500 acres of Southern California farmland.

They planned to build something that was not exactly a city. In 1950, before the work of roughing the foundations and pouring concrete began, the three men hired a young photographer with a single-engine plane to document their achievement from the air.

The photographer flew when the foundations of the first houses were poured. He flew again when the framing was done and later, when the roofers were nearly finished. He flew over the shell of the shopping center that explains this and many other California suburbs.

The three developers were pleased with the results. The black-and-white photographs show immense abstractions on ground the color of the full moon.

Some of the photographs appeared in *Fortune* and other magazines. The developers bound enlargements in a handsome presentation book. I have several pages from one of the copies.

The photographs celebrate house frames precise as cells in a hive and stucco walls fragile as an unearthed bone.

Seen from above, the grid is beautiful and terrible.

13

Four of the young man's photographs became the definition of this suburb, and then of suburbs generally.

The photographs look down before the moving vans arrived, and before you and I learned to play hide-and-seek beneath the poisonous oleander trees.

Architectural critics and urban theorists reprinted the photographs in books with names like *God's Own Junkyard*. Forty years later, the same four photographs still stand for the places in which most of us live.

The photographs were images of the developers' crude pride. They report that the grid, briefly empty of associations, is just a pattern predicting itself.

The theorists and critics did not look again, forty years later, to see the intersections or calculate in them the joining of interests, limited but attainable, like the leasing of chain stores in a shopping mall.

14

In the Los Angeles basin, the possibility of rain is ignored until the rain falls. Since it hardly ever rains, ignorance has prevailed as climate.

15

The local newspaper in 1956 used a picture to show how much had changed. This picture "Harvesting, 1900."

It shows a team of mules, a combine harvester, the field, and the men. The mules are sawteeth of black; the combine is a grand contraption in gray; the field is all design.

You cannot make out the men. They are patterns in the photograph.

16

My father's kindness was as pure and indifferent as a certain kind of saint's.

My father did not have a passion for his giving; it came from him, perhaps after much spiritual calculation, as a product might come from a conveyor belt.

The houses in this suburb were built the same way. As many as a hundred a day were begun between 1950 and 1952, more than five hundred a week. No two floor plans were built next to each other; no neighbor had to stare into his reflection across the street.

Teams of men built the houses.

Some men poured concrete into the ranks of foundations from mixing trucks waiting in a mile-long line. Other men threw down floors nailed with pneumatic hammers, tilted up the framing, and scaled the rafters with cedar shingles lifted by conveyer belts from the beds of specially built trucks.

You are mistaken if you consider this a criticism, either of my father or the houses.

17

Construction crews in thirty-man teams built the rows of houses. Each team of workmen was subdivided by specialty.

One man with a pneumatic hammer nailed subfloors on five houses a day. The framers finished lengths of precut lumber with new, electric saws. Another crew operated a power door hanger.

Rough plaster laid by one crew was smoothed a few minutes later by another.

Subcontractors delivered construction materials in exact amounts directly to each building site. Expediters coordinated the work from radio-equipped cars.

The foreman used a loudspeaker to direct the movement of his men.

18

Mr. F laid rafters for hundreds of these houses. According to Mr. F, it didn't take much skill.

The most experienced men did the framing, by assembling pieces that had been precut at the mill. Laying rafters only required knowing how to swing a hammer all day.

By 1951, the construction bosses had hired more than four thousand workmen. They were mostly unskilled veterans still in their twenties. They learned how to lay rafters—or they didn't learn—in a day or two.

The men who put up with the pace and the monotony stayed on. They earned about a dollar an hour.

19

According to Mr. F, the speed of the work depended on a gimmick called a "scaffold jack." The jack made it possible for two men to begin laying rafters with no time wasted in setting up a freestanding scaffold.

Instead, braces cut from channel iron, each fitted with two bars of sawteeth that bit into the wood stud, could be nailed up quickly on the skeletal frame of the house.

Each jack held a short length of two-by-four. On these projecting arms the roofers laid the planks on which they stood to work.

The jacks transmitted the weight of the cantilevered scaffold planks to the studs of the house frame. The planks and the men themselves made the jack bite securely into the wood.

Simple forces supported the planks, the men, and the scaffold jacks hanging about six feet above the ground.

20

The scaffold jacks were ingenious and economical. A pair could be cut and welded together from a single, eighteen-inch length of channel iron.

The process of setting the jacks up on the studs and laying the scaffold planks took the men only a few minutes.

The jack let each completed house supply the support for the next construction step. It was like lifting yourself by your bootstraps, Mr. F said.

The scaffold jack didn't last.

In the 1960s, the standard two-by-four stud was pared down to reduce lumber costs. Today, a two-by-four is one-and-a-half inches by three-and-a-half inches.

Mr. F says a scaffold jack would snap one of these new studs in two.

21

If the workmen looked up from laying rafters, they saw a row of houses with bundles of shingles being lifted by conveyor belts to shinglers on the roof. Beyond them was a row of house frames being sheathed in tar paper and chicken wire. Beyond them was another row of houses gray with new stucco. Beyond that row would be another row of houses, only a few days older, being painted.

Behind them, nearly out of sight, would be a street of finished houses, forty-six to a block.

To the workmen, suspended on the scaffold, these finished houses must have seemed out of place and very still.

22

The Los Angeles Daily News described the construction of the houses as a huge assembly line.

23

Mr. F made the city a detailed scale model of a garage being framed.

He wanted to show school children, who sometimes tour city hall, how efficiently he had laid rafters as a young man.

His model includes a set of full-size scaffold jacks mounted on two uprights with a short length of scaffold plank between them.

The model garage is mounted on a table Mr. F built. The entire display, including the table and model, is about five-and-a-half feet high.

The roof of the scale model is about half laid, so that the pattern of rafters can be seen.

Mr. F put a Ken doll on the model scaffold to show how the roofers worked. Ken is holding a tiny hammer.

24

Daily life here has an inertia that people believe in.

In the city's most recent opinion survey, 92 percent of the residents believe this suburb is a desirable place in which to live.

Such is the attraction of suburbs. You look out your kitchen window to the bedroom window of your neighbor precisely fifteen feet away.

25

The distance between my house and yours is a separation the suburb's designers carefully planned. It is one of the principal factors in determining the number of houses per acre in a subdivision. The number of houses per acre is the subdivision's yield. This is a measure of its profitability, which is not the number of houses that can be sold, but the subdivision's population density.

Density is what developers sell to the builders of shopping centers.

26

The average number of houses per acre in prewar subdivisions had been about five.

In the suburb where I live, begun in 1950, the number of houses per acre is eight.

The houses were designed by an architect named Paul Duncan.

27

You leave the space between the houses uncrossed. You rarely go across the street, which is forty fect wide.

You are grateful for the distance. It is as if each house on your block stood on its own enchanted island, fifty feet wide by one hundred feet long.

People come and go from it, your parents mostly and your friends. Your parents arrive like pilgrims.

But the island is remote. You occasionally hear the sounds of anger. You almost never hear the sounds of love.

You hear, always at night, the shifting of the uprights, the sagging of ceiling joists, and the unpredictable ticking of the gas heater.

28

What is beautiful here?

The calling of a mourning dove, and others answering from yard to yard. Perhaps this is the only thing beautiful here.

29

What more can you expect of me than the stories I am now telling?

David Mas Masumoto

"Pruning Generations"
from *Harvest Son*

David Mas Masumoto was born in 1954 and is a third-generation
farmer as well as the author of many books, including *Harvest
Son: Planting Roots in American Soil, Epitaph for a Peach: Four
Seasons on My Family Farm,* and *Letters to the Valley: A Harvest of
Memories.* He received the James Clavell Japanese American
National Literacy Award in 1986 and the San Francisco Review
of Books Critics' Choice Award in 1995. Masumoto grows
peaches, grapes, and raisins with his father on their organic
farm in Del Rey, south of Fresno.

"Pruning Generations" is excerpted from *Harvest Son:
Planting Roots in American Soil,* which was published in 1998.
With rich and disarming detail, this memoir tells of the struggle
to take over and renew the family farm.

Grapevines do not have brilliant autumn colors, they initially
turn yellow. With a freeze near Thanksgiving, a white frost

dusts the fields and as it melts, the leaves become brown—life has been sucked from them with the cold. The brittle foliage clings to the canes and will not fall off until a good rainstorm pounds them to the ground. That's when I return to farmwork.

Next year's harvest will only emerge from one-year-old wood; the old canes needed to be cut, discarded, and replaced with the new. As a youngster I pruned thousands of vines, yet somehow this year is different. The vines look foreign, shrouded in the damp fog. The moisture stains the canes dark and paints the older bark a glossy black. Each twist of a gnarled trunk casts a deep shadow and creates the illusion of a cavern cut deep into the heart of the stump. Only four or five feet tall, the vines appear hunched over like old men.

Before I start pruning, I remove some of the oddly shaped vines with their contorted features. The worst ones resemble an S shape, decades ago yanked in one direction, pulled back years later, and then bent with yet another season. They're old and the canes grow weaker with each harvest. I open a folding handsaw and grip the wooden handle as I start ripping into the bark with its coarse steel teeth. The brittle wood breaks and peels off in thin strips, scattering onto the green winter weeds and the damp earth. My arms pump back and forth until the teeth finally grab and a familiar "haaack" sound establishes a cadence. The vine topples, and at the stump a white woody membrane is exposed, the living tissue remarkably only a few inches wide, protected by layers and layers of bark. A clear fluid bleeds from the opening, dripping onto the earth and creating a small mud puddle. Later, if there's a morning sun, the beads of moisture catch the light and sparkle.

Most of the time the fog masks landmarks. A hundred feet from our house I'm invisible and alone. I can hear sounds, a door slamming, an engine starting, voices of my mom asking Dad if he'll be in for lunch. I trudge to the farthermost field and start pruning. I can barely see around me—the sky is cast in a glaring gray. The only sounds are my footsteps sliding on the damp earth and fallen leaves and the dripping of dew from saturated vines.

Is this how my *jiichan*/grandpa first saw a grapevine—a strange creature with wild growth dangling from a dark body? The rows of vines look like a silent column of prisoners, their trunks bent and twisted, their arms held upward in surrender. The canes droop like elongated fingers with an occasional leaf clinging as a decorative ring, flapping with a slight shift in the air.

I wonder if Jiichan Masumoto, arriving in America a century ago in 1899 and having never seen a vine before, yet hungry for work, lied to get a job and told the farmer, "Yes, yes, I work," then followed the crew into the vineyard and watched the others while they whispered in Japanese, telling him what to do.

"Give me five canes and two spurs," the farmer may have told my grandfather. Five canes? Spurs? These were words he had never heard before, the language of a new world he had to learn.

Other immigrant groups arrived at a similar time in the San Joaquin Valley of California. They planted their family farm traditions from their homelands—the Germans and Portuguese brought dairies and the Italians their vineyards and wineries. But the Issei came from farming villages where rice and barley were planted each spring, followed by summer weeding and irrigation, and an early autumn harvest. During the winter, the paddies were turned and prepared for another year as they had been for centuries. Pruning vines was not natural for my grandfather.

Did he still think in Japanese? What terms did he use for things he had never seen before? Did he call a vine cane the same word he used for the branches of the wild berries in Japan? What words did he use for "to prune a vine"? It's not the same as a *bonsai* gardener's meticulous pruning and shaping, where a branch is carefully clipped and wired and a stem is trimmed and braced or a stone is roped to a limb, the dangling weight gradually drawing the wood downward, redirecting growth. Did Jiichan think in English? Wasn't learning English part of becoming an American? I grew up sometimes hearing the phrase *Hayaku!* or "Hurry up!" Farmworkers were usually paid by piecework, and the only "art" to pruning was the art of making money by working as fast as you could and racing to the next vine. Good pruners eye the thick wood and quickly hack at the rest, slashing at the mass of canes, yanking the severed limbs and tossing them in between the rows.

Grapevines last for generations; some of ours are eighty years old. The first permanent plantings on this land were in the year my grandmother, Baachan Masumoto, immigrated to America in 1918: according to records, the farmer before us planted 2,640 Thompson seedless vines that year. Jiichan may have pruned our farm's vines as a farmworker. He, along with thousands of immigrant laborers, helped to establish and maintain the lush fields of our valley. Over the decades, little has changed. Farmers still hand-prune each vine, every row needs irrigating and plowing, and the late-summer harvests demand thousands of workers to pick and dry the grapes into raisins. Technology has not replaced the human element. Vineyards still require people to care for them.

I learned to prune by watching my parents and Baachan. They'd take us kids out into the fields, bundle us up to block the winter winds and damp fog. We'd stiffly stand alongside them as they pulled and stripped the clippings from the wire trellis. Mom and Dad tackled two rows at a time, each row twelve feet apart. Most rows were less than a hundred vines long, with a single wire stretching down every column and anchored to end posts. While my older brother and sister helped my parents, I'd play and wrestle with a long branch that sometimes stretched over ten feet, first pretending it to be a snake or whip until it broke into a sword. As I grew older and bored with childish games, I was anxious to learn farmwork. I too wanted to help the family.

By ten, I was given my own pruning shears, an old set with mismatched wooden handles and a well-oiled cutting head. I was allowed to slice the center brush off from the wires, canes from the prior year that were tightly wrapped around the trellis. (Grape bunches grew and hung from these branches.)

One of the few Japanese terms I grew up with was *naka-giri,* meaning "cut the center." *Naka-giri* was a mindless, tedious task, perfectly suited for us three children. We'd slice the wood, making a series of incisions, breaking the cord into smaller sections, then pulling them from the trellis, yanking and snapping the limbs, dragging them to the spaces between the rows. Right behind us worked Mom and Dad, finishing each vine, selecting the right canes for next year.

Baachan Masumoto usually helped me, the youngest and slowest. I'm not sure if she chose to *naka-giri* with the kids or felt too slow and old for the tougher job of finishing a vine. Surely she had mastered the art of pruning after six decades working in the fields. But perhaps she now enjoyed a freedom from responsibility, knowing someone else would complete her work.

Winters in the Central Valley of California are cold but not harsh. Night temperatures drop to freezing but usually warm to the forties by midmorning. Fog dampens spirits with a gray, wet chill. Since vines are spaced only a few feet apart, the whole family could work next to each other, close enough to talk and prune under watchful eyes.

We worked without gloves, and our exposed cheeks and ears turned a rosy blush in the frigid air. Inevitably branches tangled. I'd tug and pull, trying to free the mess, until finally something would crack and a cane would whip loose. Quickly I'd turn and close my eyes, but often too late; a cry would escape my throat as the wood slapped my face: a sharp bite, then a raw sting shooting across my cheek as I grimaced in pain. I'd drop my shears and run my cold fingers across the flesh, feeling for blood. Rarely, though, did my skin break; instead my eyes watered and I gritted my teeth until the stabbing ache gave way to a numbness on the surface. With tears running down, I'd begin again, sniffling and wincing, trying to work despite the throbbing.

Through moist eyes, I'd detect a motion and find Dad working the vine ahead of me. He said nothing as his powerful shears chopped the wood into small sections, making it easier to dislodge the old growth.

I can't recall a specific lesson in how to prune. While other boys were learning to catch a ball or cast a line, I watched my father snip and cut, shaping his vines into a work of art. His canes were thick, spread evenly on both sides of the vine, making them easy to lash to the wire without breaking. He snipped and grabbed the end of a branch that wore the telltale gray of frostbite instead of the normal creamy tan. He bent the tip around toward his eyes. The wood crackled and stretched but did not snap. If he found the fiber brittle and dried, he'd chop the limb back until he uncovered the pale green tissue of life.

Grape bunches will emerge from the nodes three or four inches from the trunk but usually not more than four feet away. Stepping back, Dad would scan the entire vine, judging if the remaining canes were too short for a healthy crop, evaluating if skinny ones were worth leaving. On each vine, he also tried to leave three or four "spurs," short stubs from which new canes for next year would sprout, destined to bear another harvest. His eyes darted back and forth, searching and comparing, envisioning the future.

My first attempts to prune made the vines look as though they had passed through a shredder. The canes hung limp and lacked strong structure and definition; they seemed out of balance, as if the branches I had chosen to save did not belong. I sometimes forgot to check for the strangely beautiful but sterile gray hue of frostbite, which meant that later in the year, when sap and water flowed through the rest of the vine, my branches would snap when pulled. They would never again produce grapes. Occasionally I neglected to leave spurs, cleanly snipping off old growth before remembering I should have left a foundation for the future.

Eventually it dawned on me why my early years of pruning resulted in such poor craftsmanship. Some of it had to do with my poor skills, but a lot had to do with a father giving his young son a scraggly old vine to start with. Dad had forced me to learn with the hardest vines. I can hear the collective voice of all sage farmers: why sacrifice a good vine on an inexperienced son?

Now I prune by first selecting the strong and discarding the weak wood. Then I search for the thickest canes evenly spaced around the vine head, leaving spurs in open locations for next year's growth. Over the years I have learned to distinguish wood potentially damaged by frost. I go by color, feel, and sound. A hoary white hue becomes a sign of frostbite. Then, when I snip the end of a stem, healthy tissue will slice but dead wood will snap. Through my shears I can feel and hear the difference if my blade splinters and mangles the dried fibers with a flat "whack" instead of the crisp incision of steel as it severs a limb.

I make over fifty cuts per vine, fifty decisions within a few minutes. Despite the detailed work, I slip into a cadence, a pace that allows time for my thoughts to wander. My arms and hands recall the familiar rhythms; my muscles have retained their memory of farmwork. I yank and the wire stretches and pulls against the metal stakes. The steel creaks and moans. The branches hold fast and I cannot snap the bundled wood. I look for an opening to slip my rounded shear point into and snip the strands into short segments. I then grab and rip the wood free. The entire row shakes with my tug. With brute force I try to snap the remaining branches, but they resist. Older men use more center cuts to free the wood; younger pruners sever the growth by force.

After the first vines I stop struggling. There are too many to fight. I need to play farm games to combat the monotony. I have a friend who, as a child of a poor family, spent hours and hours in the fields. He developed a wild imagination, creating space invaders out of unpruned vines, monsters with tentacles waiting to coil around small boys. In his mind, a young vine next to an old, gnarled one was one of those petrified boys. So he attacked each vine, madly chopping away at the brush in order to defend himself. They'd attack him over and over and he'd chop and clip and slash until he had defeated the vine and only a manageable five canes remained. Then he'd let the branches dangle in defeat. Later the space police would arrive and tie up these prisoners, lashing them to the overhead wires.

I frequently play strategic games of controlling territory, approaching a ten-acre block of vines by attacking each row from the ends and then, over the next few days, advancing toward the middles, pretending to surround my opponent, then asking for unconditional surrender. Working one row at a time becomes overwhelming; I look up and see an entire field unpruned and feel discouraged. Completing the first few vines all along an avenue seems like progress—I can walk home at dusk bolstered with a sense of accomplishment. I think of the Japanese game of go—on a grid-patterned gameboard, opponents try to capture territory through a series of encounters, but losing a particular battle does not necessarily mean the loss of the game.

Did my father play games while he pruned? Did Jiichan? I never thought of them engaging in childhood games. I have trouble imagining them as children. As I prune, a loose cane snaps free and grabs my jacket. I whip around and slash at the tentacle, liberating myself with a triumphant "haaa!"

Many of the vines are old and I have trouble finding good canes. I feet like a geriatric nurse searching for good blood vessels in his patients. Yet considering their lengthy time of service and occasional abuse by young pruners, these vines just need to be reshaped. Perhaps I need to ask their forgiveness so that I can just slash away, severing deadwood, amputating arms growing out at odd angles, pruning "hard" to stimulate new, vigorous growth for the coming year.

Occasionally I'll stop at a vine that seems confused. The old growth spreads in all directions, dividing the crown into two or three distinct heads, each with its own scraggly family of canes. I can date most of the wood: the thin gray canes are one or two years old, the thick dark arms come from years past. The shape tells a story of the vine's expansion outward in a constant search for sunlight that results in twisted growth. Farmers try to check that exploration and redirect the vigor.

How did these vines get to be so disordered? Old pruning errors are evident: a worker left a strong cane branching away from the main trunk, creating a dual-headed vine. I try to correct the growth by pulling it back and braiding the wood together. The vine then responds by growing fat in other places with oddly positioned shoots, resisting my attempt at control.

A vine grows only by gradual accrual, punctuated by the annual rite of pruning. I now add to the living timeline, shaping and cutting, only to return next year and discover new growth with new patterns. I need to be planning on pruning years into the future. I begin to think of these old vines as badly bent, but not broken.

After an initial week of pruning, I'm working as a veteran. My shears glide through a canopy, snipping and clipping, pulling and tugging. My eyes dance from cane to cane, monitoring the growth from old spurs and crowns while identifying strong canes that will bear next year's harvest. The easiest vines grow vigorously, following the patterns established years ago with proper pruning. I pause and talk to myself about where to leave extra spurs, knowing my decisions will affect my work years from now. I also need to trust the lead of those before me, duplicating their efforts to sustain the legacy of a healthy vine.

It takes years to learn how to prune a vine, to grow accustomed to the diverse patterns and changes manifested in a contorted trunk. I can respond to history by leaving healthy wood and strategic spurs—my best pruning works with the past in order to shape the future.

Now I understand why they call these cultural practices. Good pruning is not a science, it's the art of working with a living entity, an annual sojourn to a familiar place with the intention of returning the next year and the year after that. But it goes beyond just the physical structure of a vine. The ghosts of many pruners before me live in my fields—this is a place where generations reside.

Gary Soto

"The Elements of San Joaquin"

Gary Soto was born in Fresno, California, in 1952. He is the author of ten poetry collections, including *New and Selected Poems* (1995), which was a finalist for both the *Los Angeles Times* Book Award and the National Book Award. He has also written two novels, *Poetry Lover* and *Nickel and Dime*, as well as the memoir *Living Up the Street*, for which he received an American Book Award. Among Soto's other awards are a Discovery / *The Nation* Prize, a U.S. Award of the International Poetry Forum, and the California Library Association's John and Patricia Beatty Award (twice), in addition to fellowships from the Guggenheim Foundation, the National Endowment for the Arts (twice), and the California Arts Council. Soto lives in Berkeley, California.

Field
The wind sprays pale dirt into my mouth
The small, almost invisible scars
On my hands.
The pores in my throat and elbows
Have taken in a seed of dirt of their own.

After a day in the grape fields near Rolinda
A fine silt, washed by sweat,
Has settled into the lines
On my wrists and palms.

Already I am becoming the valley,
A soil that sprouts nothing.
For any of us.

Wind

A dry wind over the valley
Peeled mountains, grain by grain,
To small slopes, loose dirt
Where red ants tunnel.

The wind strokes
The skulls and spines of cattle
To white dust, to nothing,

Covers the spiked tracks of beetles,
Of tumbleweed, of sparrows
That pecked the ground for insects.

Evenings, when I am in the yard weeding,
The wind picks up the breath of my armpits

Like dust, swirls it
Miles away

And drops it
On the ear of a rabid dog,
And I take on another life.

Wind

When you got up this morning the sun
Blazed an hour in the sky,

A lizard hid
Under the curled leaves of manzanita
And winked its dark lids.

Later, the sky grayed,
And the cold wind you breathed
Was moving under your skin and already far
From the small hives of your lungs.

Stars

At dusk the first stars appear.
Not one eager finger points toward them.
A little later the stars spread with the night
And an orange moon rises
To lead them, like a shepherd, toward dawn.

Sun

In June the sun is a bonnet of light
Coming up,
Little by little,
From behind a skyline of pine.

The pastures sway with fiddle-neck,
Tassels of foxtail.

At Piedra
A couple fish on the river's edge,
Their shadows deep against the water.
Above, in the stubbled slopes,
Cows climb down
As the heat rises
In a mist of blond locusts,
Returning to the valley.

Rain

When autumn rains flatten sycamore leaves,
The tiny volcanos of dirt
Ants raised around their holes,
I should be out of work.

My silverware and stack of plates will go unused
Like the old, my two good slacks
Will smother under a growth of lint
And smell of the old dust
That rises
When the closet door opens or closes.

The skin of my belly will tighten like a belt
And there will be no reason for pockets.

Harvest

East of the sun's slant, in the vineyard that never failed,
A wind crossed my face, moving the dust
And a portion of my voice a step closer to a new year.

The sky went black in the ninth hour of rolling trays,
And in the distance ropes of rain dropped to pull me
From the thick harvest that was not mine.

Fog

If you go to your window
You will notice a fog drifting in.

The sun is no stronger than a flashlight.
Not all the sweaters
Hung in closets all summer

Could soak up this mist. The fog:
A mouth nibbling everything to its origin,
Pomegranate trees, stolen bicycles,

The string of lights at a used-car lot,
A Pontiac with scorched valves.

In Fresno the fog is passing
The young thief prying a window screen,
Graying my hair that falls
And goes unfound, my fingerprints
Slowly growing a fur of dust—

One hundred years from now
There should be no reason to believe
I lived.

Daybreak
In this moment when the light starts up
In the east and rubs
The horizon until it catches fire,

We enter the fields to hoe,
Row after row, among the small flags of onion,
Waving off the dragonflies
That ladder the air.

And tears the onions raise
Do not begin in your eyes but in ours,
In the salt blown
From one blister into another;
They begin in knowing

You will never waken to bear
The hour timed to a heart beat,
The wind pressing us closer to the ground.

When the season ends,
And the onions are unplugged from their sleep,
We won't forget what you failed to see,
And nothing will heal
Under the rain's broken fingers.

for César Chávez

Dao Strom

from *Grass Roof, Tin Roof*

Dao Strom was born in 1973 in Saigon, and her mother fled the country with her when she was a baby. Strom grew up in northern California and is a graduate of the Iowa Writers' Workshop. She is the recipient of a James Michener Fellowship, the *Chicago Tribune*'s Nelson Algren Award, and several other grants. *Grass Roof, Tin Roof* is her first novel. She lives in Austin, Texas.

This excerpt is taken from the middle of Strom's semi-autobiographical novel, *Grass Roof, Tin Roof*, published in 2003. The novel travels from war-torn Saigon to the Sierra Nevada foothills of California and is composed of multiple stories from many different points of view. The first part, "Lucky," is told by an eight-year-old girl; the second, "Chickens," through the perspective of her stepfather.

Lucky

Our dogs were two large mixed-breed Newfoundlands. One black female that our father had rescued—pregnant already—from the pound, and her son, a dirty white pup with faint brown spots, the only *pup we kept from the litter. The largest—thick-furred with shorter ears and tail than his mother. Quiet but strong. We called him "Kee," the most easily pronounceable name my sister, Beth, and I could agree on at the time. She was five, I was eight. No one knew who Kee's father was. All we knew, our own father liked to say, was he must've been some kind of dog to jump over the six-foot fence at the pound to get to Jamie, the mother dog. (Beth and I didn't understand what the "to get to" part really entailed, though our father's approving chuckle as he said it comforted us.) Perhaps Kee's father had been a wolf, our father would hypothesize when Kee howled at the moon or disappeared for days into the woods below our property. We were duly impressed. We took these signs to be evidence of Kee's exceptionality, his uncontainability, his superiority—the commendable result of an enigmatic and wayward background.*

Kee had been born just before our family moved to the Sierra foothills; thus he was the same age as the house that our father was in the slow process of building. Because of his job and lack of money and having only our older brother, Thien, and a neighbor to help, only the skeleton of a first floor was standing after an entire year. Now it was October and the rain had come. Shallow puddles formed where the concrete foundation was not even. The rain seeped under tarps and warped some of the lumber. Our father worried hugely over small and large complications alike. The loss of a few pieces of lumber, spider web–size cracks in the foundation, the possibility of landslides or floods over the site. Waiting for spring, he busied himself with other projects on the property, such as stringing barbed wire for the future horse pastures and burning brush and repairing leaks in the storage shed roof. He kept Thien busy as well. Our father was like a thundercloud, swelled with many hopes and plans for our new life here, glowering and desperate to set them loose, to drum them into our heads before—as he seemed to think—it became too late.

It was 1981.

*K*ee was a beautiful and smart and gentle dog. Our father would point out the integrity in his eyes, his deep-set lupine brown eyes like all the heavy-climate breeds seemed to have—the clear, soulful gaze of a creature who has not only the capacity to live wild but also enough humility and dignity to prevent him from ever harming a thing. (Our father believed this. I think it had to do with his own experience of war, of what he knew he might've been capable of had certain situations arisen—which they had not—in Korea in the 1950s.) Dogs like these, he would tell us, were unknowingly burdened by their own strength, for nothing in their domesticated lives would ever truly put it to the test. Yet that combined strength and reserve was a fine, fine characteristic, he would say, with a kind of trapped passion, and even when I was only eight it struck me he was not speaking just of dogs. He was speaking rather of something vital and exacting that had compelled him to hold himself aloof, always—from a more messily, shamelessly, and duplicitously emoting larger population, as his descriptions made the rest of the world out to be.

I understood the elusive characteristic he spoke of was what had driven him forward—and outward—through his own life. He had fled his family and another country years ago, in the early 1950s, by joining first the Danish marines and then the U.S. Army. "You have no idea, no idea what I've been through," he would tell us. And he wished now to nurture this characteristic in us children—now that we were his—this kernel of something like goodness or kindness or acumen, it is hard to name in just one word. But I would try to recognize it for myself in some sights or moments I believed my father might commend my noticing—an unusually shaped pine tree on a hillside (it must be something unique perhaps), or the warmth I felt as I began to fall asleep, before I had fallen too far no longer to be aware of the pull of sleep (it must be something inscrutable and intensely personal, then).

But to continue about our animals: we kept dogs and cats because we adored them, we kept chickens for eggs and slaughter. Our father considered chickens to be mainly brainless creatures, and no matter what the extent of their unique talents or strengths or markings, they could never become refined. This was the important difference between chickens and dogs and applied even to our favorite hen, whom we called "Lucky" because occasionally she laid an egg with two yolks. Still, we had to keep in mind she was brainless, ill destined. Our father was the kind of man who held to a hierarchy of nature, who placed his faith only in the indifference of evolution.

One morning, he woke early and walked down the hill to the chicken coop. He had to search for the hens' eggs, which often they tried to hide in corners of the coop or in holes scratched in the dirt underneath. Lucky had found a spot in the crook of the roots of an oak tree some way away, and from under her he pulled out (later, this is how we would always recall this) the largest egg any of our chickens ever laid and Lucky's last complete one.

Our mother was sitting on the trailer steps, smoking her cigarette, looking at the morning view of the mountains. She was small-boned and youthful-looking but possessed a manliness—her flat chest and short hair, her petite, muscular legs, her forward, bright manner that could come as a surprise from someone of her stature. She had (in those years) a lack of self-consciousness that we as children were not aware was unusual for an adult. She was also a willing companion to our father's adventures: the house-building, the purchase of our trailer, our new lifestyle in the foreign countryside. She was unafraid to pick up a shovel, she proudly sported the cowboy boots he'd suggested she buy for the terrain up here.

"On mornings like this, I think we very lucky," she said happily. Her English was still heavily accented.

"Yes," agreed our father as he came up the driveway, toting eggs in the stretched-out hem of his T-shirt. "Look at this." Proudly, he showed our mother that morning's largest egg, brown-speckled and big as one of her fists.

He carried the eggs into the trailer, where he placed the large one on the counter for us children to find when we woke. The rest he placed in the fridge. My sister and I were sleeping tangled like kittens in the sheets of the fold-out bed in the trailer's small dining area, our brother in the loft above us, one skinny arm dangling loose and naked over the side into the crisp morning air. Trailer life for us was like an extended camping trip, after our first few years in the States in apartment complexes and working- to middle-class suburban neighborhoods; we knew it was impermanent, this new, less structured life, and so had set ourselves loose into it, without complaint, with casual abandon, with an eye to discovery. Each routine activity seemed new and alive to us. For instance, we took our baths outside now with the use of a cup and a plastic yellow baby tub, or on a stump. We went to the bathroom outside as well, at the base of the nearest large old oak tree with a roll of toilet paper that we carried back and forth from the trailer (some mornings we made a game of passing the toilet paper off to one another as we rushed out to pee). Mastering the mundane in these new ways dominated much of our attention, and we congratulated ourselves on it every day, our survival of the daily—the mishaps and ingenuities and tiny ridiculous triumphs we'd managed. Or our parents did, at least, while our brother sulked in dismay at having to live like this at all, and my sister and I thought nothing of it, really, for we were too young to know any better. When our father and brother came home from surplus sales and unloaded bathroom appliances in the dirt in front of the skeleton of our house, we climbed into the dry tubs and pretended they were boats. We lounged on the toilet seats and ate lunch. We played outside all day and slept solidly through the night.

It was warm inside the trailer at night and only slightly chilly in the mornings, when we would wake to find the covers kicked off or stolen. Dimly, through the haze of half sleep, I could hear my father that morning filling the dogs' food bowls—the opening and closing of the cupboard door, the crinkling of the dog-food bag. He set the bowls on the counter. He opened the built-in refrigerator that faced the sink. Then came the sound of eggshells cracking, two over each bowl of dog food. Raw eggs helped keep the dogs' coats shiny and healthy. For a moment our father paused, his gaze on us stirring in our sheets. As he did many mornings, he reached down and rearranged the sheets to cover our bare chests. He placed my brother's arm back in the bunk beside his body.

Then he exited the trailer and set the dogs' bowls down on the hard dirt outside, and the dogs came to him, butts and tails wagging, snouts nuzzling against his hands and legs.

Our mother took us into town to do laundry and shop for groceries that afternoon. Our father stayed home to string wire around the chicken coop and make a pen so the chickens would not wander. The dogs lay panting in the shade under the twisted oak trees while our father squatted by the coop and planned his pen, and when he got up the dogs stood, too. They sniffed the ground, shoved their noses around under the fallen leaves.

Our father went up the hill to the storage shed to get some wire. Suddenly he heard a loud squawking and the sound of wings beating and scuffling in the dirt. He ran down the hill in time to see Kee attacking one of the chickens. He shouted and swung his arms at the pup, who cowered backward with his tail low and let go of the chicken. Our father stepped closer to inspect the damage. Lucky lay listing to one side in the strewn leaves, making strangled clucking noises and flicking her feathers. Our father did not see any blood yet, so he leaned closer and placed his hand under the chicken's soft belly feathers and gently he lifted her. The hen's stomach lay beneath her in the leaves with an egg not completely laid. The egg was broken, its yolk like a filmy yellow eye within the stomach. Our father realized Kee must've been trying to reach the egg.

Of course. Kee would've never deliberately injured the chicken.

Our father said out loud, "Well, I'm sorry, Lucky." He decided he would have to finish it for her. He pressed down on her back with one hand and twisted with the other.

As he was carrying Lucky down the hill to bury her, he spotted Kee hiding under the trailer. The poor pup was already punishing himself. That dogs were capable of shame seemed evidence to our father of an awareness not typically expected of dogs—an awareness of responsibility, or the ability to discern (and thus not act on, if the dog were well trained enough) an impulse. "A test of love and duty" was the lesson he *would draw for us out of what had happened that day. And he did not mean love in the mushy sense we wanted to give it, of course; he meant love only as a condition irrevocably tied to how one did or did not act dutifully in a given circumstance. When he told us, he told us carefully, even clinically, what had happened to Lucky. "Love," he said scornfully (when we speculated that Kee had felt bad because "he loved Lucky and knew we did, too"), "bah. Don't let it trick you."*

"Not so lucky!" laughed our mother to our brother in the background as they unpacked groceries in the trailer's tiny kitchen space—for she was callous about chickens, understood the butchering of them to be purely practical.

"The egg wasn't ready to be taken yet," explained our father. He gently told us about the logistics of chickens' stomachs.

"Why did Kee do it?" I asked.

"Because he likes the eggs I've been feeding him and he wanted more," said our father. "He wanted more but it was too soon."

His head hunched, Kee was looking at us through the trailer screen door.

"But he's a smart dog, " said our father, "to have figured out where the eggs come from."

Chickens

The relatives were waking. Hus Madsen could hear them moving around inside the van and the storage shed where they had slept in their sleeping bags. Hus took his cigarettes and headed down the hill to smoke and admire the view. The mid-August sun was rising over the mountains and the silver line of the American River wound soundlessly through the bottom of the Coloma Valley, wheat-yellow this time of year, and pocked with faraway houses and squares of plowed land and the cloud-like green puffs of live-oak treetops and the darker, bramblier heads of the black and blue oaks. Hus walked down the steep driveway, kicking up fresh red dirt with his boots, and stepped onto the concrete foundation he'd had poured the previous week. He stood there and looked out over the Coloma Valley with his arms folded across his chest.

Down there was where gold had first been discovered in California, in 1848, by some other unsuspecting new landowner. *One can only hope*, Hus liked to joke.

Behind him, from the top of the driveway, he heard the dogs' collars jingling and their paws scraping excitedly on the ground as the trailer door banged open against the sharp morning air. He began to hear the voices of the relatives. They had arrived just two days ago to visit the Madsens' new land in the foothills of the Sierra Nevada, and it was only the second time Hus had met them in the five years he and Tran had been married and living in Sacramento. The relatives spoke in slow, broken English, or rapidly and loudly in their native tongue, which he didn't understand a word of. Hus had insisted, when he married Tran, that they speak only English in their home. He believed it was more important for the children to speak the language of the country they were growing up in than for them to cling to a culture they had left. It was what he had done himself upon coming to America, twenty-eight long years ago, and if they were to succeed in this society, fluent, natural-sounding English was what they would have to learn as well. As far as he could tell, Tran agreed.

They had both agreed the past would be something best gotten over without much grief, or elaboration to one another or the children.

Of the three children, only the youngest was Hus's by blood. The other two had come with their mother from Vietnam, just four months before Hus had met them. They had escaped on one of the last vessels out of Saigon (and there had been all kinds: famed helicopters, DC-3s, DC-10s, whole squadrons of fighter planes, naval, marine and army air carriers, little rat-trap fishing boats, overloaded rowboats), before the capital fell to the

Communist forces. Tran and her two children had been moving between refugee camps, from Guam to San Diego to Sacramento, and while in the last camp, called Hope Village, Tran had written an article about her and her children's experiences that was published in *The Sacramento Bee*. Hus had just relocated from San Francisco to Sacramento through a transfer of air bases (he was now in the civil sector, putting his architectural degree to work) when he read Tran's story. He had heard many of these stories lately, and his sympathies were with the Vietnamese people, the dislocated; he believed these people could prosper if only given the right chance and circumstances. And then it had occurred to him. He had no one else. He was forty-four years old, still living with only a cat. He was not an unattractive man. Women had often said things to him, and men in bars even, long ago, when he'd been first feeling his way around the States. They had told him he might try Los Angeles, that he looked like he should be on TV. The few involvements he'd had with women, however, had been messy and disruptive, or just plainly confounding to him. He had given up. Those women, he thought, were not serious about anything and were too demanding of men; they did not know how to respect—or let alone—the deeper, more important facts about a person. They had refused even to try to understand the hardships he'd been through, or the distance he'd had to put between himself and his former life and home. They listened with consternation when he spoke about his childhood during World War II, and their questions, when they asked them, seemed always unimaginative ("Do you miss your mother? Was she a good cook? Was she pretty?") and designed to elicit only light-hearted answers. As he read Tran's story in the paper, though, something stirred in him, a sense of recognition that was more than personal, that was strangely nostalgic already; he thought, now here is a woman who has done some necessary fighting of her own. Here is a woman for whom life has not been easy, yet she has endured, she possesses character. Sitting up late that August night in 1975 in his small two-room apartment, Hus found himself writing a letter to send to her via the newspaper, typing as if another's hands were guiding his own hands over the keys. He wanted to do something for this woman who was a fighter. What could he do, he asked in his letter. His intentions at this stage were purely pragmatic, he'd thought. But when they met his heart went out to her and to himself also.

They were married two weeks later.

They drove in a rented car out to Virginia City, Nevada, and after the brief proceedings made their way into a shop called the Silver Time Saloon, where they tried on authentic pioneer costumes from the 1800s and had their picture taken. The photo was tinted to appear old, as if they had already shared history together—and a prototypical American one, at that. They spent their honeymoon in a hotel in Virginia City. Then they drove their rented car back to Sacramento the following day. Hus brought back gifts for the children, who'd been staying with some volunteers from Hope Village. Now the new family moved into Hus's apartment near downtown Sacramento. And when U.S. citizenship was officially granted to them all three years later, he encouraged the children to come up with American versions—or at least American spellings—of their former names. The little girl agreed to *April*, the month of her birth (she was too young to choose for herself and didn't fully understand anyway); the boy, however, was less agreeable and insisted on remaining Thien—although *Tim* was a close and nice enough alternative, Hus had tried explaining—but the boy could not be persuaded.

The girls were coming down the hill, holding hands with Huong, the girl cousin, who was maybe seventeen. He couldn't remember all of the seven cousins' names, and couldn't pronounce them all, either. Hus knew Huong because he thought her the most pleasant and considerate. When they ate dinner, the boys left their plates on the table, and Huong did all the cleaning. As she came down the hill now with his daughters, he called out, "Well, good morning! Come and look at the view. I'll bet you've never seen a view like this before. Views like this were, in large part, what he'd been after in moving the family up into the hills, away from the congested, suburban way of life in Sacramento. He held his cigarette away from his lips and made a sweeping gesture at the landscape beyond, as if it were his own painting he was showing.

His daughters, he noticed, were dressed in the flimsy, strapless dresses the relatives had brought as gifts. The girls had been wearing these foolish outfits ever since the relatives had arrived two days before. Even on women with full figures, the dresses would've looked nothing more than cheap, Hus thought. April, the seven-year-old, wore a glittery purple dress, and Beth, four, was in a satiny blue one. Neither had anything up top to hold up the dresses, and the fabric bagged out over their torsos, often slipping to expose a babyish nub of nipple. Tugging at the dresses, they came tottering toward him down the steep drive in high-heeled shoes that were far too big as well. Hus hadn't known what to say about these gifts without seeming rude, so he had decided, from the beginning, not even to acknowledge the dresses.

"Hi, Daddy, hi, Daddy."

"Aunt Mary and I made the girls look very pretty," said Huong, smiling brightly. She was wearing a tiger-striped bathing suit and a floppy straw hat.

"Why don't you show your cousins how to take a bath?" Hus said to the girls.

"We'll show you the way we take a bath in the country!"

"Good idea," said Hus.

He watched as the girls hobbled over to the wooden rack holding gallon jugs of water and showed their cousin how to feel for the warmest. The rack had black sandpaper nailed to it to absorb the sun's heat. They each picked up a gallon jug and started back up the hill. It was good, he thought, to see his four-year-old lugging the heavy gallon of water as well as her older sister and cousin did. He heard April explaining, "See, the sun heats up the water."

He called after them, "Make sure you lather first!"

He spotted his wife coming out of the trailer. Tran was wearing cut-off jeans with cowboy boots. She was laughing and speaking Vietnamese with her sister, the one they called Aunt Mary. Often Hus could not tell, with this language, whether the speakers were angry or happy. The tones of it were so garrulous and aggressive and shrill. Aunt Mary's husband, whom they all referred to as Uncle John, was smoking a cigarette outside the trailer, his shirt unbuttoned to well below his chest. His eyes were narrow, his brown skin mottled, and he had a straight, black moustache. He wore a gold necklace and was a skinny man, at least a head shorter than Hus. Hus had never understood men who wore necklaces. He believed men who adorned themselves to be vain, in an untrustworthy way. Uncle John saw Hus and waved his hand. "Come, eat!" the man said in his thick accent. He nodded his chin and again waved his cigarette in the air.

Hus put a hand on his stomach and shook his head. "No, thank you," he said loudly. "I have to go check on the pups." He pointed to the doghouse on the hill. Then he stepped off the foundation and dropped his cigarette, grinding it into the dirt with the heel of his boot.

Since the doghouse sat on a slope, at night the puppies sometimes rolled down the hill in their sleep and fell into the deep trench that had been dug for the septic system. Hus counted the puppies in and around the doghouse, then walked along the edge of the trench, searching. Usually he would get Thien out of bed in the mornings to do this. That morning, two puppies whined and clawed at the fresh dirt at the bottom of the trench.

Hus felt some irritation that the boy had not been out here first thing to help the puppies. But Thien was a teenager, fourteen now, and what more could one expect, these days especially? Hus hopped down into the trench and picked each puppy up by the scruff of its neck. They kicked their legs and yelped. They were so young that they had not yet opened their eyes. As he held them up and looked into their soft faces, he realized how, in or out of the trench, the world was still dark for them. Hus wondered, could they sense him helping them even when they couldn't see him? And later, when their eyes opened and they could see, would they recognize him as the man who had helped them?

Hus carried the two puppies back up to the doghouse where the mother dog was nursing, and carefully set them down.

Heading back up the hill, he heard voices and splashing. At the side of the trailer around the stump the girls usually stood on when Tran bathed them, the cousins were loosely gathered, bathing, each with a gallon of water, and the girls were instructing them, teetering on their high heels and still tugging at those dresses. The cousins wore their bathing suits, the boys small and scrawny in their swim trunks. They giggled and stomped and shook themselves as they poured water over their heads. They looked a little like chickens. Hus was struck by the realization that these people were his relations.

He walked toward them, lighting another cigarette, and he called out to them that it worked best if they poured the water slowly. "Just enough to get you wet first," he said. "Then put the gallon down, and lather up and shampoo. Then, rinse. Out here in the country, we have to conserve water." As they paused to look at him, he made lathering motions around his body to illustrate what he meant. They smiled and laughed. They put down their jugs while they rubbed shampoo in their hair. Then, one of the boys picked up a jug and splashed water at his brothers. They began to shriek and laugh and chase each other around. Hus waved his arms. "Hey, hey," he called, "we have to conserve water here. No horsing around now."

This was Hus's design for their sewage system: a large septic tank buried deep in the ground and twenty feet of pipe running the length of the trench across the hillside, attached at one end to the porthole of the septic tank and the other—when it was ready—to the sewage pipes beneath the house. In the meantime, however, Hus planned to leave one end of the pipe loose, so it could be dragged up the hill and attached to the waste tank underneath the trailer at least once every week. Thien, wearing thick rubber gloves, would be in charge of this chore. Hus had already shown him the lever that opened the trailer's sewer tank valve, how it released the smaller tank's contents into the long pipe, through the trench, and into the larger septic tank.

Thien had stared glumly, silently, at the coils of pipe as Hus explained all this to him. Hus had tried to make a joke of it, nudging the boy's shoulder and commenting, "Hey, you may hate it now but one day you'll realize, this might well be one of the most interesting experiences of your life! How many kids get a chance to man a septic tank every week, anyhow?"

Of Tran's two children before Hus, only Thien had been old enough to be aware of the changes they had gone through coming from Vietnam and his mother's remarriage. While Tran's daughter had accepted Hus easily enough, Thien was gloomy and reticent. Hus worried that the boy might be unresilient, one of those simply fated not to adapt well to changed environments. Hus had tried to teach him about fishing, cars, model airplanes—things Hus thought should have interested a boy. But Thien always seemed to listen rather unenthusiastically, though in private, Hus soon discovered, Thien worked intently on the model airplanes Hus brought him, or pored over the photos of cars in books and drew countless pictures of them. Hus took it personally, this stubborn, reclusive enjoyment of his gifts. It startled Hus, how effective an insult from a child could be.

The septic tank—a huge, black, submarine-shaped hunk of iron and aluminum—now sat at the top of the driveway. Today Hus and Thien were to drag the tank down the hill and maneuver it into the hole they had dug for it next to the trench. With two thick coils of braided rope, they fastened a harness around the body of the tank. The cousins were playing soccer with a deflated ball on the concrete foundation, the girls running barefoot after them with the hems of their ridiculous dresses flapping, and Tran had set up lawn chairs in front of the trailer for Aunt Mary and Uncle John, who were lounging in the summer morning sun with glasses of iced tea to watch the touted septic tank event (Hus had been proudly expounding on the details of this task to the relatives since the day they'd arrived). As Hus and Thien finished attaching the harness, a black Chevrolet truck appeared at the top of the driveway, its engine was cut off, and a man climbed out.

"Howdy, there." The man greeted them in the comfortable drawl Hus had grown used to hearing in these hills. People talked much the same way they walked around here, he had noticed, in ambling, calmly investigative tones, so unabashedly, enviably John Wayne American.

"Hi, there," said Hus, with a little peremptory nod. Hus couldn't recall having seen this man before, though he recognized the truck from having passed it occasionally on the roads. The man was tall and wiry, not much younger than Hus, dressed in dirty blue jeans and a white pocketed T-shirt with a red design of horses raging across the front. His muscles showed like knots through the thin fabric of the T-shirt, and his forearms were dark with tattoos. The skin on his nose was peeling slightly, his hair was curled tightly against his head, the same unlively brown as tree bark, and he had a beard. His appearance made Hus think of the black house he sometimes passed on one of the nearby roads, with the Harley-Davidson motorcycles always parked out front, the lawn furniture decrepit. Hus had been entertaining a suspicion that a cult lived there.

The man walked down the driveway with his long hands dangling loosely.

Hus stopped halfway up. "Hello," he said expectantly.

The man slowed and stood a guarded distance from Hus. He looked at Hus, then behind him at the relatives and the children and Tran. He hooked one thumb in his belt loop and rubbed his beard with his other hand. When he spoke, his voice was surprising, deep and mellow and natural. "Hello, neighbor," he said. "It's a beautiful morning, isn't it?" And there was something cheerful and knowing to the way he clipped his words, making *isn't it* sound more like *itn'dit*.

"Certainly is," said Hus.

The man stroked his beard, glancing around amiably enough. "Now I hope I'm not interrupting your party or anything here, sir, but I am conducting a little personal investigation of my own. If you like, maybe you could help me. You see, sir, my dog was shot last night." His eyes shifted, and that was when Hus noticed his motionless eyebrows, betraying the smile on his lips. "She was a damn fine dog, too, never would hurt a fly. A little mean-looking and big, sure, but still no one had the right to go and shoot her in the night like that. Now this morning, I'm just going around to ask people if they seen or heard anything unusual about eleven-thirty or so last night. That's when I heard all the commotion."

"I'm afraid I heard nothing out of the ordinary last night," replied Hus.

The man stood quietly for a moment, one hand still on his chin and the other hooked on his waist, and studied Hus. "Well, sir, she was a nice dog is the fact," said the man, "and she wasn't so easily replaceable, you see, as she was partway wolf. I raised her from a pup, after some roaming free agent hopped the fence on one of my German shepherd dogs, made her a mama." Then slowly, lowering his hands, in gentle, amused disbelief he said, "You mean to tell me you didn't hear nothing when I heard a great big commotion of barking and strange voices and real live gunfire? You may be on the other side of the hill, sir, but if you've noticed, sound carries across this lake. And if there was people out driving, they'd have surely driven past this piece of the road, too. I would think so."

"I assure you I heard nothing, " said Hus.

"Well, then," said the man, "could I ask you, then, what you and these folk were up to at about that time last night?"

"We were asleep," Hus replied briefly. "I'm sorry I can't help you anymore. Good luck, however." He turned his back to walk away, but the man raised his voice to call out after him.

"Well, sir, I have to tell you I've been hearing maybe otherwise. Some other fella gave me your address, says you're the new people here. And he's seen your truck drive by my place a number of times."

Hus's eyes swept over the relatives, who had come up the driveway and were standing now midway up the dirt road, staring at him. He turned to face the man again, but the image of the relatives had stuck in his mind and he saw himself as the man must have seen him, with all his brown-skinned, slant-eyed company in a scattered line behind him, dressed in their cheap secondhand clothing, the scrawny boys in their swim trunks and Huong in her floppy hat and tiger-striped bathing suit, his wife squatting on the ground with her knees in her armpits, in that way he tried to discourage, as she smoked her cigarette. Hus could read the man's disgust at the sight, and felt a shameful anger flare up inside himself. He understood all too well that feeling of repulsion. Suddenly there was a pain in his stomach. He was terrifically sensitive to stress and different foods and had recently developed an ulcer. Sometimes when the pain occurred, it made him furious at everything, regardless of his true intentions. Hunger and lack of discipline could do this to dogs as well, he often thought. Especially those not-entirely-domestic breeds.

"Now I don't mean to jump to conclusions," said the man, "but I don't know many other people around here who would go out in the night and shoot a man's dog for no good reason."

"As I already said, we were asleep."

"How do I know that for sure?" The man took a step forward and held his palm up toward Hus. Hus felt a flash of apprehension shoot through his body like heat. He saw the man's other arm hanging at his side, swaying, as if it had been caught by surprise. His skin looked smudged beneath the tattoos, which were a faded, inky, dark green tint—and for some reason this led Hus to think the man must be an alcoholic. "What proof have you got?" the man was demanding, the drawling tones of his voice now in anger sounding fatuous.

"You can ask anyone here," said Hus.

"And anyone here could be goddamn lying to me," said the man. "How am I to know what people like you might like to do for sport?"

"You are an insensible man," said Hus as calmly as he could, "and you are wasting my time." Behind him then he heard a soft, petulant "Hey!" He twisted around—conscious that the man was looking, too—and was met by the sight of his wife standing a few feet behind him with her hands on her hips and her feet spread. In her broken English she was exclaiming, "I his wife! He was asleep with me last night, I know!" Her eyes were beady beneath her thick glasses.

The man made a hooting noise. "Oh, mama," he chuckled.

Hus was mortified, on whose behalf more he was not sure. Tran's face, too, was red and her gaze flinched beneath the man's mocking attention. Her mouth was fast becoming a thin, disappearing, injured little line.

Hus broke. "What did I just tell you!" he turned and shouted at the man. As Hus strode forward, he was vaguely aware of the fact he had not just told the man anything to justify his shouting this question. The man jumped immediately backward into a fighting stance, fists raised and bobbing in front of his face, and said, "Yeah, c'mon, you sucker." For Hus there could be little satisfaction in striking an opponent who behaved like this. In Hus's experience it seemed this was the way most American men fought—with a scrabbling, brutal, at-all-costs type of strength that was effective but lacked any finer sense of—how else could he put it—*athletics*. He had encountered it first in the U.S. Army.

Hus stopped two feet in front of the man and chose the option of pointing at him firmly and menacingly. "You get off my property this instant," demanded Hus. "Or I swear you'll regret it. You do not know what you're dealing with if you don't get your filthy person off my property this instant." The blood had drained from his face, and he felt cold. He didn't want the girls to see him like this.

The man was still bobbing up and down in front of Hus. "You chicken, man? You afraid I might knock you on your chicken shit ass?"

They stared at one another until the man pulled himself upright, with a glowering, unfinished look. Hus didn't budge. The man spat over his shoulder, glared at Hus once more, then turned with an abrupt, jerking motion and strode back to his truck. He climbed into the cab and turned over the ignition, and the truck roared. Its grill hissed. The man rested his tattooed forearm on the window frame and leaned his head out. "Listen, I won't forget this, you hear me?" he shouted. Then he put the truck in gear and backed out of the driveway, tires spitting pebbles.

Hus turned and walked stiffly back to the septic tank. His wife and the relatives and the children were all looking at him. Thien was kicking at the septic tank with the toe of his sneaker. Tran, her face flushed, still had her hands on her hips.

"That not a very friendly man," said Aunt Mary, who stood in front of her lawn chair. She looked with concern toward Tran.

Hus said, "She's all right now. She just has to learn that not everybody in the world is friendly." He caught his wife's glance and noticed a darkness in her expression. He didn't know if this was because of what he had just said or if she was upset about the whole incident. He told himself irritably that she did not understand, that she shouldn't have stepped in and given the man more to make fun of.

"I just try to help," she said, seeming to read his thoughts, "that all, but you no appreciate anything I do." She headed back toward the trailer and Aunt Mary, her back to Hus as she spoke. Sometimes when she got upset she was like a child herself, Hus thought.

"You *do not* appreciate." He automatically corrected her grammar. "Of course I appreciate your efforts, but I don't think you understand what people like that are truly like."

His wife did not respond. She spoke in Vietnamese with her sister, and again Hus couldn't tell if they were quarreling or not. Tran was speaking in a curt voice, and Uncle John joined in, also with a raised voice. Hus watched them for a few moments. He tried to chuckle. Loudly, he interjected, "Tell them, Tran, that's not how everyone out here in the country is." He realized this would be the story the relatives would tell when they went back to San Diego. They would tell other Vietnamese people they knew, this is what people in the country are like, and this is what Tran Trinh's new husband is like.

"Tell them now, Mom," Hus said cheerfully.

The man returned about half an hour later, carrying a bottle of wine. Hus and Thien had dragged the septic tank to the edge of the driveway and were beginning to ease it down the slope. The relatives were gathered around watching, and Hus felt he was educating them by allowing them the chance to watch this work being done. Though he didn't know exactly what to make of their loud and animated, even joyous, exclamations at some moments, as when the tank began to teeter sideways on the slope, or when the ropes caught on an overhead tree branch—what were they cheering in hopes of, he wondered, a rescue or a fiasco? The girls sat above them in a tree with their prized secondhand Barbie dolls that'd been given to them by some previous neighbors in Sacramento (otherwise Hus would not have allowed them to have Barbies). The girls had strung ropes in the branches of the oak tree and were straddling each their own branch, pretending the branches were ponies.

The mother dog was barking as the man came down the driveway.

He raised his arms over his head as he approached. "I came back to apologize, is all," he announced, and held the bottle of wine out to Hus. "I was jumping the gun earlier and I just wanted to come say how sorry I am for making a mess of your morning like I did."

Hus looked at the bottle. He was reminded of his ulcer, the reason he no longer drank alcohol.

"That's fine," said Hus. "Tran," he called to his wife, "why don't you come take this?"

Tran came over from the trailer and took the bottle, smiling politely. Hus thought he should tell her later never to smile so sweetly at a man like this.

The man wiped his hands on his jeans. "My name's Will, by the way. William Bentley. I live over toward Crooked Mile Court. I do apologize for this morning, truly." His voice was measured and controlled once more, but now Hus heard a falseness in it. He shook the man's hand reluctantly, finding it thin and sticky.

"Hus Madsen," he said. "My wife, Tran."

"Hello, missus." The man tipped his head slightly. "I do hope you excuse my rotten behavior this morning."

"Well, we all okay now," said Tran brightly. Hus looked at her.

"So, you folks all Chinese or Japanese?" said the man conversationally. "I knew a Chinese family back in Tracy where I used to live for a while. They were nice people. The missus was a real good seamstress, actually. She could patch any rip in a matter of minutes. She sewed some pretty dresses for my wife." The man glanced around briefly. "Now all of you don't live in there, do you?" He nodded toward the trailer.

"No, it's just my wife and I and our three, the boy here and the two little girls," said Hus. "My wife's side of the family is visiting from down south." Hus made a gesture to Tran, to send her back to the trailer. She went, seeming oblivious.

"And they're Chinese, too, huh?" said the man.

"Vietnamese," corrected Hus.

"Is that so?" The man declared this with genuine surprise and a spark of something else. He met Hus's eye only briefly as his glance skated over the relatives. "Well, Hoss," said the man (and Hus didn't bother to correct his pronunciation), "I was on my way over to ask if you wanted to accompany me on a little visit to somebody. You see, I went over to a man named Curt Hopkins's place just now, and the way he was acting, it occurred to me he might well be the culprit I'm looking for. And I just thought I might enlist a little help talking to him." The man paused a moment, then focused again on Hus. He did not disguise the growing nastiness in his tone. "But I see you're probably much too busy for that right now."

The dog had approached them and was nuzzling Thien's legs as Thien, at the other end of the septic tank, dropped the piece of rope he'd been holding and knelt beside the dog to absently stroke her head. The dog panted and wagged her tail happily.

"Yes," said Hus, "we have far too much work to do here right now. I'm sorry about your dog, however."

"Well, I thank you," said the man, bowing with a mock salute, two fingers to his forehead. "Enjoy that wine, now." Then he turned his back and left them.

Hus and Thien got the septic tank down the hill and maneuvered it into position above the hole. They had to brace themselves against the weight of the tank, Hus in front pulling the rope over his shoulder and leaning so far forward his knees almost dug into the ground, and Thien at the back of the tank, pushing. Hus wondered if Thien was pushing hard at all. Soon they would have to pull backward on their ropes to keep the tank from sliding too fast into the hole in the wrong position. The girls had climbed down from their tree and were running about, chasing the chickens out of the way of the oncoming tank, waving their dirty, half-dressed Barbie dolls in front of them. Hus was afraid the girls might fall into the hole or the trench, and it was making him nervous and distracted. "Get out of the way now! Now!" he shouted, when he heard the truck again.

William Bentley walked to the edge of the driveway and stood with his feet spread and his fists on his hips. "Hey!" he called down. "I gotta talk with you, Hoss!"

Hus wiped his brow with his forearm and released the rope. He moved calmly back up the length of the tank to its end, and stopped beside Thien. They both shielded their eyes and looked up the hill at the man. Hus folded his arms across his chest. For a scant moment it felt as if they were in this together, father and son, both of them sweating and dusty.

"What's the problem?" Hus called.

"I got a problem with my here dog that was shot last night," yelled the man.

"I thought we discussed this already," said Hus.

"I gotta say now, Hoss, I believe you've been lying to me."

Hus took a deep breath. He stared for a moment at his dirty, worn work boots.

"Yeah, I believe you been lying to me," the man repeated, "and Curt Hopkins isn't the one who done it, and I know because he proved it to me by giving me some other pertinent news—"

"You need to get off my property right now," said Hus, raising his voice.

The man paced a few steps back and forth at the edge of the driveway. "What you got here on your property, Hoss"—he gestured at the relatives and their kids standing around—"I know better than to trust a man who's running a refugee camp on his property. I know what's normal or not. And I know if anyone shot my dog, it was someone on this here property."

"No one here shot your dog." With contained vehemence, Hus got this out.

"Yeah?" The man nodded his chin in the direction of the trailer, where Uncle John was standing. "What about him? I know something you oughtta know, Hoss. I know that boy of yours is damn sneaky enough to have sent someone out to shoot my dog last night, behind your sleeping dumb-ass back, Hoss."

Hus stared incredulously at the man. A short distance behind the man was Tran on the doorstep of the trailer. She had poured herself a glass of wine and was holding it with both hands, looking at the man's back. Beside Hus, Thien shuffled his feet. Hus wondered suddenly, how had he gotten himself into this situation, into this life? "If you don't get off my property, I am going to have to call the police."

"Oh, no, I'm not leaving yet," shouted the man. "I'm not leaving until you tell me yes, my people shot your poor dog, and then you give me some money to repair my damages. I want at least five hundred dollars, you hear me? Five hundred. Because my dog was a *rare* animal, goddamn it." The man paced. He then strode back to his truck, reached into the bed, and dragged something out, something that Hus could not see clearly until the man had heaved it over his shoulder, carried it onto the driveway, and thrown it down on the rocks. The large white dog's body was limp and the bullet wound was visible in the middle of its rib cage, where the fur was stained red.

Hus glared at the man, furious.

"I'm leaving her for you now, see? She's all yours now."

Suddenly, Hus was on the driveway, shoving the man aside and reaching for the dog. He lifted its cold furry body and felt the weight and softness of it against his forearms and chest as he began to walk with it up the driveway.

The man shouted, "Hey!"

They all watched Hus. He continued to walk, not knowing himself what he would do, down the road. It occurred to him what he was at that moment: a forty-nine-year-old man carrying a dead dog down a dirt road. How had this ever become an impasse at which he had arrived, and what did it say about his future? Everything he had done—for years—had long been motivated by the wish to separate himself from any risk of conflicts such as these, and from people whose prejudices were based, like this man's, on fear or rage or spite. This was the consequence of righteousness, it seemed to Hus, his own as well as this man's. But how could Hus not view this man as a lazy worthless person, after he had thrown his own dead dog on the ground? Surely this was a person not capable of understanding a desire for peace, a man who had allowed his dog to be shot in the first place. As Hus continued to walk, it dawned on him that the man had probably shot his dog himself. Drunk and mad at the dog for harassing the neighbors, or mad at having been accused by the neighbors of some harassment or other by the dog, this man, William Bentley, had probably on an impulse gone out and shot the dog, then regretted it. And by morning, he had convinced himself that someone else must've come and shot the dog. This was what Hus believed, the farther he walked holding the dog, as if its contact with him were imparting to him this version of the story.

The man yelled after him, "You lousy son of a bitch! You go and keep her!"

Hus stopped in the middle of the dusty road. He looked around at the trees and the brilliant blue sky and the sunshine. He gently set the dog's body down in the tall, dry grass and star-thistle on the side of the road. Then he turned around slowly, his eyes sweeping over the tangled oaks and pines descending in thickening clusters down the hill on one side; he saw his family and relatives scattered up the road watching him, slowly trailing after him, the man pushing through them and swinging his arms. On the other side of the road was a driveway that led to the Nerwinskis' house. A retired old couple, the Nerwinskis were nice enough to allow the Madsens to fill their plastic gallon jugs with water from their outdoor spigot once a week or so, and they also had a telephone the Madsens could borrow. In the pastures alongside their long, gently winding driveway, the Nerwinskis' sheep were grazing.

The man caught up to Hus and stepped over the dog's body in the grass without glancing at it.

"You bastard fucker." The man slammed his fist into his palm, but Hus did not feel threatened. "What do you think you're doing?"

"I think it's time you removed yourself and your dog from here. I think you've overstayed your welcome by now, don't you?"

Hus's family and the relatives trickled down the road toward them. Thien and two of the cousins came and stood a few feet behind the man, glancing from Hus and the man to the dead dog. Hus saw the girls and Huong holding hands at the back of the crowd. They looked pitifully disheveled in their silly strapless dresses, and they were barefoot now, like urchins.

"I've got something to say to you, Hoss," the man said quickly. "I've seen your boy going by my place on his motorbike before. And I just found out that last week there was a boy out on a motorbike chasing my dog around with a BB gun. I was told that just today when I was out asking questions of my good neighbors."

Hus didn't believe him. "To be honest with you, it's probably best your dog was shot. It was most likely mistreated and vicious because of your mistreatment." He caught sight of Thien staring open-mouthed at the man. Hus felt the pain in his stomach flare to his ribs. He straightened his back and tried to stand taller. He faced Thien with a piercing look.

Thien's gaze immediately dropped to his feet.

The man laughed.

"The dog was chasing me," Thien mumbled, "but it was a long time ago, I was on my motorbike one day and I fell off because he was chasing me and he almost bit me."

"And then you fired at this animal with your BB gun, did you?"

Thien shrugged, not looking up, and shifted his feet in the grass. "I didn't hurt his dog. He made me fall off my bike. And it happened a long time ago."

The man stood between Hus and Thien, looking from one to the other triumphantly. He folded his arms and narrowed his eyes with what looked like concentration. Maybe, Hus thought, it was best in life to just suspect everyone of holding out on you.

"And what were you doing driving around with your BB gun on your motorbike? Don't you know how stupid that is? That is a stupid, stupid thing to do!" Though he knew he should not berate the boy in front of a stranger, Hus could not contain himself—it was with kids as it was with dogs sometimes, he thought, that you had to punish them on the spot or they might not remember what you had caught them at. Hus leaned toward Thien. "*Stupid!* I would expect you to know better, Thien. Is that what you do? Answer me. Why were you driving around with your BB gun on your motorbike? Is this something you do regularly?"

Thien shook his head. His shoulders moved up and down.

Hus again demanded an answer.

"Yeah, you tell him now," added the man. Hus ignored him, but he was irked by the feeling of the man joining him.

"Do you, Thien," Hus repeated meticulously, "drive your motorcycle around with your BB gun?"

Thien muttered, "I wasn't, I didn't have it with me. I came back and got it, all right?" He glared briefly at Hus, then looked away.

Tran was beside them now, trying to step in. "Let me talk to him, Daddy," she said, addressing Hus as she usually did in front of the children.

"No, he needs to learn," said Hus. "So you came back and got your gun. You meant to come back and specifically shoot at this dog. That is what they call premeditated, do you understand? That kind of thinking, and the choice that you made is equal to a crime, do you realize? How do I know you didn't decide to do this again last night? I can't be sure of anything now, can I?"

"No, you can't," the man agreed.

"I fell off my dumb bike, okay? I almost got bit. That dumb dog was trying to bite me. But I never *shot* him!" Thien's face twisted up and he crossed his arms tightly over his chest and hunched his shoulders. He began to cry.

For a moment the only sound was Thien's sniffling. Hus didn't know what to say next. He stood staring at the boy with his eyes so fiercely focused, they ached. He stepped back in the grass.

"You do a thing that stupid again and you'll be sorry," said Hus. But he meant it not as a threat—he just wanted Thien to learn something, something about life, this. He said sternly, "You don't make dumb moves like that. Let me tell you."

Thien was crying and wiping his eyes.

"Go on home now," said Hus, and Thien turned quickly away and shouldered past his mother, who was reaching for him. She glared at Hus, and Hus believed they were all, the relatives and kids, glaring at him in the same hateful manner. Even the man was leering. Hus felt sick to his stomach.

"Aw, shit," said the man suddenly. "What the hell are you yelling at him for? He's just a kid. He didn't shoot my dog. Sure, I believe someone here did, but it wasn't that poor kid. You should be yelling at that other guy." He gestured toward Uncle John.

Tran spoke up. "Yes, you being too hard on Thien. I think you being unreasonable. We go home now, we forget everything."

Hus could hardly believe what he was hearing. He watched as Tran headed back up the dirt road, and Aunt Mary and the cousins started to follow. Hus noticed his younger daughter, Beth, was crying, and Huong knelt beside her. The older girl, April, was glancing between Hus and Tran, and Hus saw her dark hair swinging against her neck. It looked cheerful and non-chalant and so innocent, that motion. Uncle John and a few of the older boys were hesitating, still interested in the conflict.

"You got some problems," said the man, "beyond the five hundred dollars you still owe me. "

Hus looked at him with pity. "You take your animal and leave now. You disgust me. You are a low and common form of human being." He gestured toward the driveway across the road. "I am going to go call the police. You can decide what you're going to do next."

Hus stepped over the dead dog and crossed the road. The man didn't stop him. The fight was over for both of them. Hus walked up the Nerwinskis' driveway. The sheep grazing in the pastures raised their heads briefly as he went by. He stepped onto the Nerwinskis' porch and rang the doorbell. The wind chimes dangling from the eaves tinkled like water rippling—and for one second an image of a snow-covered mountain meadow crystallized in his mind with excruciating clarity. Mr. Nerwinski let him in, nodding pleasantly. The TV murmured in the living room and Hus could hear the sound of some crockery being set down in the kitchen, could see a section of the sheep pasture through the open front-room window, as perfect as a painting on the wall itself. Mrs. Nerwinski came out of the kitchen to join her husband.

Sweaty and dusty, Hus's clothes emitted a bad odor. "There's a man harassing my family" was all he could say. "May I use your telephone?"

The old couple directed him to the phone and he tramped across their clean floor, tracking clumps of dirt from his boots.

As he laid his hand on the phone, he caught sight of the dirt. His stomach turned painfully and he abruptly moved his hand to it, frowning. The couple looked alarmed, and Hus could not answer immediately when they asked what was the matter. Mr. Nerwinski brought Hus a chair. It was a simple, sturdy wooden chair, Hus noted as he sat down, leaning back and breathing heavily. He was unable to thank them or apologize right away, either. Mr. Nerwinski went back to stand with his wife, and Hus saw them, the old couple, in the middle of their living room, watching him with wondering eyes. He saw them among their weathered furniture and full bookshelves and framed pictures on their walls, pictures of children young and grown, and a strange melancholy washed over him. He remembered then an incident from his youth. It was winter, and he was at the train station awaiting his father's return from a business trip, when an older boy approached and began taunting him about his family. Hus had become so angered he had beaten the other boy until all he could see was the blood red against the white snow, and his own hands bleeding and red from the cold. Slowly, the roll of pain in his stomach subsided.

"It's nothing," said Hus. "I'm very sorry. I'll be just a minute." He tried to chuckle to ease his awkwardness.

Mrs. Nerwinski smiled tenderly and shook her head. "Poor young man," she said.

Hus raised his chin. "No, no, I'm fine," he said and nodded briskly. He sat with his back straight and reached for the phone again, but knew he would not make the call. He laid his other hand on his thigh, and tried to keep his face from clouding.

The man and the dog and all of Hus's family were gone when Hus came down the Nerwinskis' driveway. He walked back up the road home by himself. He felt drained and mentally exhausted, but there was peace in the tangles of wild oats that grew beside the road and in the sound of sparrows in the trees.

When Hus reached the top of his driveway, Tran and the others were standing about the trailer. They stopped talking when they saw him. April and Beth ran to him, exclaiming, "Daddy's back!" and he patted their heads and said, "Yep, we're all home now." He picked up Beth and carried her on his hip. When he reached the trailer he set Beth down, nodded briefly at Tran, and went inside. He poured water from the gallon jug by the sink over his hands and rubbed them together, then wiped them dry on his jeans. He spotted the bottle of wine on the counter and thought they should probably throw it out.

Outside again, his family and the relatives were gathered around the front of the trailer. They all looked at him, their eyes dark and blank, except for the girls, who were bumping hips in the dirt and twirling their dresses around their legs. Thien was standing with his arms crossed, staring off down the hill even as Hus spoke.

"Everything's all right now," he said, and gave a reassuring chuckle. He wondered if they still cared what he thought or not, and half hoped they did not. "He won't be coming back, that man," he said, feigning confidence. Then he added, addressing the girls, "It's time to feed the animals now. There's no reason to forget that." The girls ran to get the dog dishes and he added, "Make sure you give them fresh water, too."

Hus looked at his wife. She was pulling on the galoshes she used to walk in the chicken coop. She didn't like to walk on the chicken droppings in her good boots. Hus waved at her. The relatives had begun to talk again among themselves; Hus wondered whether they were discussing him. He needed to keep busy, to get away.

"No, no, Mom," he said, making a face. "I'll do it. I'll feed the chickens today." Outside the coop, he scooped up a cup of poultry feed and entered the chicken pen. As he scattered the yellow kernels around his feet in handfuls, the chickens surrounded him, scratching and clambering frantically over each other and the tops of his boots. He closed his fist, stemming the flow, then stepped over their backs to another part of the pen to scatter the rest of the feed.

Greg Sarris

"The Magic Pony"
from *Grand Avenue*

Greg Sarris was born in 1951 and grew up in Santa Rosa. He is
a professor of English at the University of California, Los
Angeles, the chairman of the Federated Indians of the Graton
Rancheria (formerly known as the Federated Coast Miwok),
and an important literary voice exploring American Indian life.
Sarris has written several books, both fiction and nonfiction,
including *Keeping Slug Woman Alive: A Holistic Approach to
American Indian Texts* and *Grand Avenue,* a novel in short stories
that was adapted into an HBO film.

"The Magic Pony" is the first story in *Grand Avenue,* published in 1994. Set in a small city in northern California, the
novel's ten connected stories focus on Santa Rosa's poorest
neighborhood and, most notably, a group of Pomo Indians
who live in dilapidated army barracks.

My name is Jasmine, but I'm no sweet-smelling flower. Names are just parents' dreams, after all. I'm thirty pounds too big and even more dull-faced than my mother, since I make no effort to camouflage it with powder and lipstick. My cousin Ruby is pretty, but it's not the kind of pretty boys see. She's thin and clothes hang on her just so, like her mom, my Auntie Faye.

Us Indians are full of evil, Auntie Faye said. She told lots of stories about curses and poison. We call it poison. Not that we're bad people. Not like regular thieves and murderers. We inherit it. Something our ancestors did, maybe, or something we did to bring it on ourselves. Something we didn't realize—like having talked about somebody in a way they didn't like, so they got mad and poisoned you.

She knew a lot about poison. She said she had an instinct for it. She'd nod with her chin to a grove of trees. "Don't walk there," she'd say. Her eyes looked dark and motionless, like she was seeing something she didn't want to see and couldn't look away from. She traced poison in a family. Take the receptionist at Indian Health, who has a black birthmark the size of a quarter on her cheek. Faye said the woman's mother stole something from someone, so the woman was marked from birth. It happens like that. It can circle around and get someone in your family. It's everywhere, Faye said.

Which is why she painted a forest on the front room wall and painted crosses over it with pink fingernail polish, to keep poison away. She wanted us to touch one of the crosses every day. "You'll be safe," she said.

I knew she was half cracked. I never believed any of her nonsense. I knew what Mom and my other aunts said was true: Faye had lost it. She was plumb nuts. And Ruby, who was fourteen, my age, wasn't far behind her. Ruby talked to extraterrestrials who landed on the street outside. She'd read books in the library and come out acting like some character in the book: Helen

Keller or Joan of Arc or some proper English girl. She made no sense. Nothing about Ruby or Faye made sense, but I lived with them anyway.

I wasn't normal either.

I wanted to hear Auntie Faye's weird stories. I wanted to know what the extraterrestrials told Ruby. I wanted to sit at the kitchen table that Faye set each day with place mats and clean silverware and fresh flowers and hear nothing but their voices in the cool, quiet air of the room. I begged my mother. "Auntie Faye said I could live there," I told her. She looked at me as if I told her I had an extra eye on the back of my head. She knew me and Ruby were friendly, but she didn't think I'd go as far as wanting to live there. Seeing how shocked she was, I begged that much harder. I cried, threatened to run away. What could she say? She didn't have a place for us, not really. We lived with Grandma Zelda. Like all of my aunts and their kids when they get bounced out of their apartments for not paying the rent or something. Only Mom seemed permanent at Grandma Zelda's. She could never keep a place of her own for long.

Grandma Zelda's apartment is like the others, a no-color brown refurbished army barracks at the end of Grand Avenue. Grandma Zelda, Faye, my other aunts—all of us lived there. It was like our own reservation in Santa Rosa, just for our clan. Each apartment was full of the same stuff: dirty-diaper-smelling kids, hollering, and fighting. But Grandma's place was the worst. It stunk twenty-four hours a day, and you never knew where you were going to sleep: on the floor, on the couch, in a chair. Babies slept in drawers. And then all the sounds in the dark. The crap with Mom and her men. And my aunts, too. All their moaning and stuff. All the time hoping none of it got close to you.

So you can see how Faye and Ruby's BS sounded to me like water trickling from a cool mountain stream, pleasure to the ears. It wasn't water that could drown you. Sometimes it was even amusing. I'd guess how their stories would turn out because they got predictable. Of course Grandma Zelda and my other aunts were shocked when I carried my things to Faye's. I knew they wouldn't stop me, and they wouldn't come looking for me either. Faye's place was just two down from Grandma's, but it might as well have been in San Francisco, fifty miles away. No one hung around Faye's. If they came over, they'd stay half a second, then leave, like if they didn't get out fast enough they'd catch a disease. I was safe.

Then Auntie Faye found a man, and one day me and Ruby came home from school and found Mom and all our aunts at Faye's like it was a everyday thing.

Billyrene. Pauline. Rita. Stella. Mom. Even Grandma Zelda. All of them were there putting on a show. Big dull-faced Indian women with assorted hair colors. They fooled with their hair and tugged at their blouses, each one hoping Faye's man would take notice. Each one had her own plan to get the man for herself. I know Mom and my aunts. Nothing stops them when they get ideas, and nothing gives them ideas like a man does. First the lollipop-sweet smiles and phony shyness, then the cattiness, the sharp words. By the time Ruby and me got there they had their claws out.

"Did you come from the mission?" Grandma Zelda asked the man, who sat next to Faye on the couch.

He didn't seem to hear her. Maybe he was overwhelmed by the line of beauties that surrounded him. Me and Ruby stood pushed up against the wall. No one saw us, not even Faye, who was looking in our direction. Her eyes weren't strange. They weren't still. She looked back and forth as people talked. I felt funny all of a sudden. I'd seen the man before. There was nothing to him, I saw that right off. He was white, ugly, orange-colored, with thick hairy arms and eyes that were little blue stones, plastic jewelry in a junk shop. It wasn't him that bothered me, really. It was Faye, the way she followed the conversation, and Mom and all them in the room. My stomach slid like a tire on an icy road.

"Did you come from the mission?" Grandma asked again. She was the only one in a dress, an old lady print, with her stained yellow slip hung to her ankles.

"What kind of question is that?" Mom snapped. She smiled at Faye's man, as if telling him not to pay any attention to the idiot old woman.

"Frances," Grandma said, "all I meant was is he Christian?"

Faye laughed, trying to make light of all the talk. She gently elbowed her man to let him know to laugh too.

I turned to Ruby. With all that was going on in front of her, her eyes were a million miles away. It aggravated me that she stood there in never-never land. I grabbed her arm and whispered, "That man's going to be your new father."

She didn't focus, so I said it again, this time loud and clear.

"That man's going to be your new father."

Grandma Zelda looked in our direction. "Hush up," she snapped. She didn't really see me and Ruby. We could've been Rita's three-year-old twins for all she knew. She didn't hear what I said either. No one did.

Then Billyrene piped up, Billyrene in her aqua stretch pants and a white blouse that didn't cover her protruding belly. "Lord knows Faye don't meet men in the mission. Not like some people here." She was looking straight at Mom and Pauline and Rita, giving them an evil gap-toothed smile.

On and on it went. Then out came the beer. They drank awhile, then left. Faye and her man went with them.

I hadn't cooked a meal since I left Grandma Zelda's eight months before. Even with this guy in Faye's life, she hadn't missed cooking for me and Ruby until that night. Tuna casserole, that's what I ended up making, just like I used to for everybody at Grandma's. Ruby set the table. We ate and didn't say anything to each other. Not until we were doing the dishes. I was washing, she was drying. I was thinking about Faye and Mom and my aunts, all their catty talk. Faye would laugh but she had to know how bad it can get, especially if they're drinking. If they don't beat on one another, they'll go after somebody else. Like the time Pauline and Mom got into it over who used all the gas in Pauline's pickup. They were hollering at each other in Cherri's Chinese Kitchen. Cherri, the owner, tried to settle them down, and Mom hit her over the head with a Coke bottle. The cops came and took Mom, the whole thing. I was picturing all that when I looked at Ruby, who was drying dishes calm as you please. She might as well have been standing next to a sink on the moon. "Your mother's crazy," I blurted out. "She's a freak and so are you."

She finished wiping a plate and placed it in the cupboard. Then she reached for another plate from the dish rack.

"Did you hear me?" I yelled. My aggravation had turned into pure pissed-off. She paid no attention to me. "Damn you, you freak!" I cupped my hand into the sink and splashed her with the hot, dirty dishwater. She was stunned. The dishwater hit her in the face, all over the front of her. But she did just what you'd expect. She got a hold on herself. She dried the plate, even soaking wet as she was, and set it in the cupboard. Then she put down the towel and walked away.

She got out the Monopoly board. I knew what she was up to. She wanted me to sit down and play with her. Whenever I got upset, like with my flunking-out grades at school, she opened the Monopoly board. She cheated so I could win. She wanted me to feel better. I knew what she was up to, but I didn't say anything. I looked at her, sitting on the couch, waiting, soaking wet. I turned, picked up the towel, and finished the dishes she was drying.

The man's name was Jerry. Where Auntie Faye found him I'm not sure. The grocery store, I think. When I first saw him come into the house with her, he was carrying a bag of groceries. He was nothing special, like I said. White, ugly. He'd come each afternoon and visit with Faye. He'd come around three, about the time me and Ruby got home from school, and leave at five, when Faye started cooking supper. He always brought something: flowers, a can of coffee, a pair of candles. It went on like that for a couple weeks, until the day Mom and my aunts came into the house and him and Faye left with them.

I knew Faye was lonely. She had bad luck with men. Ruby's father died in a car crash on his way to the hospital the night Ruby was born. He had been over in Graton drinking. But Faye didn't see it that way. She said she was cursed for loving his brother first. The brother's name was Joaquin. He got killed in the Vietnam war. Six months later Faye married Ruby's father. From the way she talked, I don't think she ever stopped loving Joaquin. She never dated after Ruby's father died. I know because I used to hear Mom and my aunts go on in that dirty woman-talk way about Faye not having a man, and until Jerry came I never saw a guy near the place. It wasn't that Faye couldn't get a man. Just the opposite. She didn't look like Mom and my aunts. She wasn't heavy, plain-looking. She was slender and wore clothes like a lady in a magazine. Everything just so, even the dark pants and white blouse she wore around the house.

But Faye's loneliness was about more than not having a man. It was bigger, more than about Joaquin and what happened to Ruby's father, I saw it in her eyes when me and Ruby left each morning for school. Her eyes got wide, not really focusing on me and Ruby but just staring. She'd be sitting at the table, plates of toast and half-empty bowls of cereal all around, and from the door, where me and Ruby said good-bye, she looked so small, sitting there dressed just so.

When she told stories about poison she looked lonely, scared. She'd sit me and Ruby at the table and tell us what certain pink crosses on her painting meant. She had painted the big green forest first, the dark trunks and thick green leaves, then kept adding crosses here and there with fingernail polish, a pink color she never used on herself. Each cross had a story of its own. When she talked her eyes narrowed. They seemed to squeeze like two hands trying to hold on to something. It was always about what happened to somebody, like the one about our Cousin Jeanne's Old Uncle. It's why Jeanne and them don't live in the barracks with us, why they split off from the family a long time ago, when everybody was still on the reservation. Her Old Uncle—I guess he's our Old Uncle too—liked this woman from Clear Lake, but she was married. He liked her so much he put a spell on her husband. Old Uncle could do things like that, poison people. But the poison turned on him. Something happened. It got his sister. One night she was playing blackjack; the next morning she was as cold and still as a rock in winter. That's how our great-aunt died, Faye said. She held a pointing stick, the kind teachers use with a rubber tip, and aimed near the center of the painting. "And it's why your Cousin Jeanne has cancer," she told us. "She inherited it. His misuse of power, it's living yet."

When she talked about Ruby's father or Joaquin, she pointed to a cross near the bottom of the forest, on the right-hand side. "Man sickness," she said. "Man poison."

Somehow because of that cross and the way she talked about it I figured she'd never have a boyfriend. Maybe she thought she was poisoned when it came to men, so she'd never have one. After Jerry started coming, she stood by the painting with her fingers on that cross and whispered, "Oh, Father, help against this poison. Keep me safe from it. Don't let it turn on me." I couldn't hear her, but I knew what she said. If me and Ruby got the urge to steal something, we had to say these words and touch the cross with the stealing story. If someone wanted to hurt us, beat us up for something, we had a cross for that too.

I never thought much about Faye praying on the man-sickness cross until after Jerry and Faye left with Mom and them that day. Jerry started coming around more, not just in the afternoons but late at night, after supper, and Mom and my aunts visited more and more. I thought about my own words, what I said to Ruby that day about the ugly man becoming her new father. Faye told me more than once I had a mean mouth sometimes and I should watch what I say. Never mind that her daughter made up the tallest tales on earth. She never said nothing about that. I don't remember if there was a cross for me to touch regarding my mean teasing mouth; what I said turned out true. The man moved in.

Me and Ruby moved out of the bedroom where we used to sleep on the bed with Faye. Now we slept on the couch, with our heads at opposite ends. "You can camp out on the couch," Faye said one night, as if it were something we had asked to do and she was letting us. Our legs met in the middle, and every time one of us moved or turned we got kicked. I thought of Faye in the bed with Jerry. The door was closed. I couldn't hear anything. Still, I couldn't sleep. I tried squeezing my eyes shut, but I kept seeing Faye with Jerry, disgusting things. Either way, with my eyes opened or closed, everything was dark, a perfect empty backdrop for all I was seeing in my mind. I looked to the painting above us, over the couch. The crosses glowed faintly in the light coming through the front window. "Ruby," I whispered, "maybe your dumb mother can find a cross that'll get us a bed."

Of course she didn't answer me. I sat up and looked at her. She was awake, staring, the window light in her eyes. I knew she heard me.

"Damn you," I said and yanked the blankets off her. She didn't move. She was probably in deep communication with a Martian that was signaling her from the back side of the barracks. Hours later I was still awake. Ruby was asleep. I sat up and covered her with the blankets. I woke up that way in the morning, sitting up.

Faye didn't pray at her painting anymore. She dusted it with her feather duster the way she dusted the top of the TV. She'd remind us to think of the crosses when we left for school each morning, but that's about all. No more stories about poison and what can happen to people. No more holding hands after one of the stories, which is what we always did. She'd finish the story, put down her pointing stick, and then we'd hold hands over the table while she said the prayer about Father God helping us against the poison.

Now she talked about ordinary stuff. The ladies she knew at the cannery. Specials at the grocery store. What was in the window at the secondhand shop on Fifth Street. She talked about getting a new place, a house someplace where me and Ruby could have our own bedroom, maybe even out of Santa Rosa. She had it planned. She wasn't going to work at the cannery anymore, where she was laid off half the year. She was going to be a nurse's aide in a convalescent hospital. Jerry knew someone who could get her a job. Once she talked about tenderness, its merits; it makes people smile, she said. It makes them have faith in others. It makes people feel connected. Then she threw her head back and dropped her shoulders, like she'd got goose bumps all of a sudden. "It's like a light's inside you." Jerry was there, and I felt embarrassed, like I was hearing what I didn't want to imagine seeing behind the bedroom door at night.

Jerry was always there, since he was out of work. Temporarily, Faye said. He helped Faye with the shopping and stuff and he still brought her things, flowers and once a coffee mug with red hearts on it. Lots about him bugged me. Like the way he chewed his food. He mashed it, curling his lips out so you could see the food in his mouth. He asked if me and Ruby were cheerleaders. That was funny. I wanted to ask him if he thought we looked like cheerleaders.

But I didn't.

Faye was happy these days. She used to get moody sometimes, just stare into space, and she'd snap at you if you talked to her. Now she was always up, and just by the way she acted you knew she wanted everybody else up too. She'd look at you and there was something in her eyes, something behind the brightness, that was scary. You wouldn't want to cross her. Seemed like Mom and my aunts saw this in Faye's eyes too. They came to the house almost every day now; there was none of their bitchy talk. Everybody was nice, the way Faye wanted. Her and Mom and Grandma went on and on about how they could help Pauline get her two younger kids out of Juvenile Hall. Stuff like that. It made me nervous. I know my aunts. There was something behind their niceness, something like what I saw in Faye's eyes.

Me and Ruby spent more and more time doing things. It was toward the end of the school year. The days were longer. We took walks. We'd go to the fairgrounds, up to the slaughter-house on Santa Rosa Avenue, and even to the mall. Anywhere except the library, which I couldn't stand. I'd put up with any-thing, her stories about extraterrestrials, anything to keep her head out of a book. That's why I got caught up in the horse thing, the magic pony.

It was a regular horse, a small pinto gelding, not much bigger than a pony. She called it a pony. It was at the slaughterhouse with the other horses. One of the things me and Ruby did those days was sit in the rusted-out boxcar by the slaughterhouse and watch the horses. She had them all named: King Tut, Cleopatra, Romeo and Juliet, the Duke of Earl. We didn't talk about what happened to them when the owner took them from the front corral, where we watched them, to the back corral: a loud buzzer, then the gun blast. Sometimes the horses got lucky. If they were gentle and sound, rich people bought them for their kids.

One day this pony darted out from a group of bigger horses by the trough. He was munching a mouthful of hay, and he kept running here and there, snatching hay from the troughs. He moved so fast the others didn't see him. After a while he walked to the cement tub by the fence for a drink. That's when Ruby flew off the boxcar to pet him. True, he lifted his head and whinnied at her. He probably would have done that for me if I had gotten there first. But Ruby didn't see it that way. He communicated with *her*.

That night in bed I heard everything. Far as she was concerned, the pony wasn't black and white but pure silver and gold. A horse who never drank water. He lived off the morning dew and the pollen of spring flowers. A magic pony that carried princesses into fields of poppies and purple lupine. He soared on wind currents over this town with wings stretched wide as an eagle's. He told Ruby he needed a home.

Faye and Jerry were gone, out with Mom and them. I was trying to sleep. I didn't want to be awake when they got home. Ruby wouldn't quit this horse business. "Shut up," I finally said.

Strange thing, though, the horse could do tricks. We went to the slaughterhouse every day. Before long Ruby was in the corral with it, riding it and everything. Smoke, the owner, a tall black man, gave her a bridle. Even he was surprised to see the pony back up and kneel down on command. He let Ruby take the pony into the open field across the street, where the last flowers of spring were blooming, poppies and lupine. He said the pony might've been in the circus. He didn't know much, except the man who dropped the pony off said it had foundered. "Too bad," he said. When he told me this, we were leaning on the fence watching Ruby and the pony in the field. His words fell like dust and piled on my shoulders. I didn't know what foundered was, but I looked back to Ruby just then, and in the early evening light, she seemed to be floating, nothing holding her as she glided above the dried oat grass and flowers.

I told her to forget the pony. I opened her dictionary and pointed to the word "founder." "Nobody's going to want that pony," I said. "You know what's going to happen." I expected her to argue with me, to point out that the stiffness in the pony's front legs was barely noticeable. But she didn't. She took the dictionary from me, set it on the table, and said matter-of-factly, "That's why he told me he needed a home. I have to find him one."

She couldn't think of anything else. Day and night she figured and planned. For two weeks she approached everybody who came to the slaughterhouse, telling them how the pony was magic. She'd jump on its back, without a bridle, and show folks how well trained he was. The pony would back up and kneel with just a little tug on its mane. By this time Ruby could get the pony to do anything. People watched, young pretty-looking girls and white shirt-and-tie fathers. They'd clap, cheer Ruby on, but they always ended up looking at other horses. Finally it occurred to Ruby what I had been telling her all along. Smoke told people about the pony's legs.

Then she went to Jerry, which was the dumbest idea ever. "If he's my father now, he can help me get the pony," she said. Jerry didn't have a pot to piss in, for as things turned out he was living off Auntie Faye's unemployment from the cannery, just like me and Ruby. The flowers he brought Faye he picked out of people's gardens, and the other things, like the coffee mug, he found in trash bins or stole from garage sales. One morning I saw him pocket me and Ruby's lunch money. I didn't tell Faye. I feared that person I had seen behind her happy eyes. But I told Ruby. I reminded her of that and of Jerry's money problems. She didn't listen.

"I want the pony," she told him one night.

He was sitting at the kitchen table, having a beer with Faye and Mom. It was late, after supper. I watched from the couch that I had just covered with a sheet and blankets for bed. Ruby stood only a couple feet from Jerry, determined. Jerry didn't answer her. He seemed surprised, as if he had looked up and just seen Ruby for the first time.

"Ruby," Faye said. "You know we're moving soon. That takes extra money. Jerry and me are saving. Wait until after we move." Her voice was muffled, far away, like a seagull calling over crashing waves. I noticed she sounded like this when she drank.

Ruby looked straight at Jerry. "I want the pony."

Mom took a swallow of beer and set down her bottle. "Ruby," she said, "you should talk it over with Grandma. She could help maybe from her social security check." Mom acted as if she were really interested. She thought she was important these days since she'd found a job at a convalescent hospital.

Jerry, who was still looking at Ruby as if he didn't know her, turned suddenly to Mom. "Your mother's old," he said. "She needs her money." He looked at Ruby. "Go to one of the farmers around here."

Ruby was up against a wall. Finally she quit. She came back and sat on the cot next to the couch. Later, after Mom left and Faye and Jerry went in the bedroom, she said, "See, Jerry did help me. He told me what to do." She was lying on top of the cot, still dressed. She stared at the ceiling, already seeing a thin Indian girl with long straight hair standing before a farmer's open front door.

We walked five miles down Petaluma Hill Road to the dairies. We went to front doors and into noisy milk barns and smelly calf pens, looking for farmers who might want the pony. Ruby never said hello. She didn't introduce herself. "There's this pony," she'd say and go on and on. Most people let her finish before they asked us to leave. One farmer was interested. He was a fat, whiskered man in dirty pants that hung halfway down his white ass. He signaled us to follow him so he could hear us over the loud milking machines in that barn where he and two Mexican men milked enormous black-and-white cows. We went into a dark, windowless room. Metal pipes fed a huge shiny tank, where they kept the milk. The farmer leaned against the wall and folded his hands over his belly. His fingers were thick and hairy.

"You can see him at the slaughterhouse," Ruby said.

"What's wrong with him? Gotta be something wrong with him," the man said. I didn't like the way he took time between his words, and I felt his eyes on Ruby, though I didn't look. I took her hand and gauged my distance from the door.

Ruby took her time answering him. "He needs a home," she finally said. "He gets around good, and he can get up and down with me on him."

The man told us his daughter wanted a horse. Then he said, "I'll go look at him. Meet me back here next week, same time."

I yanked Ruby out the door.

On the way to the main road, we passed a farmhouse where a girl about ten years old stood watering a vegetable garden.

"See, Jerry was right," Ruby said.

"At least he has a daughter," I said. "I still think he's a pervert."

I knew Ruby wouldn't listen to me, but I didn't like the idea of us going back to that dairy. I didn't like that dark room. I felt trapped.

It's not that I hate men. I just know them too well. I've been around Mom and my aunts and seen what they bring home. I've seen it all. The stuff that goes on in the dark, the stuff you're not supposed to see but end up seeing anyway. Like when I saw Auntie Pauline's man pulling off my Cousin Angela's pants in Pauline's pickup, Pauline's daughter who's my age, the one in juvee. Or when that guy Armando hit Auntie Rita in the chest. Or Tito, Mom's last man: the way he tried to get at me at night when Mom was asleep. You develop a sixth sense for it. You see things you don't want to see. You run right into it. It isn't always something heavy like with Pauline's man and Angela. It can be something simple, innocent-looking.

Like the way Mom and Jerry were sitting in Pauline's pickup outside the supermarket. You could say there were a lot of groceries on the seat, or maybe a dog or a child that caused them to have to sit so close together. You knew, though, that they could have put a dog or a child between them. But it's more than their sitting that way; it's something about them that is still, something about the way they quietly turn their faces to each other,

Mom looking up so that her eyes meet his, that tells you the whole story, not just in this moment but in all of those in the dark, where Faye hadn't seen them. And you can hear the excuse: "Jerry and me are picking up some things at the store."

I watched them from behind a car in the parking lot. First, I saw Pauline's pickup, the red Toyota, then the back of Mom's head, her teased orange-red hair that was supposed to be blond. I knew the whole story even before I had time to think about it. My stomach turned. I wanted to heave. I started up Milton toward Grand. I yanked my hair just so the pain would take my mind off things. It wasn't that I was shocked by Mom and Jerry or the things people do, sex and all that. I was worried about what was going to happen at home.

Already things were nuts. Faye's place was no different now from Grandma Zelda's or Pauline's. Me and Ruby ate canned soup on the couch for dinner. In the mornings we made our own toast and poured our own cornflakes, since Faye didn't get up with us anymore. The door stayed closed, locked. Ruby did nothing but obsess over the pony. She didn't even do her school-work now. I couldn't talk to her. Her eyes were like a pair of headlights on the highway, staring straight ahead, zooming past me. She spent all her time at the slaughterhouse, waiting to see if the farmer or anyone else came to see the pony and making sure Smoke didn't move him to the back, behind the white barn. "The farmer could come while we're in school," I said. But she wouldn't budge. She wouldn't leave the pony's side. The after-noon I saw Mom and Jerry in Pauline's pickup I had left her braiding the pony's scraggly mane.

When I got a hold of my senses, I thought of telling Ruby. I was sitting on Grandma Zelda's porch step. I had come to Faye's first, but when I got to the open screen door and heard all the folks yapping inside, I continued along the row of barracks to Grandma's and plunked myself down. I could hear the loud laughter at Faye's two doors away.

It was a couple of hours before Ruby came up the path at twilight. I jumped up and ran to meet her, feeling desperate to let out everything in my swelled brain. But I ended up saying nothing. I stopped, seeing her face as she turned to go inside, and knew that if I told her what I had seen, her eyes would only look harder and move away from me.

In the days ahead I wanted to talk to Ruby, not just about Mom and Jerry. The weather would have been enough to carry on about, far as I was concerned. But nothing. No way. I'm one to shout, shake her up with what I say, but I could've screamed at the top of my lungs and it would've done as much good as trying to stop a hundred-mile-an-hour train with a whisper. I couldn't stand being in the house. I wanted to kill Mom while she sat nice as could be talking to Auntie Faye. I wanted to pour gasoline on Jerry and watch him burn to black ashes. I stuck by Ruby. I lived at the slaughterhouse with her. But it seemed to make no difference. I was alone.

We went back to the dairy after a week, just like the farmer said, same time. "We're not going in that back room," I said. But there was no need to worry. The farmer must've seen us coming up the road. He met us in front of the milk barn. He pulled up his sagging pants, then adjusted his stained green cap to cover his eyes.

"That little Indian pony," he said, "I went and seen him. I don't know what you girls was thinking. He's useless."

Of course Faye would find out about Mom and Jerry. For me waiting was like standing on a tightrope, not knowing when I'd fall or where I'd land when I did. I didn't have to wait long. On the last day of school, after me and Ruby got home at noon, Faye explained everything.

Suddenly things were back to the old routine. Faye was sitting at the kitchen table with her pointing stick. She motioned with her chin for me and Ruby to sit down. She was plain-looking again, pale like she was before she'd met Jerry. Her eyes were distant, preoccupied. The table was set, with flowers in a mayonnaise jar. When she lifted her pointing stick to gesture at the painting on the wall, I saw she had drawn circles around many of the crosses and connected them with lines from one to another. She had used what looked like a black crayon.

She pointed to the cross circled near the bottom of the painting. "Man sickness," she reminded us and got up and went to the painting. "Man poison." She looked to Ruby. "Your father and also Joaquin, his brother. I loved Joaquin first."

She followed a line that connected this cross to one that was circled near the center of the painting. She was straightforward, a history teacher giving a lecture for the hundredth time.

"This one here," she said, now looking at both of us, "is Old Uncle's poison. Misuse of power. Do you see how they connect here?"

I sat motionless.

"I'll tell you," she said. She let her pointer hang by her side. "This is what happened. You know I loved Joaquin first. Isn't that right?"

We nodded in agreement.

"You know I loved him. Yes, but I never should have." She paused and swallowed hard, color coming to her pale cheeks. "I stole him from your Cousin Jeanne's mother, Anna. I stole him from Anna. I stole him in the worst way. I plotted with my sisters, your aunts, Billyrene and Pauline. We embarrassed her. We told Joaquin that Anna was poison because she and her mother lived with Old Uncle, who poisoned our aunt. It worked. It split them up. Anna and her mother disappeared. We didn't see them for many years, until we moved here. But that's not the point. What really happened is that Old Uncle's poison found me. Misuse of power. I opened a hole in my heart and it found a place to live."

She took a deep breath and pushed back her hair with her free hand. "I killed two men." She pointed to the two circled crosses and traced the line between them, back and forth. "Each man I love I kill. Each man I touch because the poison in me does that. Now my own sisters are full of the poison. It's growing in them and they're using it against me. They plotted and took Jerry."

Faye walked over and set the pointing stick on the table. "Now drink your orange juice," she said.

I heard her push the toaster down behind us and I smelled the toast. But it wasn't until I saw the buttered toast on the table that I realized how far Faye had gone with her story. Things weren't back to normal. Faye had gone off the edge. "Now hurry or you'll be late for school," she said.

Later that day I followed Ruby to the slaughterhouse to try and talk to her. "Look," I said, "this is serious. Your mother's nuts." Ruby had hardly said a word to me the whole week. "Listen to me," I said. We were standing just outside the corral. "Damn you, you stupid fool, wake up."

She slipped through the board fence to where the pony was waiting for her. Its white ears were perked up and it whinnied, just as it did every time it saw Ruby. She stroked its neck and led it to the front of the corral, by the main road where passersby could see them. The buzzer went off in the white barn; then I heard it, a gunshot. I climbed over the fence and made my way past the bigger horses to Ruby and the pony. She had her arms around its neck, tightly, and its head was over her shoulder facing my direction.

"OK," I said. "I'm sorry. Anyway, it's my stupid mother's fault. I'm sorry." I don't know how many times I said it. But she never turned around. Even the pony ignored me, never perked up its ears. I felt like a fifth wheel. Like I had no business there in the little world that was all their own.

Faye got her time straight, a good sign. When me and Ruby got home, after dark, she scolded us for staying out so late. "Dinner's cold," she said. She was truly angry. She shoved the food she had prepared into the oven and slammed the stove door shut. Ten minutes later me and Ruby were sitting at a table set with flowers, eating pork chops, fresh green beans, and a baked potato with sour cream, my favorite. Ruby talked on and on about the pony, crazy stuff about how it could fly and disappear, and Faye forgot about us being late.

When we finished eating, Faye went to the painting and so did Ruby. Faye wiped her mouth with her folded paper napkin and then got up, and Ruby followed her, as if Faye wiping her mouth was a signal. How else did Ruby know what Faye was doing? Usually Faye went and stood by her painting before dinner or in the morning or early afternoon. Then I saw Ruby's eyes. Walking to the painting, she looked back at me. She looked at me so I knew she was looking, and I felt like I did earlier with her hugging the pony. Only I felt worse now; I saw more, even after she looked away and joined Faye, starting in on Father God for help. I saw that Ruby wasn't in never-never land. She was always here. She was always aware of me next to her. Faye was OK too. How could she not know how hard her life had been and that my mother, her sister, had just stolen her man? Ruby knew and Faye knew, just like me. But they believed in something—Faye her crosses, Ruby the pony—and I didn't. I clung to them, and they let me.

We slept together that night. Faye told stories about when she was a girl living on the reservation. She told us the Indian names of flowers. She told us about wild birds. "*Cita*," she said. "Bird. *Cita, cita.*" I fell asleep and must've slept hard because I woke up late, without Faye or Ruby.

I went to the front room, and just as if it had jumped out at me, I saw Faye's painting—or what was left of it—before I even saw Faye. It was black, totally black, the color she had circled the crosses with the day before. Black, except for the edges here and there where you could see a bit of green from the trees underneath. It was as if I were waking up just then, as if in the bedroom I hadn't been awake at all. The fragile peace I had felt shattered like thin glass into a million pieces.

I turned to Faye, who was sitting at the table. Nothing was set, no breakfast dishes, nothing, and the flowers from the mayonnaise jar were laid out around a butcher knife, a halo of green and yellow and purple around the silver blade.

"Faye," I said. "Auntie Faye."

She didn't look at me but kept staring at the painting. It took a minute, and then she started talking. "I must kill Frances—"

"My mother?" I asked.

"I must kill Frances. Otherwise she'll kill Jerry. She's full of poison. She'll kill Jerry. Tonight I will kill her. She is hate. The poison is hate."

"Auntie Faye," I called, but she didn't see me.

I realized talking about it was useless when I saw her eyes. The fearful person I had seen behind her bright eyes the past few weeks had come out now; she was that person. She had told stories to save herself—now she was telling them to excuse herself. Hatred. Jealousy. Anger. Evil. All I had seen in my mother's and my aunt's eyes at different times was here in Faye's. I looked back at the black wall, where Faye was looking, then ran out of the house.

I went to the slaughterhouse. Ruby wasn't there so I ran through the corral and shouted up into the hay barn, where the horses were eating. I hollered and hollered. Nothing. Only the yellow bales of hay stared at me. I went around the back, behind the big white barn across from the front corral, and that's when I spotted the pony. He was there along with a crippled bay mare standing on three legs, a few unshorn sheep, and an emaciated whiteface cow. A large eucalyptus tree shaded the cramped pen. "Ruby!" I hollered. "Ruby!"

Smoke appeared in the door above the chute. "She ain't been around today," he said. "Ain't seen her. Now get, you shouldn't be back here."

First I thought Ruby had run away. But that wasn't like her. I figured she had seen how the pony was in the back. Any day could be its last. Ruby wouldn't give up. She wouldn't run. She'd work harder. She'd go back to the dairies. She'd go farther down Petaluma Hill Road, all the way to Petaluma.

So that's what I did—went back to every dairy we had stopped at, asking everybody along the way if they had seen her. I made up stories, like she needed medicine. I described her, but no one had seen such a girl. I walked clear back to town. One last place, the library—but no luck. The only place left was Faye's.

Faye hadn't moved. All afternoon while I'd been running back and forth to the slaughterhouse looking for Ruby and checking to see if the pony was alive, Faye never looked away from her painting to see me coming and going. I slammed the door. Once I even shook the table. I thought of reaching for the knife, but it was too close to Faye. She might snap, and I'd be within her reach.

I plunked myself down on the couch, and as the afternoon wore on I began hating Ruby. She had abandoned me. Faye was worse than useless. She was worse than gone. I thought of running over to Grandma Zelda's and telling her or Mom. But then what? Have them come down and get stabbed? I thought of calling the police, but why start trouble when it hadn't started? I guess, too, that I didn't want anyone to see Faye like this. They would take her away. I waited and waited. I wanted Ruby to come home, for things to be fine. Maybe Faye would flip back to her old self, I thought, if I just waited.

Faye must have gotten up so quietly I didn't notice. She was standing at the kitchen table looking toward the screen door. Slowly, deliberately, she walked to the door and stopped. "Jasmine," she said, "come here." Her voice was cool, even.

I went to the door.

"A miracle," she said.

And then I saw the sky, where Faye was looking. It was lit by a huge ball of fire, yellow, purple, golden, and red. I was stunned by the sight of it. Then I heard the sirens, and before I could think, I knew. Ruby had set the barn on fire.

I tore past Faye, around the crowds gathered outside the barracks. I ran up Santa Rosa Avenue, past the flashing lights. Horses were everywhere, all over the street, stopping traffic, halting police cars and fire trucks. I was stopped by police and yellow tape, but in the thick of lights and uniforms, through the haze of smoke, I saw a plain-looking girl being escorted to a police van.

There was nothing to do but go back and tell what had happened. There was nothing to hide now. I felt heavy, tired. The first people I saw were Auntie Pauline and my cousins. They were standing on Grand. Then I went in and told Faye. "I know," she said. "I know." She was sitting on the couch.

Funny thing, no one asked me how I knew it was Ruby. Everybody collected in Faye's. They waited for the police car. Something my family always does when there's trouble—wait together. Wait for the details. Auntie Pauline. Auntie Billyrene. Grandma Zelda. Auntie Rita. Mom and Jerry. Auntie Stella.

As it turned out, there wasn't a lot to the story. Ruby had opened the gates and then set the hay barn on fire. She let the horses go. Of course I was the only one who understood the details. I don't mean about how she hid out and poured gasoline on the hay and all that, which we found out later, after she was released from juvee and came back to Faye's. I mean about why she did it. What led up to it. I understood it plain as day even while I was sitting there next to Faye, waiting with everybody else for the police to come with Ruby.

There was nothing I could do. Faye was a crying mess on the couch, and the cops had Ruby. Face it. Face reality, which I always did, which I told myself I should never have stopped doing. I had been hiding at Faye's. With her and Ruby I had been fooling myself. See the road ahead, I kept saying inside my brain. But when I saw Ruby come through the door, a uniformed policeman on each side of her, I stopped. My heart turned and never righted back.

"Jasmine," she blurted out, seeing me. "He's free. He flew away."

I said what made no sense. I said it like a prayer. "Everything's going to be all right, Ruby."

Joan Didion

from *Where I Was From*

A fifth-generation Californian, Joan Didion was born in Sacramento in 1934 and raised in the Central Valley. Although an accomplished novelist, her renown springs from her essays, which combine highly personal commentary with an apocalyptic view of American politics and culture. Her books include *The White Album, Democracy, Slouching Towards Bethlehem, Run River,* and her most recent book, *Where I Was From,* a deeply critical collection of essays about California myth, history, and culture. Her literary career officially began in 1956, when she won first prize in *Vogue's* Prix de Paris. Since then she has won and been nominated for a number of awards, including the Edward MacDowell Medal in 1996. She lives in New York with her husband, John Gregory Dunne.

This selection is excerpted from *Where I Was From,* published in 2003. The book mercilessly dissects popular notions about Didion's home state, exploring everything from its original settling to the Spur Posse scandal of the early 1990s.

J osiah Royce, who was from 1885 until his death in 1916 a central figure in what later became known as the "golden period"
of the Harvard philosophy department, was born in Grass
Valley, not far from Sacramento, grew up there and in San
Francisco, and in some sense spent the rest of his life trying to
make coherent the discontinuities implicit in this inheritance.
"My native town was a mining town in the Sierra Nevada—a
place five or six years older than myself," he said at a dinner
given in his honor at the Walton Hotel in Philadelphia in 1915.

> My earliest recollections include a very frequent wonder
> as to what my elders meant when they said that this was
> a new community. I frequently looked at the vestiges left
> by the former diggings of miners, saw that many pine logs
> were rotten, and that a miner's grave was to be found in a
> lonely place not far from my own house. Plainly men had
> lived and died thereabouts. I dimly reflected that this sort
> of life had apparently been going on ever since men dwelt
> thereabouts. The logs and the grave looked old. The sun-
> sets were beautiful. The wide prospects when one looked
> across the Sacramento Valley were impressive, and had
> long interested the people of whose love for my country I
> heard so much. What was there then in this place that
> ought to be called new, or for that matter crude? I won-
> dered, and gradually came to feel that part of my life's
> business was to find out what all this wonder meant.

Here we come close to a peculiar California confusion: what
Royce had actually made it his "life's business" to do, his work,
did not resolve "what all this wonder meant." Instead Royce
invented an idealized California, an ethical system in which "loyalty" was the basic virtue, the moral law essential to the creation

of "community," which was in turn man's only salvation and by
extension the redeeming essence of the California settlement.
Yet the California community most deeply recalled by the
author of this system was what he acknowledged to have been
"a community of irresponsible strangers" (or, in another reference, "a blind and stupid and homeless generation of selfish
wanderers"), a community not of the "loyal" but of "men who
have left homes and families, who have fled from before the
word of the Lord, and have sought safety from their old vexa-
tious duties in a golden paradise."

Such calls to dwell upon the place and its meaning (and, if the
meaning proved intractable, to reinvent the place) had been
general in California since the first American settlement, the
very remoteness of which was sufficiently extreme to raise questions about why one was there, why one had come there, what
the voyage would ultimately mean. The overland crossing itself
had an aspect of quest: "One was going on a pilgrimage whose
every suggestion was of the familiar sacred stories," Royce
wrote. "One sought a romantic and far-off golden land of promise, and one was in the wilderness of this world, often guided
only by signs from heaven....The clear blue was almost perpetually overhead; the pure mountain winds were about one; and
again, even in the hot and parched deserts, a mysterious power
provided the few precious springs and streams of water."

Each arriving traveler had been, by definition, reborn in the
wilderness, a new creature in no way the same as the man or
woman or even child who had left Independence or St. Joseph
however many months before: the very decision to set forth on
the journey had been a kind of death, involving the total abandonment of all previous life, mothers and fathers and brothers
and sisters who would never again be seen, all sentiment banished, the most elementary comforts necessarily relinquished. "I
had for months anticipated this hour, yet, not till it came, did I

realize the blank dreariness of seeing night come on without house or home to shelter us and our baby-girl," Josiah Royce's mother, Sarah, wrote of the day in 1849 on which she set off for Sacramento with her husband and first child.

The blank dreariness, Sarah Royce wrote.

Without house or home, Sarah Royce wrote.

Suffice it to say, we started, my great-great-grandfather William Kilgore wrote.

This moment of leaving, the death that must precede the rebirth, is a fixed element of the crossing story. Such stories are artlessly told. There survives in their repetition a problematic elision or inflation, a narrative flaw, a problem with point of view: the actual observer, or camera eye, is often hard to locate. This was Josephus Adamson Cornwall's goodbye to his mother, as related by a son who seems to have heard the story from his mother, Nancy Hardin Cornwall, she of the fixed and settled principles, aims, and motives in life, who had not herself been present: "Just ready to go, he entered his mother's parlor. She went out with him to his horse to say the last words and to see him depart. She told him that she would never again see him in this world, gave him her blessing, and commended him to God. He then mounted his horse and rode away, while she followed him with a last look, until he vanished from sight."

Who witnessed this moment of departure? Was the camera on Josephus Cornwall's mother, following her son with the last look? Or on the son himself, glancing back as he vanishes from sight? The gravity of the decisive break demands narrative. Conflicting details must be resolved, reworked into a plausible whole. Aging memories will be recorded as gospel. Children recount as the given of their personal and cultural history what neither they nor even their parents could possibly have known, for example the "providential interposition" that was said to have saved Josephus Cornwall's life when he was an infant in Georgia: "It was a peculiarity of that section of the state that mad dogs were very common. One day when his parents were busy he was left in the house alone in his cradle. A mad dog entered the room, walked around it and went away, but never molested him." What witness saw the mad dog enter the room? Did the witness take action, or merely observe and report, trusting the "providential interposition" to save the baby?

Yet it was through generations of just such apparently omniscient narrators that the crossing stories became elevated to a kind of single master odyssey, its stations of veneration fixed. There were the Platte, the Sandy, the Big and Little Sandys. There was the Green River. Fort Hall. Independence Rock. The Sweetwater. There were the Humboldt, the Humboldt Sink, the Hastings cut-off. The names were so deeply embedded in the stories I heard as a child that when I happened at age twenty to see the Green River, through the windows of a train crossing Wyoming, I was astonished by this apparent evidence that it actually existed, a fact on the ground, there to be seen—entirely unearned—by anyone passing by. Just as there were stations of veneration, so there were objects of veneration, relics of those who had made the redeeming journey. "The old potato masher which the Cornwall family brought across the plains in 1846" was not the only family totem given by my grandmother's cousins to the Pacific University Museum in 1957. "After consulting with certain of the heirs," Oliver Huston wrote, the cousins had also determined "that it will be advisable to turn over to the Museum at that time the small desk sent Grandfather in 1840 by William Johnson from Hawaii, and also certain mementoes of Grandmother Geiger," specifically "the blouse which formed part of her wedding costume" and "the old shawl or shoulder wrap she wore in her later years." So Saxon Brown, the heroine of Jack London's curious "California" novel *The Valley of the Moon*, could hold in her hands her mother's red satin corset ("the pioneer finery of a frontier woman who had crossed the plains") and see pass before her, "from East to West, across a

continent, the great hegira of the land-hungry Anglo-Saxon. It
was part and fiber of her. She had been nursed on its traditions
and its facts from the lips of those who had taken part."

As repeated, this was an odyssey the most important aspect of
which was that it offered moral or spiritual "tests," or challenges,
with fatal consequences for failure. Josiah Royce's parents, traveling with only their two-year-old daughter, three other emigrants, and a manuscript list of landmarks that stopped at the
Humboldt Sink, found themselves lost on the Carson desert,
"confused, almost stupefied," "dazed," "half-senseless," suffering
for a period "the same fatal horror of desolation and death that
had assailed the Donner Party in the Truckee pass." Children
who died of cholera got buried on the trail. Women who
believed they could keep some token of their mother's house
(the rosewood chest, the flat silver) learned to jettison memory
and keep moving. Sentiment, like grief and dissent, cost time. A
hesitation, a moment spent looking back, and the grail was for-
feited. Independence Rock, west of Fort Laramie on the
Sweetwater River, was so named because the traveler who had
not reached that point by the Fourth of July, Independence Day,
would not reach the Sierra Nevada before snow closed the
passes.

The diaries of emigrants refer to the Sierra Nevada as "the
most dreaded moment," "the Great Bugaboo," the source of
"sleepless nights," "disturbed dreams." *Without house or home:*
Sarah Royce and her husband and child abandoned their wagon
and made it through the Sierra, with the help of a United States
Army relief party, only ten days before the passes closed. Even
while the passes remained open, there would be snow. There
would be the repeated need to ford and again ford the Truckee
or the Carson. There would be the repeated need to unload and
reload the wagons. There would be recent graves, wrecked wagons, and, at Donner Lake, after the winter of 1846–47, human as
well as animal bones, and the trees notched to show the depth of

the fatal winter's snowpack. This is the entry in William Kilgore's diary for August 1, 1852:

> Ice and frost this morning. Four miles to Red Lake. This is…the head of Salmon Trout, or Carson River. It is a small lake and is within one mi. of the summit of the Sierra Nevada. From this lake to the summit the ascent is very great, some places being almost perpendicular.… Four mi. from the summit we cross a small creek, a tributary of the Sacramento.…At this creek we stop to noon. Here we help inter a young man who died last night of bilious fever. He was from Michigan. His name was Joseph Ricker. His parents reside in the state of Maine. Here we ascend another ridge of this mt. It is higher than the one we have just passed, being 9,339 ft. above the sea. From the foot to the summit it is five miles, and in ascending and descending we travel over four miles of snow, and it from two to 20 ft. deep.…21 miles today.

To read these crossing accounts and diaries is to be struck by the regularity with which a certain apprehension of darkness enters the quest, a shadow of moral ambiguity that becomes steadily more pervasive until that moment when the traveler realizes that the worst of the Sierra is behind him. "The Summit is crossed!" one such diary reads. "We are in California! Far away in the haze the dim outlines of the Sacramento Valley are discernible! We are on the down grade now and our famished animals may pull us through. We are in the midst of huge pines, so large as to challenge belief. Hutton is dead. Others are worse. I am better." By this point, in every such journey, there would have been the accidents, the broken bones, the infected and even the amputated hands and feet. There would have been the fevers.

Sarah Royce remembered staying awake all night after a man in her party died of cholera, and hearing the wind whip his winding sheet like "some vindictive creature struggling restlessly in bonds." There would have been the hurried burials, in graves often unmarked and sometimes deliberately obliterated. "Before leaving the Humboldt River there was one death, Miss Mary Campbell," Nancy Hardin Cornwall's son Joseph recalled. "She was buried right in our road and the whole train of wagons was driven over her grave to conceal it from the Indians. Miss Campbell died of mountain fever, and Mother by waiting on her caught the fever and for a long time she lingered, apparently between life and death, but at last recovered. Miss Campbell was an orphan, her mother having died at Green River."

There would have been, darkest of all, the betrayals, the suggestions that the crossing might not after all be a noble odyssey, might instead be a mean scrambling for survival, a blind flight on the part of Josiah Royce's "blind and stupid and homeless generation of selfish wanderers." Not all emigrants, to take just one example, cared for all orphans. It was on the Little Sandy that an emigrant named Bernard J. Reid, who had put down two hundred dollars to secure a place on an 1849 crossing, saw first "an emigrant wagon apparently abandoned by its owners" and then "a rude head-board indicating a new grave," which turned out to be that of the Reverend Robert Gilmore and his wife Mary, who had died the same day of cholera. This account comes to us from Reid's diary, which was found by his family in the 1950s, entrusted to Mary McDougall Gordon for editing, and published in 1983 by the Stanford University Press as *Overland to California with the Pioneer Line*. On turning from the grave to the apparently abandoned wagon, Reid tells us, he was "surprised to see a neatly dressed girl of about 17, sitting on the wagon tongue, her feet resting on the grass, and her eyes apparently directed at vacancy."

She seemed like one dazed or in a dream and did not
seem to notice me till I spoke to her. I then learned from
her in reply to my questions that she was Miss Gilmore,
whose parents had died two days before; that her brother,
younger than herself, was sick in the wagon, probably
with cholera; that their oxen were lost or stolen by the
Indians; and that the train they had been traveling with,
after waiting for three days on account of the sickness
and death of her parents, had gone on that morning, fearful, if they delayed longer, of being caught by winter in
the Sierra Nevada mountains....The people of her train
had told her that probably her oxen would yet be found,
or at any rate some other train coming along with oxen
to spare would take her and her brother and their wagon
along.

"Who could tell the deep sense of bereavement, distress and
desolation that weighed on that poor girl's heart, there in the
wilderness with no telling what fate was in store for her and her
sick brother?" Reid asks his readers and surely also himself. Such
memories might have seemed difficult to reconcile with the con-
viction that one had successfully met the tests or challenges
required to enter the new life. The redemptive power of the
crossing was, nonetheless, the fixed idea of the California
settlement, and one that raised a further question: for what
exactly, and at what cost, had one been redeemed? When you
jettison others so as not to be "caught by winter in the Sierra
Nevada mountains," do you deserve not to be caught? When
you survive at the cost of Miss Gilmore and her brother, do you
survive at all?

Robert Hass

"Palo Alto: The Marshes"

Robert Hass was born in San Francisco in 1941. His books of
poetry include *Sun Under Wood, Human Wishes, Praise*, and *Field
Guide*, which was selected for the Yale Younger Poets Series. He
is also the author or editor of several collections of essays and
translations, including *The Essential Haiku: Versions of Basho,
Buson, and Issa*, and he has also co-translated several volumes of
poetry with Czeslaw Milosz, most recently *A Treatise on Poetry*.
Hass has been honored with a MacArthur "genius" fellowship
and a National Book Critics Circle Award (twice), and from
1995 to 1997 he served as U.S. poet laureate. He is currently a
chancellor of the Academy of American Poets and a professor in
the English department at the University of California, Berkeley.

1

She dreamed along the beaches of this coast.
Here where the tide rides in to desolate
the sluggish margins of the bay,
sea grass sheens copper into distances.

Walking, I recite the hard
explosive names of birds:
egret, killdeer, bittern, tern.
Dull in the wind and early morning light,
the striped shadows of the cattails
twitch like nerves.

2

Mud, roots, old cartridges, and blood.
High overhead, the long silence of the geese.

3

"We take no prisoners," John Fremont said
and took California for President Polk.
That was the Bear Flag War.
She watched it from the Mission San Rafael,
named for the archangel (the terrible one)
who gently laid a fish across the eyes
of saintly, miserable Tobias
that he might see.
The eyes of fish. The land
shimmers fearfully.
No archangels here, no ghosts,
and terns rise like seafoam
from the breaking surf.

4

Kit Carson's antique .45, blue,
new as grease. The roar
flings up echoes,
row on row of shrieking avocets.
The blood of Francisco de Haro,
Ramon de Haro, José de los Reyes Berryessa
runs darkly to the old ooze.

5

The star thistles: erect, surprised,

6

and blooming
violet caterpillar hairs. One
of the de Haros was her lover,
the books don't say which.
They were twins.

7

In California in the early spring
there are pale yellow mornings
when the mist burns slowly into day.
The air stings
like autumn, clarifies
like pain.

8

Well I have dreamed this coast myself.
Dreamed Mariana, since her father owned the land
where I grew up. I saw her picture once:
a wraith encased in a high-necked black silk
dress so taut about the bones there were hardly ripples
for the light to play in. I knew her eyes
had watched the hills seep blue with lupine after rain,
seen the young peppers, heavy and intent,
first rosy drupes and then the acrid fruit,
the ache of spring. Black as her hair
the unreflecting venom of those eyes
is an aftermath I know, like these brackish,
russet pools a strange life feeds in
or the old fury of land grants, maps,

and deeds of trust. A furious dun-
colored mallard knows my kind
and skims across the edges of the marsh
where the dead bass surface
and their flaccid bellies bob.

    9

A chill tightens the skin
around my bones. The other California
and its bitter absent ghosts
dance to a stillness in the air:
the Klamath tribe was routed and they disappeared.
Even the dust seemed stunned,
tools on the ground, fishnets.
Fires crackled, smouldering.
No movement but the slow turning
of the smoke, no sound but jays
shrill in the distance and flying further off.
The flicker of lizards, dragonflies.
And beyond the dry flag-woven lodges
a faint persistent slapping.
Carson found ten wagonloads
of fresh-caught salmon, silver
in the sun. The flat eyes stared.
Gills sucked the thin annulling air.
They flopped and shivered,
ten wagonloads. Kit Carson
burned the village to the ground.
They rode some twenty miles that day
and still they saw the black smoke
smear the sky above the pines.

10

Here everything seems clear,
firmly etched against the pale
smoky sky: sedge, flag, owl's clover,
rotting wharves. A tanker lugs silver
bomb-shaped napalm tins toward
port at Redwood City. Again,
my eye performs
the lobotomy of description.
Again, almost with yearning,
I see the malice of her ancient eyes.
The mud flats hiss as the tide turns.
They say she died in Redwood City,
cursing "the goddamned Anglo-Yankee yoke."

11

The otters are gone from the bay
and I have seen five horses
easy in the grassy marsh
beside three snowy egrets.

Bird cries and the unembittered sun,
wings and the white bodies of the birds,
it is morning. Citizens are rising
to murder in their moral dreams.

for Mariana Richardson (1830–1891)

lê thi diem thúy

from *The Gangster We Are All Looking For*

lê thi diem thúy was born in 1972 in Phan Thiet, South Vietnam, and left the country on a boat with her father in 1978. She grew up in Linda Vista, San Diego, and her childhood there became the basis of her first book, *The Gangster We Are All Looking For.* She is an author and a performance artist and has been awarded a fellowship by the Radcliffe Institute for Advanced Study at Harvard University.

This excerpt is characteristic of the tone and style of *The Gangster We Are All Looking For*, published in 2003, which has best been described as "elliptical." It follows a Vietnamese family shrouded in mystery through the difficult, drifting life of new immigrants to San Diego, as told through the eyes of the six-year-old daughter.

We live in the country of California, the province of San Diego, the village of Linda Vista. We live in old Navy Housing bungalows built in the 1940s. Since the 1980s, these bungalows house Vietnamese, Cambodian, and Laotian refugees from the Vietnam War. When we moved in, we had to sign a form promising not to put fish bones in the garbage disposal.

We live in a yellow house on Westinghouse Street. Our house is one story, made of wood and plaster. Between our house and another one-story house are six two-story houses. Facing our row of houses, across a field of brown dirt, sits another row of yellow houses, same as ours, watching us like a sad twin. Linda Vista is full of houses like ours, painted in peeling shades of olive green, baby blue, and sun-baked yellow.

There's new Navy Housing on Linda Vista Road, the long street that takes you out of here. We see the Navy people watering their lawns, their children riding pink tricycles up and down the culs-de-sac. We see them in Victory Supermarket, buying groceries with cash. In Kelley Park they have picnics and shoot each other with water guns. At school their kids are Most Popular, Most Beautiful, Most Likely to Succeed. Though there are more Vietnamese, Cambodian, and Laotian kids at the school, in the yearbook we are not the most of anything. They call us Yang because one year a bunch of Laotian kids with the last name Yang came to our school. The Navy Housing kids started calling all the refugee kids "Yang."

Yang. Yang. Yang.

Ma says living next to Anh's family reminds her of Vietnam because the blue tarp suspended above Ahn's backyard is the bright blue of the South China Sea. Ma says, isn't it funny how sky and sea follow you from place to place as if they too were traveling.

Thinking of my older brother, who was still in Vietnam, I ask Ma, "If the sky and the sea can follow us here, why can't people?"

Ma ignores my question and says even Anh reminds her of Vietnam, the way she sets out for market each morning.

Ba becomes a gardener. Overnight. He buys a truck full of equipment and a box of business cards from Uncle Twelve, who is moving to Texas to become a fisherman. The business cards read "Tom's Professional Gardening Service" and have a small green picture embossed on them, a man pushing a lawn mower. The man has his back to you, so no one holding the card can tell it's not Ba, no one who doesn't already know. He says I can be his secretary because I speak the best English. If you call us on the business phone, you will hear me say: "Hello, you have reached Tom's Professional Gardening Service. We are not here right now, but if you leave us a message, we will get back to you as soon as possible. Thank you."

It is hot and dusty where we live. Some people think it's dirty but they don't know much about us. They haven't seen our gardens full of lemongrass, mint, cilantro, and basil. Driving by with their windows rolled up, they've only seen the pigeons pecking at day-old rice and the skinny cats and dogs sitting in the skinny shade of skinny trees. Have they seen the berries that we pick, that turn our lips and fingertips red? How about the small staircase Ba built from our bedroom window to the backyard so I would have a shortcut to the clothesline? How about the Great Wall of China that snakes like a river from the top of the steep hill off Crandall Drive to the slightly curving bottom? Who has seen this?[…]

Ma shaved her head in Linda Vista because she got mad at Ba for gambling away her money and getting drunk every week during *Monday Night Football*. Ba gave her a blue baseball cap to wear until her hair grew back and she wore it backward, like a real badass.

After that, some people in Linda Vista said that Ma was crazy and Ba was crazy for staying with her. But what do some people know?

When the photograph came, Ma and Ba got into a fight. Ba threw the fish tank out the front door and Ma broke all the dishes. They said they never should've got together.

Ma's sister sent her the photograph from Vietnam. It came in a stiff envelope. There was nothing else inside, as if anything more would be pointless. Ma held the photograph in her hands. She started to cry. "Child," she sobbed, over and over again. She wasn't talking about me. She was talking about herself.

Ba said, "Don't cry. Your parents have forgiven you."

Ma kept crying anyway and told him not to touch her with his gangster hands. Ba clenched his hands into tight fists and punched the walls.

"What hands?! What hands?!" he yelled. "Let me see the gangster! Let me see his hands!" I see his hands punch hands punch hands punch blood.[…]

When the eviction notice came, we didn't believe it so we threw it away. It said we had a month to get out. The houses on our block had a new owner who wanted to tear everything down and build better housing for the community. It said we were priority tenants for the new complex, but we couldn't afford to pay the new rent so it didn't matter. The notice also said that if we didn't get out in time, all our possessions would be confiscated in accordance with some section of a law book or manual we were supposed to have known about but had never seen. We couldn't believe the eviction notice so we threw it away.

The fence is tall, silver, and see-through. Chain-link, it rattles when you shake it and wobbles when you lean against it. It circles our block like a bad dream. It is not funny like the clothesline whose flying shirts and empty pants suggest human birds and vanishing acts. This fence presses sharply against your brain. We three stand still as posts. Looking at it, then at one another—this side and that—out of the corners of our eyes. What are we thinking?

At night we come back with three uncles. Ba cuts a hole in the fence and we step through. Quiet, we break into our own house through the back window. Quiet, we steal back everything that is ours. We fill ten-gallon garbage bags with clothes, pots and pans, flip-flops, the porcelain figure of Mary, the wooden Buddha and the Chinese fisherman lamp. In the arc of our flashlights we find our favorite hairbrushes behind bedposts. When we are done, we clamber, breathless. Though it's quiet, we can hear police cars coming to get us.

We tumble out the window like people tumbling across continents. We are time traveling, weighed down by heavy furniture and bags of precious junk. We find ourselves leaning against Ba's yellow truck. Ma calls his name, her voice reaching like a hand feeling for a tree trunk in darkness.

In the car, Ma starts to cry. "What about the sea?" she asks. "What about the garden?" Ba says we can come back in the morning and dig up the stalks of lemongrass and fold the sea into a blue square. Ma is sobbing. She is beating the dashboard with her fists. "I want to know," she says, "I want to know, I want to know...who is doing this to us?" Hiccupping she says, "I want to know, why—why there's always a fence. Why there's always someone on the outside wanting someone...something on the inside and between them...this...sharp fence. Why are we always leaving like this?"

Everyone is quiet when Ma screams.

"Take me back!" she says. "I can't go with you. I've forgotten my mother and father. I can't believe...Anh Minh, we've left them to die. Take me back."

Ma wants Ba to stop the car, but Ba doesn't know why. The three uncles, sitting in a row in the bed of the truck, think Ma is crazy. They yell in through the rear window, "My, are you going to walk back to Vietnam?"

"Yeah, are you going to walk home to your parents' house?"

In the silence another shakes his head and reaches into his shirt pocket for his cigarettes.

Ba puts his foot on the gas pedal. Our car jerks forward, and then plunges down the Crandall Drive hill. Ma says, "I need air, water…" I roll the window down. She puts her head in her hands. She keeps crying, "Child." Outside, I see the Great Wall of China. In the glare of the streetlamps, it is just a long strip of cardboard.

In the morning, the world is flat. Westinghouse Street is lying down like a jagged brushstroke of sun-burnt yellow. There is a big sign within the fence that reads

COMING SOON:
CONDOMINIUMS
TOWN HOUSES
FAMILY HOMES

Below these words is a copy of a watercolor drawing of a large pink complex.

We stand on the edge of the chain-link fence, sniffing the air for the scent of lemongrass, scanning this flat world for our blue sea. A wrecking ball dances madly through our house. Everything has burst wide open and sunk down low. Then I hear her calling them. She is whispering, "Ma/Ba, Ma/Ba." The whole world is two butterfly wings rubbing against my ear.

Listen...they are sitting in the attic, sitting like royalty in the dark, buried by a wrecking ball. Paper fragments floating across the surface of the sea.

There is not a trace of blood anywhere except here, in my throat, where I am telling you all this.

Paul Beatty

from *The White Boy Shuffle*

Paul Beatty, poet, performance artist, and novelist, was born in
1962 in West Los Angeles. He received an M.F.A. in creative
writing from Brooklyn College and an M.A. in psychology
from Boston University. His books of poetry include *Big Bank
Take Little Bank* and *Joker, Joker, Deuce.* He is also the author of
the novels *Tuff* and *The White Boy Shuffle.* He currently lives in
New York.

In this early chapter of Beatty's debut novel, *The White Boy
Shuffle,* published in 1996, the teenaged narrator, Gunnar,
reflects on his years as the "cool black guy" in a mostly white
neighborhood in Santa Monica.

M y earliest memories bodysurf the warm comforting time-
lessness of the Santa Ana winds, whipping me in and
around the palm-tree–lined streets of Santa Monica. Me and— *Stylistic*
white boys Steven Pierce, Ryan Foggerty, and David Schoenfeld *Fragment*
sharing secrets and bubble gum. Our friendship was a buoyant
one based on proximity, easy-to-remember phone numbers, and

the fact that Ryan always had enough money for everybody. We were friends, but didn't see ourselves as a unit. We had no enemies, no longstanding rivalries with the feared Hermosa Beach Sandcastle Hellions or the Exclusive Brentwood Spoiled Brat Millionaire Tycoon Killers. Our conflicts limited themselves to fighting with our sisters and running from the Santa Monica Shore Patrol. My co-conspirators in beach terrorism and I suffered through countless admonishments from overzealous officers lucky enough to grab one of us in some act of mischief that was always a precursor to a lifetime of incarceration bunking with society's undesirables. "Young man, try to imagine a future behind bars."

"What you in for, young buck?"

"I garnished the potato salad of this obese family of Orange County sea cows with sand crabs."

"Premeditated?"

"Hell, yeah! The entire clan beached themselves fully clothed twenty feet from the water. Tourists. Fucked up the local vibe."

"Hey, that's worth a couple of years, easy. Chow's at six o'clock."

After I was escorted home by the police "one too many times," my mother made me join Cub Scout Pack #251, starting me on the socialization treadmill toward group initiation and ceremonial induction. I was kicked out after three meetings for failing to learn the pledge, but the experience stayed with me. It was as if somebody assigned a den mother to point out the significance of campy blue uniforms with buttons in every imaginable place, flags, and oaths. My salt-air world began to subdivide into a series of increasingly complicated dichotomous relationships. Thankfully, I still remember when my worldview wasn't "us against them" or "me vs. the world" but "me and the world."

I was an ashy-legged black beach bum sporting a lopsided trapezoidal natural and living in a hilltop two-story townhouse on Sixth and Bay. After an exhausting morning of bodyboarding and watching seagulls hovering over the ocean expertly catching french fries, I would spend the afternoon lounging on the rose-wood balcony. Sitting in a lawn chair, my spindly legs crossed at the ankles, I'd leaf through the newest Time-Life mail-order installments of the family's coffee-table reference library. *Predators of the Insect World, Air War Over Europe, Gunfighters of the Old West*; I loved reading about red ant–black ant wars, dog-fights at fifteen thousand feet, and any cowboy "who was so mean he once shot a man for snoring." The baseball game would crackle and spit from the cheap white transistor radio my father gave me for my seventh birthday. The tiny tweeter damp with drool from Dodger play-by-play man Chip Parker salivating over Rusty Lanahan's agility around the bag and how despite allega-tions of spousal abuse the first baseman with the All-American *punim* remained a shining role model for the city's youth. If I still swore on my mother, I'd swear that between pitches I could hear the fizzing of the sun setting behind me, cooling down with a well-earned bedtime dip in the Pacific. I liked to twist the glossy Time-Life photos in the fading yellow light. When the praying mantis's chalky lime green changed to ghostly white and a B-26 Marauder bomber's drab army olive melted away into a muddy dark brown, it was time for dinner. The call of the irate mother could be heard over the roar of the airplanes flying off the page.

"Gunnar, set the fucking table."

"'kay, Ma."

Before making my way to the silverware drawer, I'd lean over the balcony, squinting into the dusk, and look out toward the nearly empty waterfront six blocks away. The elongated shadows of beachcombers and their metal detectors skimmed across the dimpled and paper-cup–laden sand in hopes of finding lost sand-wich baggies full of quarters stolen long ago from the bottom of parents' dresser drawers. Lifeguard Station 26 is boarded up and shut down for the evening. The sandy-colored hairy-legged life-guard walks quickly toward his classic convertible VW Beetle, his cherry-red vinyl shorts and windbreaker barking, "Caution! Dangerous riptide!" and fluttering in the strong sea breeze. Two shimmering wetsuit-clad surfers straddle fiberglass DayGlo boards bobbing offshore, waiting for the last good wave of the day to take them home. The sandpipers play tag with the receding tide, scampering just outside the stretching reach of the waves dying at their knobby feet. Every once in a while the birds call time out to take water breaks, sticking their thin beaks into the moist sand. The sun stops fizzing, though Chip Parker remains excited, haranguing the listening audience about left-fielder Nathaniel Galloway's powerful Negroid hindquarters and seguing smoothly into the ad copy for Farmer John's ham, "hickory smoked just the way you like it."

The lights at Dodger Stadium and the streetlamps flicker on, and throughout Santa Monica the obedient kids wave goodnight to their delinquent friends as the community goes into the seventh-inning stretch. "Jesse Stewart retires the side in order, one, two, three. And after six it's the Dodgers three, the Mets one." Life was full of Cracker Jacks, root-root-rooting for the home team, and fucking with my mother.

"Gunnar! Set the table!"

"Ma? You know what?"

"What?"

"That's what."

"Very funny. Set the table or I'll wash your sharp-tongued mouth out with the whetstone."

I was very funny, in a sophomoric autodidactic knock-knock-who's-there sort of way. I learned timing, Zen and the art of self-deprecation from the glut of Jewish standup comics on cable TV, who served as living Chinese acupuncture charts of comedic pressure points: dating-yin, parents-yin, daily absurdities-yang. The ancient texts of Bennett Cerf and the humorous anecdotes from Grandma's waterlogged *Reader's Digest*s were, if not the I Ching, at least Confucian hymnals.

I was the funny, cool black guy. In Santa Monica, like most predominantly white sanctuaries from urban blight, "cool black guy" is a versatile identifier used to distinguish the harmless black male from the Caucasian juvenile while maintaining politically correct semiotics. If someone was planning a birthday party, the potential invitees always asked, "Who's going to be there?" The conversation would go:

"Shaun, Lance, Gunnar..."

"Gunnar? Who's that?"

"You know, the funny, cool black guy."

Some kids had reps for shredding on skateboards or eating ear wax. My forte was the ability to hold a straight face and pull off the nervy prank. I learned early that white kids will believe anything anybody a shade darker than chocolate milk says. So I'd tell the gullible Paddys that I was part Gypsy and had the innate ability to tell fortunes. Waving my left index finger like a pendulum over their sticky palms, I'd forecast long lifetimes of health and prosperity. "You'll have a big house in the hills. Over here on the love line is your tennis court. Right here by the life line is your heliport. Now where do you want your pool?" The unsuspecting dupe would point to a spot usually midway between the mystic cross and the creative line, and I'd spit a wad of saliva somewhere near the designated area. "There's your pool."

I was the only cool black guy at Mestizo Mulatto Mongrel Elementary, Santa Monica's all-white multicultural school. My early education consisted of two types of multiculturalism: classroom multiculturalism, which reduced race, sexual orientation, and gender to inconsequence, and schoolyard multiculturalism, where the kids who knew the most Polack, queer, and farmer's daughter jokes ruled. The classroom cross-cultural teachings couldn't compete with the playground blacktop lessons, which were cruel but at least humorous. Like most aspects of regimented pop-quiz pedagogy, the classroom multi-culturalism was contradictory, though its intentions were good.

My third-grade teacher, Ms. Cegeny, liked to wear a shirt that read:

~~Black~~
~~White~~
~~Red~~
~~Yellow~~
~~Brown~~

Human

Whenever she wore it she seemed to pay special attention to me, Salvador Aguacaliente (the silent Latin kid who got to go home early on Cinco de Mayo), and Sheila Watanabe (the loud-est Pledge of Allegiance sayer in the history of American education), taking care to point out the multiculturalist propaganda posted above the blackboard next to the printed and cursive letters of the alphabet: "Eracism—The sun doesn't care what color you are."

On hot stage-three smog-alert California days Ms. Cegeny would announce, "Okay, class, put away your pencils and take out your science books. Turn to page eighty-eight. Melissa, please read starting from 'Fun with Sunshine and Thermodynamics.'" Melissa Schoopmann would begin in her deliberate relentless monotone. "This may sound funny…to the novice…third-grade scientist,…but sunshine is cool.…Without it…the earth…would be…as lifeless as a…Catholic funeral on a…rainy, dreary day." I'd try to fall asleep, but it was too hot even to daydream. My sweat-soaked Suicidal Tendencies *You Can't Bring Me Down* tour shirt clung to the inversion layer of grit on my skin. Melissa droned on. "Dark colors…such as…black absorb sunlight…and light colors…such as…white reflect sunlight." I looked up and down my skinny dark brown arms and turned to my lab partner, Cecilia Peetemeyer, the palest kid in school. Cecilia's skin was so transparent that one week during health Ms. Cegeny used Cecilia's see-through skim-milk-white limbs to show the difference between arteries, capillaries, and veins.

"Cecilia, are you hot?" I asked.

"No."

"Shit."

"Gunnar, what was the last thing Melissa read?"

"Uh, she said um. She said dark colors soak up the sun's rays through processes called conduction and convection and the lighter colors of the spectrum tend to alter the path of the radiation through reflection and refraction."

"Good, I thought you weren't paying attention. Melissa, please continue."

Everything was multicultural, but nothing was multicultural. The class studied Asian styles of calculation by learning to add and subtract on an abacus and we then applied the same mathematical principles on Seiko calculators. Prompting my hand to go up and me to ask naively, "Isn't the Seiko XL-126 from the same culture as the abacus?" Ms. Cegeny's response was "No, we *gave* this technology to the Japanese after World War II. Modern technology is a Western construct." Oh. To put me in my place further, Sheila Watanabe hummed "My country 'tis of thee, sweet land of liberty" loud enough for the whole class to hear.

One year during Wellness Week a MASH unit of city health workers set up camp in the gymnasium to ensure that America would have an able-bodied supply of future midlevel managers ready to lead the reinforcement brigades of minimum-wage foot soldiers to their capitalistic battle stations. A free-enterprise penologist was a physically fit one. We answered the patriotic call one girl and boy at a time. Allison Abramowitz and Aaron Aaronson were the first to go. Brave warriors, they left with no send-off party save the frightened faces of their classmates. Ten minutes later Allison returned unharmed. She skipped over to her desk, sat down, and covered a sly I-know-something-you-don't smile with her hand. Kent Munson quickly asked for permission to sharpen his pencil. He dropped the pencil next to Allison and asked her what happened. She hissed, "None of your beeswax," sending Kent slinking back to his seat defeated. When copycat and cootie-infested Katie Swickler tried the same technique, Allison greeted her with a message whispered in her ear. Then girls throughout the classroom giggled and smiled at Katie, thanking her for the reassurance. It was as if they were communicating through gender-specific telepathy, leaving us guys looking more confused than usual.

Then Aaron Aaronson walked in, his face drained of color, his arms stuck tightly to his sides, and a newly acquired tic violently tossing his head back at a sickeningly acute angle every two seconds. Zombiefied, he walked a few steps into the classroom, stopped, and shouted, "Oh shit, you guys. They touched my balls and made me cough."

Ms. Cegeny ignored Aaron's pederastic pronouncements, called two more names, and continued her lecture on the importance of living in a colorblind society. "Does anyone have an example of colorblind processes in American society?"

Ed Wismer raised his hand and said, "Justice."

"Good. Anything else?"

Millicent Offerman, who as teacher's pet spoke without raising her hand, shouted out, "The president sure seems to like people of color."

"Anyone else think of anything that's colorblind? Gunnar?"

"Dogs."

"I believe that dogs are truly colorblind, but they're born that way. Class, it's important that we judge people for what?"

"Their minds!"

"And not their what?"

"Color!"

The response to Ms. Cegeny's call was mostly soprano. I know none of the boy altos were into it—too busy cursing ourselves for wearing the same drawers two days in a row. Colorblind? I hoped the doctor would be totally blind, or he might pull down my underwear, see the brown skid marks on my white Montgomery Ward cotton briefs, and recommend me for placement in special education.

Eventually Ms. Cegeny called my name and I left to be examined by a quiet nurse and a doctor so old he may have cowritten the Hippocratic oath. I was weighed and measured. The doctor banged on my knees with a rubber tomahawk, then asked me to pull down my drawers. Ignoring my stains, he wrapped his trembling and wrinkled hand around my equally wrinkled scrotum. I didn't flinch. Which surprised him.

"Anyone ever do this to you before, son?"

"No."

"Do you know what I am doing, son?"

"Touching my balls."

"Do you know why? Cough."

"Ah-hem. To practice your juggling?"

"Oh, you're one of those funny cool black guys, aren't you. No, I'm testing you for a hernia. Cough."

"Ah-hem! How do you test the girls?"

"I pinch their nipples and ask them to whistle. Pull up your pants and we'll test your sight."

I sat on a stool and read the eye chart with no problems. The nurse placed an open book on my lap and asked if I saw any numbers in the pattern of colored dots. I pointed out the yellow-orange eight-six in the sea of gray dots and asked the nurse what I was being tested for. The doctor stopped shaking long enough to interrupt the nurse and answer, "Colorblindness."

"Our teacher says we're supposed to be colorblind. That's hard to do if you can see color, isn't it?"

"Yeah, I'd say so, but I think your teacher means don't make any assumptions based on color."

"Cross on the green and not in between."

"They're talking about human color."

"So?"

"So just pretend that you don't see color. Don't say things like 'Black people are lecherous, violent, natural-born criminals.'"

"But I'm black."

"Oh, I hadn't noticed."

I went back to class and told the still-nervous boys in the back rows whose last names began with the letters L through Z that the physical wasn't too bad other than when the doctor measures your dick with a ruler and calls out to the nurse, "Penis size normal," or "teeny-weeny," or "fucking humungous." Ann Kurowski, who was twice as blind as Helen Keller but determined to go through life without wearing glasses, asked me if I remembered the letters on the bottom of the eye chart. I told her "F-E-C-E-S" and opened my primer to the story about a war between a herd of black elephants and a herd of white elephants.

I don't remember what the elephants were fighting about— something about hating each other for the colors of their sponge-rubbery skins. It wasn't as if the black elephants had to use the mosquito-infested watering hole and rely on white elephant welfare for their quinine. After heavy casualties on both sides, a cease-tusking was called. The elephants, as wounded and bedraggled as elephants could possibly be, headed off into the hills, only to return to the plains years later as a harmonious and homogeneous herd of gray elephants.

I never could figure out why that story was so disquieting. Maybe it was the unsettling way Eileen Litmus would loudly slam shut her reader and stare at me from across the room as we completed the assignment at the end of the story.

1. *Why did the elephants not get along?* A folded note would soon find my hand under the desk.

2. How come the elephants came back gray? I'd open the note, trying my best not to rustle the paper. The scrawl read:

> Fuck the stupid elephants, I like the tortoise and the hare story much more better. I challenge you to a race. Meet me after school for a race from the baseball diamond to the handball courts and back. Do you accept the challenge or are you a pigeon-toed wuss? P.S. You have big ears so you must be an African elephant.

3. Can we apply this story to real life? I'd look up and see Eileen's hand raised high in the air, her eyes' radar locked on mine. "Ms. Cegeny! Ms. Cegeny! Gunnar's passing notes!" Ms. Cegeny would squeak her pudgy sandal-shod feet over to my desk and read the entire note to the shrieking delight of the class. As punishment for my misdemeanor, I'd have to stand up and read aloud my answer to the last question regarding the elephant story.

4. What do you think will happen to the elephants in the future? "Just like some human babies are born with tails or scales, some unfortunate baby elephants are going to be genetic flashbacks and come out albino white and summer's nap black. Then the whole monochrome utopia is going to be all messed up."

My first crush was on Stan "the Man" Musial, an old second baseman with a corkscrew batting stance who played for the St. Louis Cardinals in the 1940s and 1950s. Eileen Litmus was my second love. She had a vindictive sense of humor, power to left-center, and was faster than winter vacation, three qualities I admired in a third grader. Despite our age, Eileen and I were easily the fastest kids in the school. Kids would bet movie money on who would win our Friday marathons around the schoolyard backstops. The "Ready, get set, go!" often caught me flatfooted, staring at her lean figure, my arms frozen in prerace Tiberian

Olympic-statue readiness. The sudden *whoosh* of Eileen's departure would roust me from my trance, her thick dirty-blond hair streaming behind her like jet vapor, denim hip-huggers blurring past the tetherball courts. Pumping my arms and puffing my cheeks like I'd seen the track stars do on TV, I'd try to make up ground just so I could catch a glimpse of her round tan tomboyish face. If the grass near the hopscotch boxes was soggy and she wore the heavier Nike Cortezes, not the lighter Adidas running shoes, I stood a chance of catching her near the handball court, the inner thighs of my corduroys rubbing and buzzing down the stretch. Usually Eileen crossed the finish line first, wading into a welcoming committee of high fives and hugs from the girls. The boys wreathed me with humiliation. "Dude, why did you let her win? I lost four grape Pixie Stix. What the fuck is wrong with you, man? You're supposed to be fast. When's the last time a white sprinter won a race? Would you bowl with a white bowling ball? No, you wouldn't."

After a long schoolday of moralistic bombardment with the aphorisms of Martin Luther King, John F. Kennedy, Cesar Chavez, Pocahontas, and a herd of pacifist pachyderms, my friends and I were ready to think about color on our own terms. We'd make plans to spend the weekend at the beach, sunning in the shoreline's warm chromatics and filling in childhood's abstract impressionism coloring books with our own definitions of color, trying our hardest not to stay inside the lines.

Blue

Those without bikes rode on the handlebars. We pedaled side by side in wobbly tandems, yelling our blue profanities, sharing our blue fantasies. We bombarded the windows on the Big Blue municipal bus with wet baby-blue toilet-paper grenades. We splashed in the postcard blue of the ocean and stuck out our Slurpee blue tongues at the girls two towels over. Eileen's light-saber blue eyes cut through me like lighthouse beacons lancing the midnight.

Psychedelic

When you're young, psychedelic is a primary color and a most mesmerizing high. Santa Monica was full of free multihued trips. The color-burst free-love murals on Main Street seemed to come to vibrant cartoon life when I passed them. The whales and dolphins frolicked in the clouds and the sea lions and merry-go-round horsies turned cartwheels in the street. The spray-any-color-paint-on-the-spin-art creations at the pier were fifty-cent Jackson Pollock rainbow heroin hits that made your skin tingle and the grains of sand swell up and rise to the sky like helium balloons. Looking into the kaleidoscopic eyes of a scruffy Bukowski barfly sitting in the lotus position along the bike trails fractured your soul into hundreds of disconnected psychedelic shards. Each sharp piece of your mind begging for sobriety.

White

Santa Monica whiteness was Tennessee Williams's Delta summer seersucker-suit blinding. The patchy clouds, the salty foams of the cresting waves; my friends, my style—all zinc oxide nose-cream white. My language was three-foot swells that broke left to right. "No waaaay, duuuude. Tuuubular biiitchin' to the max. Tooootalllyy fucking raaad." White Gunnar ran teasingly tight circles around the recovering hollowed-out Narc Anon addicts till they spun like dreidels and dropped dizzily to the ground. White Gunnar was a broken-stringed kite leaning into the sea breeze, expertly maneuvering in the gusty gales. White Gunnar stabbed beached jellyfish with driftwood spears and let sand crabs send him into a disco frenzy by doing the hustle on his forehead. White was walking to school in the fog. White was ignoring the crossing guards and trying to outrun the morning moon. White was exhaling crystallized plumes of carbon dioxide and knowing it was the frozen exhaust of our excited minds. White wasn't the textbook "mixture of radiations from the visible spectrum"; it was the opposite. White was the expulsion of colors encumbered by self-awareness and pigment.

Black

Black was an unwanted dog abandoned in the forest who finds
its way home by fording flooded rivers and hitchhiking in the
beds of pickup trucks and arrives at its destination only to be
taken for a car ride to the desert. Black was hating fried chicken
even before I knew I was supposed to like it. Black was being a
nigger who didn't know any other niggers. The only black folks
whose names I knew were musicians and athletes: Jimi Hendrix,
Slash from Guns n' Roses, Jackie Joyner-Kersee, the Beastie Boys,
and Melody the drummer from Josie and the Pussycats.

Black was trying to figure out "how black" Tony Grimes, the
local skate pro, was. Tony, a freestyle hero with a signature
model Dogtown board, was a hellacious skater and somehow
disembodied from blackness, even though he was darker than a
lunar eclipse in the Congo. The interviews in *Shredder, Rollerbladers
Suck*, and *Stoked* magazines never mentioned his color.

Stoked: So, dude?

Tony: Yeah.

Stoked: Gnarly frontside ollie 180 fakie at the Laguna Pro-Am.

Tony: Nailed it, bro, want another hit?

Now and then we'd see Tony Grimes, our deracinated hero,
in Coping 'n' Doping Skateshop on Ocean Street next to the
Tommy Burger. "What's up, Tony?" we'd all ask coolly, yet with
genuine concern in our voices. We'd receive an over-the-shoulder
"What's shakin', dude?" and fight over who he'd acknowledged.
"He called me dude. Not you, you nimrod."

Tony Grimes strolled around the shop, a baseball cap mag-
netically attached at some crazy angle to his unkempt thick
clumpy Afro. His lean muscular legs loped from clothes rack to
clothes rack as he eyed the free shit he would take home after he
got through rapping to the manager's girlfriend.

Black was a suffocating bully that tied my mind behind my
back and shoved me into a walk-in closet. Black was my father
on a weekend custody drunken binge, pushing me around as if I
were a twelve-year-old, seventy-five-pound bell clapper clanging

hard against the door, the wall, the shoe tree. Black is a repressed memory of a sandpapery hand rubbing abrasive circles into the small of my back, my face rising and falling in time with a hairy heaving chest. Black is the sound of metal hangers sliding away in fear, my shirt halfway off, hula-hooping around my neck.

That summer of my molestation, my sister Christina returned from a YMCA day camp field trip in tears. My mother asked what was wrong, and between breathless wails Christina replied that on the way home from the Museum of Natural History the campers had cheered, "Yeah, white camp! Yeah, white camp!" and she had felt left out. I tried to console her by explaining the cheer was, "Yeah, Y camp! Yeah, Y camp!" and no one was trying to leave her out of anything. Expressing unusual concern in our affairs, Mom asked if we would feel better about going to an all-black camp. We gave an insistent "Noooooo." She asked why and we answered in three-part sibling harmony, "Because they're different from us." The way Mom arched her left eyebrow at us, we knew immediately we were in for a change. Sunday I was hitching a U-Haul trailer to the back of the Volvo, and under cover of darkness we left halcyon Santa Monica for parts unknown. Ma driving, singing a medley of Temptations hits, my sisters passed out in the back seat, twitching in exhaustion from moving and packing.

Ma's voice dropped a couple of octaves as she segued from "My Girl" into "Papa Was a Rolling Stone." I rolled down the window, trying to capture the last vestiges of the nighttime salt air, and began writing mental letters to friends I knew I'd never see again.

Dear Ryan Foggerty,

Later, man. Thanks for the ticket to the Henry Rollins/Anthrax show at the Civic Auditorium and for lending me your Slidemaster trucks and the Profane Insane Urethane wheels, I'll send 'em back to you. Rock and roll will never die.

Be cool,
Gunnar

Dear Steven Pierce,

I'll miss the weekend speedboat outings with your red-haired ex–Playboy Bunny mom and her loaded boyfriend who always wore the stupid Skipper from *Gilligan's Island* hats. I remember how you hated the way he winked at you, one hand on the steering wheel, the other stroking your mother's behind. We did the right thing by pissing in the gas tank, so what if his engine stalled and he nearly died of exposure off the coast of Mexico. I'm sorry, but Larry, not Shemp or Curly or Moe, was the funniest Stooge. "Susquehanna Hat Company"?

> Slowly I turn,
> step by step,
> Gunnar

Dear Eileen,

I never told anyone. I know you didn't.

> XXOXOXX,
> Gunnar

Of all my laidback Santa Monican friends, I miss David Joshua Schoenfeld the most. He was off-white and closest to me in hue and temperament. Strangers would come up to him and ask if he was Mediterranean. David would shake his head, his dollar-bill-green eyes trying to convey that he was a tanned Jewish kid originally from Phoenix and perpetually late for the Hebrew school bus. Every Tuesday and Thursday after bar mitzvah classes we'd meet at the public library and pore through the WWII picture books, doing our best to fight the bewitching allure of Fascist cool. Our obsession wasn't a clear-cut Simon Wiesenthal Dudley Do-Right always-get-your-war-criminal fixation. We concerned ourselves with whether it would be more fun to fantasize about world domination attired in crushed Gestapo black velvet with red trim or in crumpled green Third Army gum-chewing schleppiness.

Himmler is wearing the Aryan autocrat's summer
ensemble, designed for maximum military foreboding
with a hint of patrician civility. Ideal for a morning jaunt
through the death camps or planning an autumn assault
on the Russian front.

By sixth grade we'd read the junior warmongers' canon: *Mein
Kampf, Boys from Brazil, Thirty Seconds over Tokyo,* and Anne
Frank, and our allegiances were muddled. On the way to Laker
games we'd talk about the atrocities at Buchenwald and
Auschwitz. David's father, looking for a parking space, would
ask us whether he should feel guilty about playing the serial
numbers branded onto his father's forearm in the state lottery.
During time-outs we'd test each other on the design specifica-
tions and flight capabilities of the Luftwaffe arsenal.

"The blitzkrieg clarion the Polish heard whistling out of the
clouds in 1939?"

"Please, the Stuka dive-bombers."

"Top speed for the Messerschmitt 109 K-model."

"Easy, 452 miles per hour, climb rate 4,880 feet per minute."

"Someone's been studying."

"Knock this out. Give me the wingspan and ceiling for the
Focke-Wulf 190 D-series."

"You know that's my favorite plane of all time. Wingspan 33
feet and 5 inches, ceiling 32,800 feet. Don't Focke with me, man.
Chu wanna go to war? Okay, we go to war."

Later that night, with permission to sleep over at David's
house, we went to war. On our last reconnaissance sortie before
bedtime we found a trail of ants on a Bataan death march to
underground bunkers beneath his front porch. After five passes
with the aerosol deodorant, we applied the matches and
watched the soldier ants burn, shouting, "Dresden! Dunkirk!
Banzai!" and strafing their shriveling exoskeletons with plastic
scale-model airplanes. Then it was inside to watch our favorite

video, *Tora, Tora, Tora*, stuffing handfuls of Jiffy Pop popcorn in our mouths and cheering for the Japanese.

When David's parents were asleep we played Hiroshima-Nagasaki in the bedroom. In our astronaut pj's with the crinkly plastic soles we moved the armoire into the hall and cleared enough space for Little Man and Fat Boy to land. Fake radio transmissions from the backs of our throats: "Come in, Los Alamos kkksssk. Come in, this is the *Enola Gay*, do you read? Kkksssk."

"Loud and clear, this is Oppenheimer, copy."

"Oppy baby, is this thing goin' to work?"

"Oh yeah, equivalent to twenty thousand tons of TNT. Do you copy?"

"Roger, ten-four, over and out."

We'd simulate the atomic flash by switching the bedroom light on and off as fast as we could, catching strobe glimpses of ourselves as nuclear shadows. Frozen in our positions, we mimicked death, writing letters home, pruning bonsai trees, playing with Hot Wheels, bent over mid butt-wipe.

Before going to bed, we brushed our teeth in the cramped bathroom. I noticed that David put the toothpaste on his brush before passing it under the cold water. I, like most folks, wet my brush, then put on the toothpaste, but I copied him because he was white and I figured maybe I was doing it wrong.

The only time race entered our war was when we sat over a basket of french fries drinking root beer and debating who Hitler would kill first, David the diabolical Jew or me the subhuman Negroid. It was on our excursions to the library that I stumbled across my first black heroes: the Tuskegee airmen, the Redball Express, some WAC nurses from Chicago, Brigadier General Benjamin O. Davis, Sr., Jesse Owens, and the mess cook who shot down a couple of zeros from the sinking deck of the *Arizona*. I kept these discoveries to myself. I didn't think David would find it as juicy as when I told him that Hitler had only half a package.

Dear David Schoenfeld,

I'm still high from the model airplane glue-sniffing session in the alleyway behind Pic 'n' Save. Remember the waterfalls of vomit rushing down our chins and our contest to see who could find the largest chunks of undigested potato chips in their pool of throw-up? Fuckin' cool. David, somehow through being with you I learned I was black and that being black meant something, though I've never learned exactly what. *Barukh atah Adonai.*

> Shalom, motherfucker,
> Gunnar

I don't remember helping my mother unload the trailer, but the next morning I awoke on the floor of a strange house amid boxes and piles of heavy-duty garbage bags jammed with clothes. The venetian blinds were drawn, and although the sunlight peeked between the slats, the house was dark. My mother let out a yell in that distinct-from-somewhere-in-the-kitchen timbre: "Gunnar, go into my purse and buy some breakfast for everybody." I acknowledged my orders and got dressed. Rummaging through my personal garbage bag, I found my blue Quicksilver shorts, a pair of worn-out dark gray Vans sneakers, a long-sleeved clay-colored old school Santa Cruz shirt, and just in case the morning chill was still happening, I wrapped a thick plaid flannel shirt around my skinny waist. I found the front door, and like some lost intergalactic B-movie spaceman who has crash-landed on a mysterious planet and is unsure about the atmospheric content, I opened it slowly, contemplating the possibility of encountering intelligent life.

I stepped into a world that was a bustling Italian intersection without Italians. Instead of little sheet-metal sedans racing around the fontana di Trevi, little kids on beat-up Big Wheels and bigger kids on creaky ten-speeds weaved in and out of the water spray from a sprinkler set in the middle of the street.

It seemed there must have been a fire drill at the hair salon, because males and females in curlers and shower caps crammed the sidewalks.

I ventured forth into my new environs and approached a boy about my age who wore an immaculately pressed sparkling white T-shirt and khakis and was slowly placing one slue-footed black croker-sack shoe in front of the other. I stopped him and asked for directions to the nearest store. He squinted his eyes and leaned back and stifled a laugh. "What the fuck did you say?" I repeated my request, and the laugh he suppressed came out gently. "Damn, cuz. You talk proper like a motherfucker." Cuz? Proper like a motherfucker? It wasn't as if I had said, "Pardon me, old bean, could you perchance direct a new indigene to the nearest corner emporium." My guide's bafflement turned to judgmental indignation at my appearance. "Damn, fool, what's up with your loud-ass gear? Nigger got on so many colors, look like a walking paint sampler. Did you find the pot of gold at the end of that rainbow? You not even close to matching. Take your jambalaya wardrobe down to Cadillac Street, make a right, and the store is at the light."

I walked to the store, not believing that some guy who ironed the sleeves on his T-shirt and belted his pants somewhere near his testicles had the nerve to insult me over how I dressed. I returned to the house, dropped the bag of groceries on the table, and shouted, "Ma, you done fucked up and moved to the 'hood!"

Brian Ascalon Roley

from *American Son*

Brian Ascalon Roley was raised in Los Angeles. His fiction and nonfiction have appeared in *Epoch*, the *Georgia Review*, the *San Francisco Chronicle*, and elsewhere, and his work has been translated and anthologized. His novel, *American Son*, has been honored as a *New York Times* Notable Book, a *Los Angeles Times* Best Book, and a Kiriyama Pacific Rim Prize finalist. He is currently a professor of English at Miami University in Cincinnati, Ohio.

What follows is the opening chapter of Roley's debut novel, *American Son*, published in 2001, a story of identity, violence, and longing in the urban ghettos of Los Angeles.

*D*ear *Ika,*
I am thankful for your letter of March 15th. We appreciate your prayers, and you and your sons will of course be included in our prayers as well. Here in Manila things have been busy. Julita will soon be graduating Ateneo, and we have been renovating the house in preparation for her graduation party. Some of our walls are for the moment no longer standing and last night a typhoon rain battered the plastic

tarp the workers had put in place for protection. You can imagine my surprise when I awoke this morning to find the living room flooded! I am certain the weather must be nicer for you in Los Angeles.

It is with concern that I read of your boys' declining studies. Perhaps Gabe's biology grade can be dismissed as an aberration—one which must be punished, of course—yet the case of his older brother appears most serious. It came as a surprise to me that Tomas was expelled from Saint Dominic's, particularly given that he is accused by Father Ryan of committing violent behaviors. I still recall Tomas as the quiet and handsome boy who visited us here in Manila as a child. With his American father's blood he has the mestizo looks of an actor. No doubt if you had remained in Manila, as I had warned you to, he would have fared well and you would not now have so many worries. Here Tomas would have known what it means to be a Laurel, its responsibilities and expectations. In fact, if he had shown any delinquent propensities I would have certainly spoken severely with him myself, and made communications with his teachers. My circumstances and connections have improved since you left the Philippines, and I believe that I could have averted his expulsion.

In fact, I suspect that in writing me you may have hoped that I could communicate with his American teacher, Father Ryan, as he had formerly served as a chaplain here in Forbes Park. I will try, yet as I have no other connections in Los Angeles, I am not hopeful in this regard. I can only advise you to attempt to gain admission for Tomas into another Catholic school, a stricter one if that is possible in a place like California.

Also, you must be careful whom you let him befriend. I find it particularly puzzling that a Filipino boy such as Tomas should choose to spend his time with poor Mexican children when there certainly must be nice American and Asian children of successful people in Los Angeles.

May I suggest that you consider bringing Tomas and Gabe here to Forbes Park for a visit? I know that you do not like to take my money *for plane tickets you cannot afford, but we would be most pleased if you were to change your mind.*

We will be praying for you and your sons always.

Love,

Your brother Betino

Balikbayan
South Santa Monica
California
April 1993

I

Tomas is the son who helps pay the mortgage by selling attack dogs to rich people and celebrities. He is the son who keeps our mother up late with worry. He is the son who causes her embarrassment by showing up at family parties with his muscles covered in gangster tattoos and his head shaved down to stubble and his eyes bloodshot from pot. He is really half white, half Filipino but dresses like a Mexican, and it troubles our mother that he does this. She cannot understand why if he wants to be something he is not he does not at least try to look white. He is also the son who says that if any girlfriend criticized our mother or treated her wrong he would knock the bitch across the house.

I am the son who is quiet and no trouble, and I help our mother with chores around the house.

The client is some man from the movie business who is coming over any minute so that Tomas can help him train the dog he bought to protect his home. This morning I have been helping my brother wash and train his dogs, which he calls "guard dogs" to the people he sells them to, but which you should really call *attack dogs* since we use methods he learned from cop friends he knows on the LAPD. Each time I come to the cage, they clamber against the rusted wire, throwing themselves against the links and barking for my attention. All week I have been replacing the old wood boards, rotted and nearly broken from the dogs' thrown weight. Despite my efforts, the wood bends and threatens to buckle and snap under their weight. The door pushes outward as if the cage has inhaled a great amount of breath. I unlatch its aluminum bolt, then let it come open a few inches— and stop it with my shoe. The dogs nudge at the stopped door. My hand slips inside and meets their wet noses and warm fur and the warm wet feeling of their tongues and drool.

Cut it out, I tell them.

They do not listen to me. They are far too excited, though if I were to use a German word—one my brother uses to train them to attack—they would become instantly attentive.

Quiet.

I find the one I want, Heinrich, and grab his collar and tug him out between the other dogs. They look disappointed, and some even wail. I give Greta and Johan and Sigmund quick pets and hush them, then shut and relatch the cage. They bark at my back, though they soon realize I am not going to let them out and they settle down. It is all I can do to keep hold of Heinrich's collar as I lead him across knee-deep grass to the training area. He ignores my shushing until I finally get impatient and tell him to quit it in German. *Las das sein!* He immediately quiets and stands at attention, ears perked. Though it is easier this way— and he follows me obediently now—I prefer not to use these commands since he changes from an affectionate pet to an alert and serious guard dog. He becomes all duty.

We find my brother at the shed, pulling out the burlap and plastic armor which he wraps around his arms for protection.

Tomas looks up at us. The sunlight makes his pale scalp, shaved like a Mexican gangster's, glow through his black, three-day-old stubble.

What took you so long?

The dogs all wanted to get out.

They always want to get out.

I look down. Sorry.

He turns to the dog. Heinrich stands stiffly, pressed against my leg. His ears prick as he looks at Tomas.

Don't look so excited to see me, Heinrich.

As Heinrich senses that Tomas does not yet need him to be alert, the dog's muscles relax and he pulls away from me—his fur sliding gently along my jeans—and he hurries to my brother. Tomas reaches over and hugs him and scratches behind Heinrich's ear. The tattoo on the back of my brother's neck—a black rose whose stem is wrapped by vinelike barbed wire— emerges from beneath his stretched T-shirt collar. He always wears a sleeveless T-shirt so people can see the tattoos along his muscled arms. The tattoos are mostly gang, Spanish, and old- lady Catholic. As he leans forward, the thin fabric of his shirt moves over his Virgin of Guadalupe tattoo that covers his back from his neck down to his pants. She wears a black robe and has deep, olive eyes. Crushed beneath her feet are the Devil's horns.

My brother is bent over, tongue-kissing Heinrich.

Good boy.

He looks up from Heinrich and regards me. You better wash him. The client's coming soon.

I did wash him. I washed all the dogs.

He doesn't smell like it.

You know I did, Tomas. You saw me.

Well then maybe you'd better do a better job.

I grit my jaw. You shouldn't complain. It's not like you pay me.

Fine, he says. Don't help if you don't want to. Sit inside and watch TV all day for all I care.

He turns away, letting Heinrich trot after him. I do not want to follow him, but I do not want to go back into the house either. Finally I do come alongside the house, batting aside the overgrown old trellis vines, and emerge onto the front yard. My brother sits on the porch. He is waiting for the client, the dog scrambling around on the threadbare grass before him, chasing a worn tennis ball Tomas threw onto the street. With sunlight coming through dusty overhanging branches, the street resembles an ocean bottom beneath a sunny kelp bed.

I linger at the lawn's edge. He ignores me for a while, then calls out, Why you standing all the way over there?

I keep my mouth closed and my arms crossed.

Stop sulking.

I'm not sulking.

Sit down. If the client sees you standing there like that he's gonna think you're my houseboy.

This is a lie, of course, but my face goes hot, which is what he was after. I do not want to sit after what he has just said, so I stand there for a moment. But I feel foolish, so I walk past him and enter the front door, to see if our mother needs any help inside.

II

All morning our mother has been cleaning up the kitchen so she can look out the window as Tomas prepares Heinrich for the client's arrival. I know it is hard for our mother to imagine the quiet boy he used to be. Right now Tomas is playing around with a false canvas arm. The dog leaps on it viciously, shaking it like a white shark thrashing a tenderloin on a harpoon, and on each impact she flinches. The client finally arrives around noon. He is a screenwriter or a producer or something. Mom studies this man who wears ratty black jeans meant to make him look casual, polished wing-tip shoes, and a maroon silk shirt. He nervously eyes the dog that will soon go home with him.

Who's this man, Gabe? she says to me without turning from the window. Her finger touches the glass.

I don't know. Some producer or something.

Hmmm, she says suspiciously. Does he own a nice mansion?

I wouldn't know.

She wipes the countertop she has already cleaned three times, her finger still bearing her wedding ring even though my father left us a few years ago and Tomas and the relatives think she should not wear it. She touches her earlobe and sighs. Well, I don't see why such a man needs a dog to guard his house. He's not such a big celebrity. Who does he think he is?

Maybe he's married to one.

Of course not. You tell your brother to come in before your aunt arrives and sees this dog attacking him.

The first time the client arrived he asked why my brother named the dog Heinrich. Tomas always gives the dogs German names and trains them with foreign words. He tells the celebrities and rich people he sells them to that they have pedigrees that go back to Germany, and that they descend from dogs the Nazis used. He likes to tell them Nazi scientists did experiments in dog breeding just as they did in genetics and rocketry. He tells them this is a Teutonic art that goes back to the Prussian war states. All this is a lie, of course. But the clients seem to like the explanation, even this movie producer who has a Jewish name. He paid six thousand dollars for the one dog and it was not even the best in the litter.

The celebrities also like that Tomas wears tattoos that tell you he belongs to the Eighteenth Street Gang. Tomas is six-three and you can see the definition of his muscles through his shirt. Sometimes he takes his shirt off. Not too many young white people have a huge tattoo of the Virgin Mary on their back and a gold crucifix dangling from a chain against their chest. He never tells his clients he is not Mexican. Sometimes he buys pit bulls in Venice or downtown where all the black people have them chained in their alleys and when you drive through the alleyways you can hear them barking for miles. The sound echoes between the buildings. He can buy them for forty dollars there and then place an ad in a West LA newspaper like the *Evening Outlook* and sell them for a couple hundred dollars. Sometimes he gets them from Compton or East LA, but he never lets me go with him anywhere east of Crenshaw. They are cheap nasty dogs and not even the best guard dogs, but ever since they started killing children everyone seems to want one. Selling them is an easy way to get money; Brentwood and Santa Monica people will come with cash (our neighborhood is at the poor end of Santa Monica, bordering Venice, so it does not scare them) and they do not expect the pit bulls to be trained. You do not buy one to be a nice pet, or a safe one. You chain them to a tree outside your house and dare people to attempt to get inside. A lot of young white people from West LA come because they want to be cool and think owning one is like having a tattoo or being branded on a shoulder or arm. But celebrities do not buy pit bulls. They buy American bulldogs and Rottweilers and Tervurens and Bouviers and other expensive dogs that require extensive training. Purebreds. My brother used to sell Akitas, but after Nicole Simpson's dog failed her, people on the Westside stopped buying them.

Mainly Tomas prefers to breed American bulldogs—pedigrees—and he raises them and trains them and he pets them and sometimes he even has to feed the puppies from a bottle. The ones he keeps long enough he trains according to the Schutzhund method. Each time he sells a puppy he falls quiet and pretends he does not care about it leaving, that he will never see it again. He will not scratch its chin or pet it in front of a customer, but afterwards, he will go to the window and watch the customer carrying it down the steps. Sometimes he will stand there for a very long time.

The client—Rosenthal—stands at one end of the backyard as he waits nervously for Tomas to fasten on his protective armor. The dog sits patiently now, wagging his tail. Tomas walks twenty yards across the grass and turns and nods. The man calls out a word in German and the dog sprints across the yard, barking viciously, and leaps at my brother and grabs his arm. I know it hurts even with the armor on. Sometimes you get bruises that trace the shape of a jaw. The dog will hang there on your arm, like a pendulum, until the client calls out for it to stop in German. Sometimes the clients get so mixed up and nervous they forget the word. Tomas cannot say it because he is being attacked and the dog is trained not to listen to him. Once a dog missed my brother's arm and caught him in the stomach, but fortunately I was there and called out *Aus* and the dog let go and sat down obediently, wagging its tail. It had love in its eyes again, longing for my brother's attention. Spittle still dripped down its gums and neck.

III

After our father left us, our mother started calling up her brother—Uncle Betino, who lives in the Philippines—for advice on how to deal with me and Tomas. They soon got into a dispute, however, over some jewelry and old statues of the Virgin Mary their mother owned before she died. Our mother had long, distressed conversations on the telephone, and Tomas (still small then) would hover nearby while she was on the line. Sometimes she would sob. Other times she simply wrapped a strand of hair around her finger. Mostly she worried about an old piece of jewelry, a silver pendant which had been with the family for over a century and had come to Manila on a ship from

Spain. Grandma had added her own diamonds to it, and meant for it to pass down to our mother. But Uncle Betino was in control of the estate and decided to give it to his wife Millie, who had hated Grandma and treated her badly on her deathbed. For that reason our mother didn't want her to have it.

Tomas did not talk much then, and he would stand in the hallway most of the time so she would not know he was listening, though afterwards—after our mother calmed down—he told her not to give in to our uncle. He asked if she could get a lawyer, and she said it was the Philippines and you could not sue for something like that there from a man like our uncle. He lived there, he knew people, and anyway had more money than we did. Tomas thought there must be something she could do, but she would get so upset he would finally drop it. I knew he was mad by the way he moved around the house doing chores or building model rockets. Uncle Betino came to Los Angeles a year later and he took us out to dinner. Even though he and our mother had argued about the pendant on the phone, now they acted warm with each other, the way Filipinos have to even when they are angry, and our mother and Millie kissed cheeks in greeting. I shook our uncle's hand. It was dark and callused and firm. He touched the side of my shoulder as though he were going to slap it, but then gripped it warmly and looked into my eyes. It was all I could do not to lower them. It was hard to imagine him making our mother cry. After he let go, he looked around to greet Tomas. But my brother wasn't there.

Our mother found him in his bedroom, shades drawn. She made him come out but Tomas did not look into Uncle Betino's eyes and shook his hand loosely, though after feeling how hard our uncle's grip was, Tomas suddenly started clenching his hand harder. Uncle Betino's face changed and he squeezed down tighter. My brother winced, though he tried to hide it. Uncle Betino was very nice to Tomas the rest of the night. He ordered him extra spare rib appetizers. He addressed him often, though he made sure not to ask him questions Tomas could refuse to answer. In this way, my brother could just sit there quietly and not be rude. He did not say anything during that dinner, but Uncle Betino did not lose face, and neither did our mother.

That night Tomas stole our uncle's wallet but Mom found out and made him return it, and she told our uncle that Tomas had found it on the floor and was merely safeguarding it. Our uncle was not fooled, but he took it back smiling and thanked him.

Afterwards, Tomas would not do any chores around the house and barely talked to her for a week. He sat in his room watching TV and refused to do any homework, which is how he knew he could most hurt her. Two years later, our father returned from his station in Germany and Mom took him back in. On his third night home he got drunk and started smashing my model rockets and I tried to tell him to stop and he struck me. Mom tried to make him stop and it looked as if he would hit her too, but then Tomas came out of his room. He was larger than our father now. Dad stood over her making fun of Filipinos and her family and looked as if he was about to hit her, and my brother dragged him outside and tossed him onto the acorn-covered lawn. Our father picked himself up and stumbled towards his car, then leaned against the hood. He wiped his fore-head and then looked up at my brother—Mom and I saw this from the front steps—and told him he only married her because he wanted someone meek and obedient, but had been fooled because she came with a nagging extended family. He said he never intended to come back to us permanently anyway and only wanted to sleep with her, and now he had gotten what he wanted and would leave and did not care if we wanted him back or not. I doubt he really meant the worst of what he said—there was, I remember, hurt in his voice—but Tomas came up to him and shoved a fist into his side and then slammed his head into the window. After our mother drove him to the emergency room, we never saw him again.

IV

Today, Heinrich is pretty well trained—the man has been here four times already—and the dog always catches Tomas below the elbow. You have to know how to take it or you could dislocate a shoulder. Our mother pretends not to notice each time the dog leaps at my brother and digs teeth into his arm, but I always catch her staring out the window. She had not wanted him doing this, but Tomas finally managed to assure her it was safe. She relies on him to tell her how things work in America, and it has become easy for him to convince her of things. Now she likes the dogs as much as Tomas and me—in particular, Tomas's favorite breeding dog, Buster, the only one he did not give a German name since he refuses to sell her. She is a bitch, but he named her the masculine Buster because he had always wanted to name a dog Buster. Since Tomas often does not come home at night, our mother feeds Buster and so Buster no longer sleeps with Tomas but goes into her room and curls up at the end of her futon. At first she complained about the dog's smell and hair in the sheets. She still does complain, but actually she has become used to Buster's company.

Sometimes at night I will pass by her bedroom on the way to the bathroom and if the moon is out you can see Buster curled up at the edge of our mother's bed, on the sheet's wrinkled shadows; or at times even on the small edge of mattress by our mother's pillow, her hind leg hanging over the futon edge. Sometimes our mother has a hand on Buster's neck, as if she were her husband. It seems strange that our mother would like Buster so much considering what the dog did to Saint Elmo and Sister Teresa. Saint Elmo was our mother's white cat, who was sweet: everyone liked him because he would go up to strangers and rub his head against their legs, and his gums against their shoes. She called the girl cat Sister Teresa after some Spanish nun who founded the Carmelites, Mom's religious order. This cat was skittish and shiny black and liked to hide behind the couch. Saint Elmo and Sister Teresa got along with the dog all right if a person was around. But one day I came home and Buster had Saint Elmo in her mouth; the cat was still crying. Buster wagged her tail as she looked up at me, all proud, and was surprised when I kicked her and tried to get the cat out of her mouth. But it was too late.

Mom loved Teresa best of all because she was weak and skittish and afraid of things. At night our mother is afraid of the wind in the trees. She will not admit she is afraid of ghosts, but when the Santa Ana winds blow, she turns on all the lights and puts on the TV and then vacuums the house. The vacuum and lights drive Tomas crazy. He teases her, tells her she is acting like a maid fresh from Manila. Tita Dina says our mother is afraid their dead father will come back.

Why are you afraid of your dad? Tomas once asked her.

Outside the hot wind rattled branches against the house.

I'm not. She looked embarrassed and turned away from Tomas and focused on her dishes.

So why you turn on the TV and shit? You hate TV.

I don't know, she said. I don't like the sound of the wind.

So you're afraid.

No.

Was Grandma afraid he'd come back?

She paused. She did not look at him although he was close behind her.

Yes, she admitted.

He shook his head. You would think you'd want to see your relatives again, he said.

She hesitated. She looked flustered and probably thought she should not respond. Finally, she did. But he's dead.

Wouldn't you want to see me come back if I was hit by a car? he said. What about Gabe? He said this glancing over at me with an expression meant to imply I was a mama's boy.

Our mother did not like to think about this. She turned off
the faucet and walked into the living room. Tomas followed her.
So you wouldn't want me to come back? he said.

Come on, Tomas.

I'm offended.

No you're not.

I am, he said. My own mother.

You're just saying that.

You wouldn't want me to come back, he shook his head.

Maybe because Sister Teresa was careful she lasted longer
than Saint Elmo. Although Saint Elmo had occasionally bullied
Sister Teresa, they usually got along and often curled up on the
couch by the back window and he licked her face while she
licked at his leg. After he died she would sit there alone, only
occasionally jumping down to try to get you to lick her head like
Saint Elmo had. After Saint Elmo died I could not get the sound
of his cry out of my head, or the image of his panicked look in
Buster's mouth. I wanted to give Sister Teresa away to our
cousin Matt, but my mother and Tomas wanted her around. She
lasted about four more weeks.

N ow when the winds roar outside on hot Santa Ana nights,
rustling through the dry brittle leaves and branches, on
nights when your hair feels staticy against your pillow and your
legs sparkle beneath the sheets in the dark while the window rattles in its pane, Mom has a special pork biscuit to entice Buster
away from the windows. The dog thinks she hears animals and
prowlers out there, her nose pressed to the glass, though it is
only branches clattering in the trees. If our mother feeds her
enough, Buster sleeps on her bed and keeps her company.

v

S he has gotten used to seeing the dogs throw themselves at
Tomas in front of clients. But today she is especially nervous

because she expects Tita Dina and my cousin Matt for lunch. She has already patted on her makeup and used curlers to make her hair ends curl off her face, as though she were going to work. She imagines Tita Dina might think she is not the best mother.

She turns off the faucet and comes up to me where I am sitting at the Formica counter reading a magazine. Gabe, she says.

Yeah?

When will your brother be finished with this man?

I don't know.

Will it be in an hour?

I don't know.

She looks at me. Will you ask him?

Why don't you ask him? I say. I do not like to nag my brother because you never know how he might respond. Also, it was my brother's idea to invite them over in the first place. He wants to ask our cousin Matt if he knows any movie people who might want to buy dogs. Matt went to a private high school founded by Episcopalian hippies. He teaches there now, and movie people pay a lot of money to send their kids there. Our mother does not know I am worried about annoying Tomas, and she looks at me as though I were lazy and ungrateful.

It's just one little favor I'm asking.

Okay, I'll do it.

Just one little favor.

I said I would do it, Mom.

She stands there and shakes her head.

Okay.

Lately she has begun talking about moving back to the Philippines to grow old, because she has no husband to take care of her and American children put their mothers in nursing homes. We tell her we will not, but she says American wives would not have an old Asian lady living with them. Tomas says he would smack any bitch who treated her badly. Still, our mother likes to run down a list of cousins and nephews and other distant relatives who live in the Philippines and she wonders out loud whether she should call up and ask for a visit.

Right now she probably does not want to go outside, because Tomas would not want the client to see her. Also, movie types and other important people make her self-conscious about her accent. Sometimes she has me come with her to do errands so I can do the talking for her; I do not mind so long as we go someplace like the DMV, where I am unlikely to run into someone from school. At my school—Saint Dominic's—everyone thought I was white, for a while. Tomas had gone there first and he had passed as a white surfer. There were no other surfers there, but he was known as one—he even bought a board and had our mother take him to the beach three times a week—and he put Sun-In in his hair, though instead of turning blond it went all red. Then he began hanging out with Mexicans, who are tougher. He stopped surfing and dyed his hair black again. If anyone tried calling him an Asian he beat them up, and he started taunting these Korean kids who could barely speak English. Father Ryan brought him in to talk about it, to see a school psychologist. And he hated it when Tomas started wearing a big gold cross; that was what Mexican gangsters wore then. Each time my brother taunted a Korean kid Father Ryan would call our mother in to pick Tomas up, and it embarrassed her. She would lower her head and apologize, saying she was a bad mother, so finally Father Ryan had to reassure her. It angered him that Tomas made her feel ashamed. In the classroom Father Ryan called on Tomas and ridiculed his answers and made pointed comments about the way he dressed and looked. Finally, Tomas got kicked out of school for smashing a Japanese boy's car window with a tire iron. By then people had figured out I am part Filipino. Still, I do not like having her pick me up from school. She is short and dark and wears funny-looking giant purple glasses that are trendy on other people's mothers but which do not match her brown skin tone.

I emerge into the brilliant backyard, the sun on my face, while behind me the aluminum screen door clatters into its loose frame. The producer appears to be the sort of man who takes walks on Montana Avenue upright and confident, even when he passes skinny models, though today he does not look too confident. Seeing me, he acts uncertain, as if I were important and not just a fifteen-year-old brother, probably wondering if he should tell Tomas I'm here.

My brother can hear me approaching, but he takes a few drags on his cigarette before turning around. You can see the Virgin through his shirt back, the Devil's horns beneath her feet.

He turns to me. What you want?

How long are you gonna be?

As long as it takes, he says.

Tomas has not told the producer what to do with the armor he is holding, and the man awkwardly watches us, waiting to be told what to do with it. He has a bald spot I never noticed before, but in the sun you can see his pale scalp glowing through his dark thinning hair. You gonna be an hour? I say.

I don't know.

Mom wants to know.

He hesitates, giving me a look that says this is none of my business. He shrugs and says maybe an hour.

I go in and tell this to our mother.

An hour?

Yeah.

She looks at the clock. It is half past noon. From outside a German word comes through the window and then the sound of Heinrich barking.

Why? I say.

They're supposed to be here at one.

She pretends she is worried about having Tomas free to greet Tita Dina, though really she does not want her sister to see this dog attacking Tomas in our backyard.

You want me to tell him to finish up? I ask.

No, she says, returning to her dishes with trembling hands.

VI

After our father left us, Uncle Betino kept trying to get our mother to bring us back to Manila so we would be disciplined and educated and Asian, but she did not want to leave America.

Nowadays she threatens to return to the Philippines because American wives will not take care of their mothers-in-law, but the last time we went there our mother did not seem to miss the country all that much. She complained about the heat and smelly showers, even the ones in Uncle Betino's Forbes Park mansion. Relatives took us on trips to Palawan, Quezon, Visaya, and other islands, and when we checked into the hotels each night she unpacked clean sheets she'd brought from America and made us fold them over and sleep in them. She pushed the beds away from the wall so insects would not crawl onto the sheets. She warned us not to eat unpackaged food from local stores, and washed her hands after touching shopkeepers at the markets. In the evenings, when we returned to the room, she threw herself on the chair and sighed.

Manila smells like cockroaches, she said, and scrunched up her nose.

Why are you so tired? Tomas said. He was sitting on a bed, reading a book by James Michener.

It's hot.

But you grew up here, he said. You should be used to it.

Well I'm not, Tomas. She was plucking off her damp stockings, reluctant to do this in front of us.

Take a shower.

The bathroom's dirty.

Didn't you have dirty bathrooms when you were a kid?

I've lived in the States longer than the Philippines, she said firmly. I'm American now.

You don't talk like it.

She frowned. Anyway, mostly I'm tired from dealing with all these relatives and their dramas and gossips. This country's crazy.

Don't you like seeing them? You were laughing a lot over lunch.

They can be funny, that's true, she said, and a smile came to her face. But I would hate to live here again. Everything's about appearances. They're all afraid of being poor, so they act like they're rich, and talk tsismis about each other behind their backs.

We're poor back home, he said. Here we'd be rich.

She shook her head. No, Tomas. You should appreciate America. I went there so you could be an American.

Thanks a lot, he said.

That was several years ago. Last August an aunt invited us to visit her farm in Palawan, said she would pay the plane ticket. Tomas and I wanted to go. We remembered the dark river caves filled with blind chirping swallows, and their miles of ceilings lined with sleeping red-eyed bats. The maids who brought you Cokes and drivers who waited for you outside of malls. But our mother shook her head to Tita Adorie even though she was on the telephone.

No, she insisted.

I could tell the aunt was persisting, asking why, and though our mother could not give her a good explanation, I remembered our last trip there and how melancholy she had seemed.

VII

The client comes out the side buttoning his shirtsleeve at his wrist and smoothing his hair flat. In the shade of the avocado tree you cannot tell his hair is thinning. A few more sessions, and he will be able to take his dog home. He appears to be thinking and not paying attention and he does not see me sitting on the edge of the porch until he is almost upon me. Startled, he halts suddenly and there is a moment of fear in his eyes and then he recognizes that it is only me and they calm again.

Hey, he says.

I nod.

Earlier he seemed afraid of me, around the dogs and Tomas, but now that his eyes are calm I have to focus on his chin so it will look like I am holding eye contact. He appears to be waiting for me to say something, but I cannot think of anything, and he continues on and leaves.

James Quay

Interviews

As executive director of the California Council for the Humanities since 1983, it's been my privilege to oversee hundreds of public projects in which Californians attempt to document, express, and interpret their unique part of the California story. The stories chronicled by these projects are by turns proud, angry, tragic, and inspiring, but early on I was as struck by their similarities as by their diversity. California is one of those places that has an image—usually characterized as "The California Dream" or something similar—suggesting equal elements of good weather, opportunity for striking it rich, and freedoms social, sexual, and artistic. But anyone who lives here for a time knows that the boundaries of the state encompass many Californias, and that generalizations about the state are reductive and usually ridiculous.

Nevertheless, "California" does stand for something in the global imagination and, while it was easy to dismiss the usual Sunday supplement definitions of California as dream or nightmare, I began to wonder what, if anything, it meant to be a Californian. I decided to find out by interviewing Californians from different parts of the state and different walks of life—writers, artists, scientists, activists, educators, public officials—some prominent, some not.

I used the same set of questions for all of the interviews, beginning with how and why these people came to live in California and then exploring their particular identification with places or things that seem most Californian to them. The state's vaunted diversity asserted itself in the interviews, of course, but after the first dozen or so, I found that one particular word kept surfacing: hope. These people or their ancestors may have been drawn to California because of an image or a dream—something as grand as the gold rush or as simple as a job and good weather. They often encountered realities that tarnished or destroyed those initial images or dreams. But those who stayed—and everyone I interviewed has obviously stayed—spoke about the persistent sense of hope they associate with California.

So I added a final element to the interview, asking people to respond to the following idea, adapted to California from a statement scholar Samuel P. Huntington made about the United States in his *American Politics:* "Critics say that California is a lie because its reality falls so far short of its ideals. They are wrong. California is not a lie; it is a disappointment. But it can be a disappointment only because it is also a hope."

Some of the excerpts that follow are responses to that particular quotation, but all of them, I think, provide insights about the California hope that remains after we have awakened from the California dream, the one we embrace with our eyes open. I hope you enjoy them.

* * *

Claire Peeps was born in Vancouver, British Columbia, and moved to Minnesota with her family in 1960. She first saw California in 1973 while visiting her brother, who was attending Stanford University.

Four years later, she also enrolled at Stanford, later moving to Los Angeles. Claire is now executive director of the Durfee Foundation, a private charitable foundation that supports individuals and organizations in Los Angeles County.

The kind of ethos that we all grew up with was that you shouldn't be too proud to be an American, and that there was no reason to be an American because we got all the benefits anyway. You just couldn't vote. Then when I had kids, I couldn't bear it anymore—the fact that I couldn't vote—and I just couldn't bear the idea of bringing up kids not setting an example as a voting person. Even though I'd campaigned for people in the past and I had been active politically, I'd never actually voted and I'd rationalized that that was okay. But then I finally did.

I waited until the year after the immigration moratorium in '95–'96. There had been a big INS [Immigration and Naturalization Service] moratorium on processing requests for citizenship, and so there was a huge backlog. I remember the day I went in for an interview. The people there were working twelve-hour days, and they were processing fifteen hundred people a day, starting at 7:30 in the morning and going until 7:30 at night. I was sworn in at the Convention Center in downtown L.A. with six thousand people, and sixteen thousand were sworn in over a two-day period. They were doing morning and after-noon sessions over consecutive days, and there were twelve thousand visitors watching (in addition to the six thousand), so there were eighteen thousand people there in the Convention Center.

It was like the Olympics, because they called out the countries most represented in the room that day, and people waved flags and threw confetti and huge cheers went up and the singing of national anthems. And it really was such an extraordinary thing that you felt "only in California" would this happen with that intensity and those numbers. To be in a room with six thousand people, with huge numbers of them from Mexico, huge numbers from the Philippines, huge numbers from Iran...

It was very moving, but the most moving part of the whole nine-month process was taking the written test. I went to Venice High School, and I was one of sixty people who had come to take the test, and everybody was seated with two blank seats between us so there wouldn't possibly be any cheating, and we took our written test, which was like taking a driver's test. You know, multiple choice. The test was, of course, very simple from my perspective, but there were two sentences of dictation. One was "There are fifty states" and the other sentence was "Washington was the first president." Phonetically "Washington" is pretty complicated for a lot of languages, I guess.

Anyway, it caused a stir, there was a lot of whispering and muttering and shuffling of paper and anxious body language and, at the end, a lot of clustering of people to compare notes to see what that was: "What was that sentence?" The staff administering the test said they would mail out the results three weeks later but that you could stay if you wanted to, and of course everybody stayed, and I got caught up in the excitement. You couldn't possibly go home! And so they took the sixty exam booklets, and they went behind the curtain in the auditorium, and they spent about fifteen or twenty minutes and came back out and took the microphone and called people to the front to hand them their pass or fail slip, and I think most people passed.

Everybody who had been there had been taking night classes, and they'd studied for six weeks, and they'd been studying very, very hard, and there were high fives and spontaneous parties and cheers, and it was truly an amazing and moving experience. I think this is what you want in an American citizen, because these are the folks who want desperately to be here, and they are celebrating it, and all the rest of us walk around everyday and take it for granted and don't celebrate it. These folks are the ones you want voting, because they're paying attention to every detail, and they're deeply invested in this process, and they were so happy! I walked to the microphone when my name was called, and the woman shook my hand with such feeling and said, "One hundred percent! Congratulations!" You know, your heart kind of swells. I wish that everybody could go through that experience because it was wonderful.

* * *

Cruz Reynoso was born in Brea, California, in 1931. After attending Fullerton Junior College and Pomona College, he graduated from Boalt Hall in 1958. He practiced law, was staff secretary to Governor Edmund G. Brown in 1966, and was director of California Rural Legal Assistance from 1969 to 1972. Governor Jerry Brown appointed him as an associate justice on the California Court of Appeal in 1976 and as a justice on the California Supreme Court in 1982. He is currently a professor at the UC Davis School of Law, where he holds the Boochever and Bird Chair for the Study and Teaching of Freedom and Equality.

I was born and grew up in Orange County at a time when we had segregated schools. I attended a segregated school for Mexicans and Mexican Americans[...] And even now we see the great divide that so many sociologists talk about between Anglo (European) Americans and many—not all—Asian Americans on the one hand and Latinos and blacks on the other. So that's all part of our history and part of our present reality. Nonetheless, there's great opportunity and great hope. And I've seen many changes for the better that give me that sense of hope.

Now there are some issues that have seemed practically intractable and I mention particularly farmworkers. There have been many changes to the good. We have lawyers who now represent farmworkers. We have social security that now covers farmworkers—it didn't used to. We have unemployment insurance that now covers farmworkers—it didn't used to.

So we might say "look at all that progress," and yet when I see the life of a farmworker now, I can't tell you that it's any better; in fact, I think it's worse than it was when I was a kid over fifty years ago. So in half a century that's one area where we haven't made much progress in California.

But in most areas, in accepting our diversity, in providing economic opportunity to all walks of life, so much has happened in the last century.

Q: I'd like you to respond to this statement by Samuel Huntington: "Critics say that California is a lie because its reality falls so far short of its ideals. They are wrong. California is not a lie; it is a disappointment. But it can be a disappointment only because it is also a hope."

That quote strikes a chord very close to how I feel about California. There's so much here, so in some way it's a disappointment that we haven't been able to do better by our farmworkers. We haven't been able to do better by many of the African Americans who came here, particularly after the Second World War. And even today we have that social and economic divide I have mentioned, with blacks and Latinos being on the bottom rungs.

Nonetheless, I've seen a great change. Look at what's happened with the Japanese Americans that now are honored instead of being segregated. Or the Latinos who now represent nearly a quarter of the legislators, and even my credit union has both Spanish and English when you go to the ATM. Accepting our diversity has been a true part of our strength in California and has put us in a position to be leaders in the world. So I say, "Yes, there is some disappointment," but I'm a natural optimist. So I see the good things that have happened and I see the great potential.

In my own life, I describe myself as being somewhat of a troublemaker; I became a lawyer to represent people who needed representation, particularly the poor. I not only represented businesses when I started practicing law, I represented farm-workers and other poor clients. I was told later that I was one of the few rural lawyers in private practice who spent a lot of time representing farmworkers. That didn't make some people very happy, but that's why I became a lawyer. Frankly, I had thought that a person like me who has been somewhat of a troublemaker very often won't be rewarded by society, that if they open doors, others will be rewarded. That I ended up being rewarded by society has been a little bit of a surprise to me, quite frankly.

When I was a kid, I was in charge of a group of young junior high boys, and on one occasion I saw two of the boys in my group standing in front of a hall [where] a dance was going on for junior high kids. I stopped my car and asked them what's up. And they said, "They won't let us go in because we're Mexican." And I said, "Well, that can't be true because it's a school dance." I went in and talked to the fellow in charge, whom I knew. He said, "Yeah, we won't let them in because we think there might be problems." Well, I found out who sponsored it—it was a serv-ice club—and I went and found out who the officers were and I went to see all the officers to tell them what happened and that, in my opinion, that was no way to run a dance for a public school. It was my first experience being invited to leave some-body's office. So they weren't very happy to hear from me, but I just felt compelled to do that.

And that's why I say that I've been somewhat of a trouble-maker most of my life. But neither did I hear that they ever had a segregated dance after that.

We had a segregated school. I went to see the superintendent. He suggested that maybe a group of parents should go see him. After a great deal of effort, the school was desegregated.[...]So to some extent, if those of us who are disadvantaged—and I'm speaking now of groups, Latinos and blacks—have the opportunity to be more active, I think society will respond. In a democracy, particularly in a place like California, folks will respond to a strongly felt and well-organized expression of concern by a group that's been disadvantaged. And I see that as great hope.

* * *

Father Gregory J. Boyle, S.J., was born in Los Angeles in 1954. He earned degrees at Gonzaga University, Loyola Marymount University, the Weston Jesuit School of Theology, and the Jesuit School of Theology, and he served from 1986 to 1992 as pastor of Dolores Mission Church, located in the poorest parish of the Los Angeles Catholic Diocese. The housing projects in the parish, Pico Gardens and Aliso Village, have the highest concentration of gang activity in Los Angeles. He is founder/director of Jobs for a Future/Homeboy Industries, an employment referral center and economic development program for at-risk and gang-involved youth, located in Boyle Heights. This is his response to Samuel Huntington's statement:

I don't know if California's an illusion or a lie or even a disappointment. I think it's a hopeful place for a lot of people. This community is so heavily undocumented and people just come...In fact, we have and have had for many years allowed undocumented men recently arrived from Central America and Mexico to sleep in the church. We probably have had many thousands sleep there. For all the sad, bittersweet part of leaving your family, there is a sense that despite how hard it is, they're all able to make some money and able to find something. They're all able to send money back or to bring [family members] over here. Those stories are really numerous.

Maybe there's disappointment in it not being immediate, but I feel like I know such a rarified world, which is mainly the gang world. And it's still about a lethal absence of hope. It's still about kids being unable to imagine a future for themselves, and that happens in the state of California. That happens in L.A., the gang capital of the world. You wonder how that happens. People will talk about other pockets of poverty in the world and you'll say Cochabamba, Bolivia, was the poorest place in the hemisphere [but] you don't see this kind of violence. Maybe that comes from a disconnect of hope...hope denied...It's an ingredient that isn't present in a lot of other places where the promise isn't so full and out there. Of course L.A. is a different place too because it has the Hollywood part. But it's a very divided city and the disparity is really huge and it's not like New York where you can go one block and you're, you know, "Jackie Onassis lives there" and the next block you have drug selling and poverty. You really have to get in the car and go somewhere.

The intention of this place [Homeboy Industries] is to manufacture hope. Even the hope of hope. Because you want to say that somebody comes here with the hope of getting a job, even if they don't get one. We have one thousand people a month; that doesn't mean we have one thousand jobs a month. And yet I get many a thousand letters that I can't even answer from guys who are locked up who are just wanting something. "Will there be anything for me when I get out of here?" And of course the answer is probably no. I'd say yes, I say, "By all means, it would be an honor and we will do all we can and we're at your service," knowing that 65 percent of all employers won't hire them. An equally high number of landlords won't rent to them. And consequently 71 percent of all folks released from a California prison will return within a year, which is the highest recidivism rate in the country. We give them nothing in there; we have nothing waiting for them so hope is pretty tough.

You see the goodness and you see extraordinarily good hearts and fine spirits. And then you see with greater admiration people who grew up in the same city that I did and know that there was no chance that I ever would have joined a gang—an impossible concept that I would have ever joined a gang. And that fact doesn't make me morally superior to the kids who grow up in this community; quite the opposite. My life has never presented me with the types of obstacles and difficulties that are daily presented to them. And so I stand back in awe and I think that "there but for the grace of God..."; you stand in awe at the real burden of the poor.[...]

So there's a difference. Downtown separates where I was born from where I currently work. Privilege and good schools and two parents and comfort and everything we needed—a world of difference between that and here. And it's only a very few miles, ten minutes driving time. There's something about poverty here that's different. It's more insidious. It's so connected to people's imagination. That's the hard thing to do battle with because California is the land of plenty and people have that image in their mind and they can see it and the images of it.[...]These are still people whose dignity has been denied in a systemic way. These are people who are voiceless and powerless and experience themselves that way in the city.[...]

I've never met a hopeful kid who joined a gang. It's kids—misery loves company. They've encountered some sort of misery in their life and that's what has pushed them in the general direction of a gang. They're not pulled, they're not lured, they're not attracted, they're not drawn. They're in fact pushed by an inability to conjure up an image of what tomorrow will bring. That's a devastating thing not to possess, I think, because if you can't imagine a future, then your present isn't compelling. And if your present isn't compelling, these guys won't care whether they inflict harm or duck to get out of harm's way. Which is why a lot of what people think and what people try—three strikes and you're out, two strikes and you're out, try juveniles as adults—is all about the analysis that these kids aren't *scared* enough. But the truth is these kids aren't *hopeful* enough. And those are two hugely different analyses. You can't scare a kid who doesn't care. And the fact that these folks don't care is the most devastating ingredient out there.

The kids who go out and kill, not one of them wants to kill. But they all want to die and that's the most dangerous kid out there. So the antidote is somebody showing up paying attention, valuing who they are, reminding them about the truth of who they are. They are exactly what God had in mind when God made them. And then you watch them become that truth. You watch them inhabit that truth and then you see that nothing will change, that maybe everything has changed forever because they've come to embrace that truth. Quite apart from a job, quite apart from anything else. It's relational; it's people saying, "You can do it and I'm grateful to know you."

"Hope is the thing with feathers that perches in the soul and sings the song without the words and never stops at all." It's about singing the song without the words. It's about somehow just showing up accompanying them and somehow paying attention.

★ ★ ★

Pablo Espinoza was born in San Juan, Texas, in 1937. A farmworker, he picked cotton in Texas, Arizona, and California for years before settling in the San Joaquin Valley, where he worked with César Chávez and the United Farm Workers union. After leaving the UFW, he worked for the American Friends Service Committee's Proyecto Campesino until he retired in January 2002. He lives in Woodville, California, surrounded by an extended family that he estimates at 250. I asked Pablo where he would take a foreign visitor, or someone from another planet, to see his California.

I would want to show them I haven't forgotten where I come from. I would not take them to San Francisco, to Fisherman's Wharf, or L.A., to Hollywood. I want to show them there's still a lot of poverty here and the people who have not got out. I'd like to show them where poor people live in bad housing, even though conditions have improved. They're not that great yet, compared to what conditions are supposed to be. They're good, it's true, if you compare them to Texas or Arkansas or any other agriculture state. But here, there are a lot of abuses, out in the fields, with pesticides.

People think that because you're making minimum wage—you know, $6.75 an hour—they expect that that's a good wage for farmworkers. They think that what we're looking for only is to eat. You know, our children deserve to go to a good school, to a good college, to a good university. Who in the world could send their children to a good university or to a good college only making $6.75? We deserve also to live in a nice home. We deserve also to have good furniture. We deserve also to have a good car.

I would take them and show them the people whose wages are below the poverty line. And how do they manage, these people, to survive? A lot of these people, they make miracles. They stretch their dollar by eating more beans, more rice, more macaroni. You have to stretch. How do you buy more with your dollar? That's how these people stay in business. On the weekends, or whenever they've got money, instead of going to JC Penny, they go to the yard sales to see whether they can find some clothes for their kids. And that's really sad, that living here in the richest agricultural valley in the whole world we go and pick the vegetables and the fruits to feed stomachs all over the world, but we don't have enough food for our children. We don't put enough food on the table for our children. That's really sad.

I could take you to Lindsay, I could take you to Plainview. Or here—to Woodville!—where people live in houses that they should get paid to live in instead of paying rent, because any housing that costs $400 or $500 is bad housing. The organizations or community advocates or migrant advocates or housing advocates don't push too hard to condemn those houses because where will these people go? It is true. You've got very irresponsible politicians. The county board of supervisors is supposed to be responsible to provide those houses for their residents. People are forced to live in those houses, and not just one family, but two families or three families are living in very poor housing. I mean, why do we have to live in a house that is not suitable to live in and then [have] a second family, because they cannot afford to pay the monthly rent on their own house? So that's what I would show the people who would come. Because people who would come here from another planet, they don't need to see the luxuries or nice parks or the nice city.

I think anyone who came here to California [would] want to see the working conditions, where people work, where people live, what kind of schools we have. Many schools in the rural communities become daycare centers. The education is very low. We have problems getting teachers here—I know because I served on the school board. I was the first Mexican American elected to the school board here in Woodville in 110 years. Kids who already graduated from eighth grade go to their first year of high school with a fourth-grade reading level. That's a shame! So that kid, you know, it takes a long time with him or with her. I don't know if they will catch up in high school and make it up with the four years that they've got left. And make up the 220 or 218 units that you need to graduate from high school. A lot of these kids become very frustrated and become high school dropouts. They get frustrated because they just cannot make it, because things are getting harder as you move on, things don't become easy. You graduate from eighth grade—with a fourth-grade reading level—to ninth grade; things are not getting easier.

I don't know if you can walk out of your house and leave the doors unlocked and come back at 11:00 or 10:00 and find everything is okay. Here, I can leave that door open, and I come back at 9:00 or 10:00 and nobody would come here. But you go on the other side of town and nobody could say that. But I can. I've got nice neighbors, very good people, all migrants. People come from Mexico and they struggle to buy, but they are surviving. I like this house. You in Berkeley, you cannot go out and build a fire to do a cookout. I can go here and start my barbecue pit with wood. I can have music and I can have booze. I tell my neighbors, "I'm going to have some company here, and we'll have some booze, come over." I got a lot of freedom and you guys don't have that freedom where you live or where you come from. So you go to Porterville, you can't burn wood. It's just thirteen miles from here. Because those people, they lost their freedom. I know that the environmental people would not appreciate it. But, you know, I can build up the fire and I can have music without one of my neighbors going out and filing a complaint for disturbing the peace. So there are a lot of things, you know. These are my people.

I have a lot of friends, all kinds of friends in many capacities, from judges to attorneys and teachers, and I want to spend the least time with them because I feel very uncomfortable because of the education that they have. If they come from the background that I come from, then we've got a lot to talk about. But if they don't come from where I come from, then the conversation will be very short. These people, I identify with them, the farmworkers. These are my people.

* * *

Uri Herscher was born in Tel Aviv in 1941. He moved to San Jose, California, with his family in 1954. He graduated from the University of California, Berkeley, was ordained a rabbi at Hebrew Union College in 1970, and received a doctorate in American Jewish history in 1973. He is founding president and chief executive officer of the Skirball Cultural Center in Los Angeles. I asked him whether he identified himself as a Californian:

I define myself as a Californian with global ambitions. California to me is very much a place we might consider the

Ellis Island of this century. I feel very, very comfortable among immigrants, being one myself, reminding other immigrants not to forget that they were immigrants, and therefore trying their best to welcome new people to this country. I'm an immigrant at heart, and welcoming the stranger is very much at my core.

The physical California is quite special in that very rarely will you travel throughout the world and be able to water ski and snow ski pretty much at the same time. There are mountains, there are the seas, there are the in-betweens, there are the valleys; so from an aesthetic point of view, I would say that California beats most places in the world.

Well, aesthetics one can find anywhere. I think, emotionally, I feel as a Californian because my ambitions are in California. My ambitions in California are related to bringing the variety of human beings that we have in California under a more colorful shelter where everyone can feel safe and at home. So my ambition is not in dollars. The bottom line is whether we can figure out how to make California a place where immigrants are absorbed, where we take their heritages, the best of their heritages, and make a stronger cloth as an umbrella for the state and, I think, a stronger cloth for the globe as well.

I love being among different cultures. They're much more interesting than being homogeneous, and California is not homogeneous. I know that many people who'd like to go back to the California of San Marino. I do not. I see California as a state with vast opportunities, more so than any other place in the world—literally in the world. We have resources, we have people, and I see California having a work ethic defined often by new immigrants whose goal is simply to have a better life provided for their children. I think it's a great agenda, to have their children continue to pursue higher education and to pursue what their parents could not pursue. What a better place to live in, where children can outdo their parents. I like the pattern a lot, and one can find that pattern in California.[...]

I think if you're a third-, fourth-, fifth-, sixth-, seventh-generation American, you're apt to settle back and say, "Well, I've been here for a very long time, my family's been here for a very long time," and I find there to be a possibility of saying, "I don't have to move forward with the same pace that new immigrants do," and I don't find the ambition to be necessarily always deeply rooted. In other words, when you've been here for a very, very long time, you feel comfortable, and comfort is not necessarily a plus for society. I think walking the edge, taking chances, I'll do anything, is. In other words, you need me to pick up paper from the floor, I will. You want me to change the trash, I will. I'm not beyond every chore that I might face that particular day. That's a very healthy view of the world, and I do find it in California.

I don't want to suggest that California is a utopian state. It is heavily ghettoized; we are not yet all together. There are separations, especially in southern California, and we're trying to break them down. Trust is a major factor. Immigrants don't trust those who came before unless those who came before truly welcome them, and the immigrant will know when they're not welcome and will resist becoming a Californian, and will easily say, "Well, I came from Mexico. I will always be identified as a person of Mexican heritage." I want them to be identified as members of Mexican heritage, but I want them to be identified as American citizens who have taken that heritage and said, "There are certain values I brought with me that I think will only strengthen the fabric, whether that be family, whether it would be ritual, whether it would be tradition." I think we need to send out life rafts to one another so that California does not sink in any way.[...]

Q: Finally, I'd like you to respond to this statement by Samuel Huntington: "Critics say that California is a lie because its reality falls so far short of its ideals. They are wrong. California is not a lie; it is a disappointment. But it can be a disappointment only because it is also a hope."

I can't imagine hope without disappointment. There's nothing to contrast to hope if there is no disappointment. I think there are daily disappointments and therefore there needs to be daily hope. But hope alone, the word, won't change the disappointment. I think there's a word missing: it's called hard work. There are disappointments. How we deal with them will take hard work. And then the result will be a hopeful note. I think the great model, the great Biblical model, is Moses. He starts out his life, he's first found when he's weeping, and we all need to cry out to the world when we feel desperation, and Moses is feeling that desperation as a little child because his parents had to abandon him in order to rescue him. Not unusual for California. Parents send their little children here when they themselves do not come here, and those children cry out to all of us. The next stage is that Moses stammers. He's insecure about this experience in life, and he works awfully hard on finding collaborations, whether it's with his brothers or others, and his stammering ceases, and his last chapter in the book of Deuteronomy is called the Song of Moses. I think that is California, I think that is the world. That people come to this state every day who cry out for one reason or another: they're new, they're isolated, they want to become part of the community. We give them, all together, an opportunity and they stammer through it, they work hard at it, and then my prediction is that California will end up in a song, if we work hard at it.

★ ★ ★

Cindi Alvitre *was born in Orange, California, in 1955. Her mother's family came to the United States during the Mexican Revolution, while her father's family is southern California Indian, Gabrieleño /Tongva, with other lineages. Cindi is a culturalist and Ph.D. student in the Department of World Arts and Cultures at the University of California, Los Angeles.*

Change in California is very accelerated, especially in southern California as opposed to northern California. When I'm with Native people from northern California as opposed to the kind of things that we experience here, it's very different. I love San Francisco. San Francisco's got to be my favorite city. I could live in San Francisco; I'm not a city person, but I could live in San Francisco.

My father never accepted the changes. And I always remember my dad saying, "I want to go home." I'd say, "Dad you are home." "I want to go home." When we went to Catalina in the last couple years before he passed away, it had been many years since we'd really spent a lot of time there. And we were staying in this fabulous condo—we didn't pay for it—of the man who was the philanthropist paying for the Ti'at Project [a cultural revival program]. We lived at beautiful places, six hundred dollars a night or something outrageous. My dad and I are just kind of laughing, like, "Check this out." But every morning my father said in his dreams he was dreaming of a raven. And he would awaken to a raven chattering at his window. And that was what woke him up. And after three days of this he said, "We're home." He said this is home.[...]

On Catalina I have this belief—it's a personal belief of mine. Maybe it's a cultural belief too, about what the placement of the animals are. And the ravens over there are like this reincarnation of the people. And I had some very interesting experiences. I do music too, and we had just done a reburial of seventy-three individuals who had been dug up over at the ARCO refinery in Carson. It was a massacre site, one of the most devastating massacres that's ever been documented where women had their necks broken, were buried alive, and [there were] babies on the mothers' backs. And one individual, they must have taken his legs and arms and drug him and then smashed his back up against a tree so his body was bent the other way. Medicine people with their arms chopped off holding deer tibia wands, just the arm covered in ochre and crystals.

When we were doing that a medicine man from western Shoshone told me, "You go home because some of these people are going back to the island because that's where they were from. And they're going to return as something else." And when I got off the boat—there's a place on the other side of the island where we have a natural altar. It's like this extrusion of quartz, a big circle of this huge quartz—it's amazing. When I went there, there were these ravens and their behavior was not like ravens. As soon as I got back from the funeral I went there. And they were right there chattering and this song came to me. And I knew that these were the individuals that he was talking about.[...]

Wherever I travel I look at the land and the history of the land and that's how I perceive the place. David Suzuki, the physicist, made a comment once that when his family was in Japan, they acknowledged that this was the land of their ancestors. They knew where their ancestors were buried. They knew where certain historic, cultural, or significant events had occurred. There's knowledge yet they honored it. When they came to this continent, the land was no longer sacred. It was a commodity. It was something to make money from. And I think that's part of it with people. They don't see the land as a place of history of ancestor. They see it as a commodity, something to be commodified and appropriated. I think about this because I've had some students ask me, "Do you think that the California Indians will ever take over the state?" And I said, "Yeah, I believe that that could be possible." I do believe that, but my hope would be that because of our historical experience that our contributions would be the justice and the generosity and the visionaries and the path into the future.

* * *

Pai Yang was born in Laos in 1969 or 1970 and lived in the Hmong village of Lung Chang. In 1980 her family came to the United States, sponsored by a church in Rogue River, Oregon, where they were the

only refugee family in that small town. After a few months they moved
to Des Moines, Iowa. In 1990 the family moved to Fresno, where Pai is
a social worker with Catholic Charities and lives with her husband
and two children. I asked if there were anything about the Fresno
area that makes it feel like home for Hmong people.

Yes. Number one is the weather. It's very similar back home:
hot in the summer, year round. And that's the one thing that
Hmong families are most interested in, the weather. And then
the second biggest part, beside the weather, is the agriculture
town, city, state. Most families, almost 99 percent or 100 percent,
were farmers back then. And they look at Fresno as an opportunity to be very like home, and farm. A lot of Hmong families
started coming to Fresno because, they said, farming, it's one
thing that they know. A lot of them didn't have education or
work skills or work experience, but they're very good at farming.
That's [what] the majority dream that hope they're coming to
Fresno—they could farm.

But there's also a lot of sad stories to that. There's always
tragedy too, or a sad story, because when they all came, it's not
what they think. Even a farmer has to have the education, to have
a degree, and to know all about irrigation, pesticide products, how
to work the land, and et cetera. So many families came here and
they fell. They fell through. They found out that it's a lot of struggle. It didn't go as well, yet all family keep coming and hoping to
come and farm. They farmed the land with their physical
strength, not with their big machines like the big corporations.

Yeah, so that becomes a very great challenge to a lot of small
family farmers. The situation or the dream died and they ended up
asking for public assistance because they couldn't succeed. The
Hmong here, they become lingering, and not know what to do,
because in Fresno, think about it, there's no job. So if their dream
of farming didn't come true, didn't go through, they're stuck.

Q: Do you think of yourself as a Californian?

Now I think I do. I've been here almost thirteen years, so I
think the last five years, I actually am.

Q: What do you think caused it to start to happen?

I think that I was starting to accept it, that challenge, and the things that are, the way things are in Fresno, and I can't speak for all California, just Fresno here. And starting to stand up and accept that is, I believe, part of my work, because I'm a community organizer, community builder. And when you start to know the community inside out, you found that you have to take leadership to improve things that need it or things that happen the way they shouldn't. And you start organizing your community to be productive citizens and you yourself to be a productive part of that community that you're living in. I think that's when it started kicking in, saying, you know, I'm part of this community, I need to contribute by helping the community to grow, helping—my whole family, whose been here ten years already, we need to organize, we need to be organized, we need to do a lot of education, as well as health or civic involvements or just social justice, education. And I've been doing organizing for a little over six years, so I would say accepting and being part of the community over six years.

Q: Are there many in the Hmong community who would hope one day to return to Laos?

For almost a decade all of the elders, everybody, their way of thinking was that they're still refugees and this like a temporary home, that they would go back to Laos when there's peace and settle down in Laos [after] the Communism of the world is dead. But as you can see, one decade after another, that's not happening. Even now, there's still a lot of violence, killing, executions going on in Laos. And it finally hit them that they can't go back, because this is your home, this is your new country. You belong to this country and you should become citizens and be part of this country. And that sense of belonging and accepting and letting that feeling go that this is a temporary resettlement.

The elders always sang songs that say they love their freedom, the freshness of the air, the cleanness, you know? That kind of environment, where they're up in the mountains and their spirit's free. Sometimes we take our elderly up to the Yosemite or mountain area, and some of them start crying, and not just crying but start howling, you know? Because they miss the old home so much and way on the high rock where you see the whole valley, they cry, they start, I don't know the words, howling?

Q: *Like keening...in grief or mourning?*

Yeah, yeah, and loud. Just like the native Indians sometimes, when they "wo wo wo," and the elders start doing that, because they just miss that kind of environment so much.

Q: *I didn't realize the mountains were that high in Laos, but they must be quite high.*

Yeah, they're quite high...and they always say that they're the first to see the sun rise, the first to see the sun down. They lived above clouds, you know, where the clouds gather below and they live up there.

Q: *What image comes into your mind that you think of when you think of California?*

Sunny.

Q: *Sunny.*

Sunny. And if I'm speaking for just Fresno, I would say, I love that every direction you drive for two hours, you see something else.

Q: *[Pai was eight-and-a-half months pregnant when I interviewed her] Is this your first child?*

My second. *[Gesturing to a photograph]* Yeah. My first one is right there.

Q: *Ah. And how old is she?*

She just turned four last week.

Q: *Four. Very cute.*

Thank you.

Q: *So she's a Californian.*

She is. Fresno, California. Right now, you ask her, where are you from? I'm from California. And she'll point toward California.

Q: *What is her name?*

Sunshine.

Shirley Geok-Lin Lim

"Riding into California"

Shirley Geok-Lin Lim was born in 1944 in Malaca, Malaysia. She is the author of five poetry books, three short story collections, two volumes of criticism, a novel, and a memoir. Her poetry collection *Crossing the Peninsula* won the Commonwealth Poetry Prize in 1980 and *The Forbidden Stitch: An Asian American Women's Anthology* won an American Book Award in 1990. She is currently a professor in the English department at the University of California, Santa Barbara.

If you come to a land with no ancestors
to bless you, you have to be your own
ancestor. The veterans in the mobile home
park don't want to be there. It isn't easy.
Oil rigs litter the land like giant frozen birds.
Ghosts welcome us to a new life, and
an immigrant without home ghosts
cannot believe the land is real. So you're
grateful for familiarity, and Bruce Lee

becomes your hero. Coming into Fullerton,
everyone waiting at the station is white.
The good thing about being Chinese on Amtrak
is no one sits next to you. The bad thing is
you sit alone all the way to Irvine.

Laila Halaby

"The American Dream"
from *West of the Jordan*

Laila Halaby was born in Lebanon in 1966 and speaks four languages. She won a Fulbright scholarship to study folklore in Jordan, and she holds an M.A. in Arabic literature. She currently lives with her family in Tucson, Arizona. *West of the Jordan* is her first novel.

This excerpt from *West of the Jordan* is a kind of interim in the tumultuous story of four adolescent female cousins growing up in Jordan and the United States, and growing apart as they adopt the traits of the cultures that surround them.

Our house has an endless supply of visitors, as though this were Nawara.

Saturday, Ma made a party for Khadija's birthday. She knows that if she doesn't, no one else will. It's mostly family and food and dancing and gossips, which sometimes gets on my last nerve and sometimes doesn't.

Today it doesn't, and I help my mother coax a story from her sister-in-law, Dahlia.

"Dahlia, *habibti,* tell us what happened to you," Ma says.

"Maysoun, you can't want to hear that story again. Shame on you. It's over and done with and time to move on."

I pretend I haven't heard it before. "What happened?" I ask.

"*Yulla,* go on. Tell her."

"*Tayeb.* Okay, okay." Dahlia settles into her chair and begins...

It was a spring-air, flower-smell, Los Angeles kind of day—after all these years I remember it clearly. So many details to tell you: like the huge blue sky in the morning and the black sky in the night that can never get dark. It confuses the days and makes them gray, even when the sun is out.

Wait, you also need to know about my life before the incident.

All right, go ahead, Dahlia, tell us everything.

Twenty-seven years old and already a wrinkled and achy mother of four, husband injured at his job in this country with so many rules and benefits that he can stay home accumulating government assistance and watching me out of the corner of his eye, though sometimes I forget which one can see.

"Don't go to work," he tells me so many times. "It's shameful."

But I don't see it that way. What's shameful is an able-bodied man sitting at home on his no-good ass watching his wife clean and cook and do mothering things while he spends all his government assistance money on nothing: a couch with plastic covering and beer that he shouldn't be drinking in the first place.

What's truly shameful is those funny-looking four children holding their bellies and stealing candy bars from 7-Eleven because no one gives them enough of anything to take their aches away.

So one of those lovely spring mornings that smells of familiar flowers, I decide to go to work. It takes a while but it's not too long before I find a job as a nurse's aide at Desert Acres Convalescent Hospital, which means I work ten hours a day wiping drippy asses with skin so loose it's like used-up cheesecloth dripping with rotted fruit. Smells like that too. No one says thank you, only speak louder because they think if you don't speak their language, well, that it also means you don't hear very well and that you're dumb.

"Oh, girl," calls one withered white lady with skin like dough, cold and powdered. "Girl, could you adjust my bed, please."

I get stuck on the word *adjust* for a minute and look at her. Just as it clicks in my head she raises her voice. "Girl, please adjust my bed so I can sit up."

My ears are ringing, but I do what she wants. The convalescent hospital is old, with old walls and old beds and old plumbing, just like the people they've got stored up inside of it.

"Thank you, girl," she says and pats my arm, which surprises me because most of them try to avoid touching you at all, even though you have to touch them in all sorts of places that should make an arm touch not too shameful.

I guess I don't blame them. Their bodies don't work, their minds have wandered off to meet old friends and new horizons, and their own families treat them like they are idiots.

At home such a thing would never happen. At home an old person is revered and cared for. At home most women don't work. Mixed-blessing kind of place, I suppose.

One-mile walk home under spring skies to save bus fare and relax before the zoo that is my other full-time job. Feet like beaten rocks, crumbly and useless, climb up the stairs to find one, two children, half dressed and dirty, and one husband, good for nothing, sleeping passed out on the plastic couch that I hate, more because he insisted we buy it on credit they shouldn't have given us than because it is ugly and uncomfortable.

Better that way. Better no matter how irritating to find him like this. No bothering, no harassment, no when-is-dinner-going-to-be-ready kind of questions.

"Where are your sisters?" I ask Fatima, who laughs her cute little laugh that I have no patience for now.

"My sisters got to go with their uncle for ice cream," she tells me.

"Fatima, please. I'm very tired. Where are your sisters?"

"I told you, Ma, they got to go with their uncle and have ice cream."

"Who is their uncle and where did they go?" I ask, suddenly feeling a pang in my heart.

"Uncle Hector told them Ma was at work and Baba was asleep on the couch and that two could go for ice cream and two had to stay and could go tomorrow."

There is no one in our family named Hector. We have no neighbors I know by that name. In fact, I don't think I have heard the name before, which is how it comes to be that I don't sleep that night and instead go to the police station with my pile-of-shit husband who didn't even want to tell the police in the first place because he is so ashamed of himself for not being able to manage to keep an eye on his very own children. I'll be damned if I leave the fate of those two little girls in the hands of a man who can't even find a job.

I feel as though my insides are being torn out and I refuse to think of anything beside the fact that the police will find our daughters and they will be fine and Hector won't have done anything to them.

Early the next morning, which just feels like an extension of the night, I call the Desert Acres Convalescent Home.

"This is Dahlia. I won't be in today. I have a family emergency."

"You don't come today, then don't bother coming back," Helga screams into my ear in words I would understand in a whisper.

I am tempted not to go because if I didn't have this job in the first place, my two daughters would never have wandered off with Hector—and there are still no leads who he is—and I would have had time to warn them about the evils of this society.

"You go to work," my husband says. "I will find our babies if it's the last thing I do."

I pray to God he finds Hector and our girls are safe.

My crumbled feet rest on the bus, but crack more when I get there as I wash dirty ass after dirty ass—it's amazing how much waste these shriveled bodies produce—and empty their bedpans and change their sheets and all the while Hector is doing God knows what to my daughters.

Despite the exhaustion and panic and continuous feeling that I will throw up, I see the day for what it is, which is clear and beautiful—how cruel the world can be.

Later Mrs. Julienne asks me to adjust her bed.

Adjust reminds me of yesterday and of coming home dead tired with at least the anticipation of four little children waiting for me with so much excitement and how if there had been no *adjust* they would all still be there—and I burst into tears.

"Are they working you too hard?" she asks me, patting my hand.

Her doughy touch triggers an avalanche. Away with the plastic face for this total stranger, all cracks and withers, who's been in the world three times for my once. I break down.

"What's your name, honey?"

"Dahlia," I manage to squeak out between sobs.

"What a lovely name," she tells me, though a lovely name has done nothing for me so far. "Dahlia, what is the matter?"

Out it spills—in English I didn't know I knew—the rest of the avalanche. My country I may never see again. My injured idiot husband who can't even look after our children well enough to keep them from being picked off the street by crazy Hector.

To come this far only to be poorer than you were when you started poor and then to have your children stolen is more than is worth enduring.

Mrs. Julienne's skin is pale, deep pale, not just the usual dead white. "This is terrible. What are you doing here today?"

"They say they fire me if I don't come."

Without so much as a blink or one question more, Mrs. Julienne rings the emergency button for the nurse who comes in immediately.

"I am appalled. Dahlia has a personal emergency. Her two children have been kidnapped. Either you give her the next few days off as paid leave, or I will move to another hospital, taking all of your credibility with me."

The nurse calls her supervisor, who calls the director, who apologizes, calls a taxi, pays for it, and tells me to take all the time I need.

When I get home there are police cars in front of our building and I feel my heart drop to my cracking toes. They are dead, I tell myself. Don't expect anything good because they are dead.

But they aren't dead. They are playing in the living room with Fatima and Selim.

"Mommy," Lina cries as she sees me, and she and Yasmine fly into my arms.

Turns out Hector thought they were the children of someone else who he had a grudge against. He wasn't going to do anything to them, just wanted to scare their parents. When he found out they weren't who he thought, he panicked.

"I ain't no pervert," he announces on what turns out to be international television. "I took them by mistake and then I brought them back, no harm done. They have lovely manners."

Not very impressive in the brains department; he is held on kidnapping charges.

Our family scene that night is very loving and happy. My lazybones husband says he will look for work, and even if it means that *he* is the one who has to clean drippy-skin asses, he doesn't mind because his children need their mother.

The next day I stay home with my four little children who squirm around me like worms while my husband gets up at 6:00 a.m. to start his hunt. I have my doubts, but three days into this routine he comes back at noon with a smile like the Jordan River on his face and says that 7-Eleven down the block has hired him for the night shift. More than minimum wage, no heavy lifting involved, no bus transfers. We're set.

I go back to the convalescent home and learn that Mrs. Julienne's son is a health inspector so her threats have scare in them. I thank her for her kindness.

"I've been saving that threat for the perfect occasion. Thank you for giving me the opportunity to use it," she tells me, holding my hand.

Helga tells me that my job is there if I want it and even if I want it six months from now. "We saw you on the news," a few of the nurses tell me. "Congratulations that your children are back safely."

This is how we kicked the American nightmare out of our lives and bit off a little of the American dream.

This one's a happy-ending story, for a change. I remember when it happened, and I remember how Ma held my hand extra tight when we went to the mall, or other public places. But just like everything, after a while, the kick in the story goes far enough away that you go back to your normal life.

Khaled Hosseini

from *The Kite Runner*

Khaled Hosseini was born in 1965 in Kabul, Afghanistan, the son of a diplomat whose family received political asylum in the United States in 1980. Hosseini lives in northern California, where he is a physician. *The Kite Runner* is his first novel.

    The Kite Runner takes the reader from Afghanistan to California and then back to Afghanistan. This selection is taken from the middle of the novel, as the narrator, Amir, seems to be on the verge of escaping the horrors of his past and becoming truly American.

Fremont, California. 1980s

Baba loved the *idea* of America.

It was living in America that gave him an ulcer. I remember the two of us walking through Lake Elizabeth Park in Fremont, a few streets down from our apartment, and watching boys at batting practice, little girls giggling on the swings in the playground. Baba would enlighten me with his politics during those walks with long-winded dissertations. "There are only three real men in this world, Amir," he'd say. He'd count them off on his fingers: America the brash savior, Britain, and Israel. "The rest of them—" he used to wave his hand and make a *phht* sound "— they're like gossiping old women."

The bit about Israel used to draw the ire of Afghans in Fremont who accused him of being pro-Jewish and, de facto, anti-Islam. Baba would meet them for tea and *rowt* cake at the park, drive them crazy with his politics. "What they don't understand," he'd tell me later, "is that religion has nothing to do with it." In Baba's view, Israel was an island of "real men" in a sea of Arabs too busy getting fat off their oil to care for their own. "Israel does this, Israel does that," Baba would say in a mock-Arabic accent. "Then do something about it! Take action. You're Arabs, help the Palestinians, then!"

He loathed Jimmy Carter, whom he called a "big-toothed cretin." In 1980, when we were still in Kabul, the U.S. announced it would be boycotting the Olympic Games in Moscow. "*Wah wah!*" Baba exclaimed with disgust. "Brezhnev is massacring Afghans and all that peanut eater can say is I won't come swim in your pool." Baba believed Carter had unwittingly done more for communism than Leonid Brezhnev. "He's not fit to run this country. It's like putting a boy who can't ride a bike behind the wheel of a brand new Cadillac." What America and the world needed was a hard man. A man to be reckoned with, someone who took action instead of wringing his hands. That someone came in the form of Ronald Reagan. And when Reagan went on TV and called the *Shorawi* "the Evil Empire," Baba went out and bought a picture of the grinning president giving a thumbs up. He framed the picture and hung it in our hallway, nailing it right next to the old black-and-white of himself in his thin necktie shaking hands with King Zahir Shah. Most of our neighbors in Fremont were bus drivers, policemen, gas station attendants, and unwed mothers collecting welfare, exactly the sort of blue-collar people who would soon suffocate under the pillow Reaganomics pressed to their faces. Baba was the lone Republican in our building.

But the Bay Area's smog stung his eyes, the traffic noise gave him headaches, and the pollen made him cough. The fruit was never sweet enough, the water never clean enough, and where were all the trees and open fields? For two years, I tried to get Baba to enroll in ESL classes to improve his broken English. But he scoffed at the idea. "Maybe I'll spell 'cat' and the teacher will give me a glittery little star so I can run home and show it off to you," he'd grumble.

One Sunday in the spring of 1983, I walked into a small bookstore that sold used paperbacks, next to the Indian movie theater just west of where Amtrak crossed Fremont Boulevard. I told Baba I'd be out in five minutes and he shrugged. He had been working at a gas station in Fremont and had the day off. I watched him jaywalk across Fremont Boulevard and enter Fast & Easy, a little grocery store run by an elderly Vietnamese couple, Mr. and Mrs. Nguyen. They were gray-haired, friendly people; she had Parkinson's, he'd had his hip replaced. "He's like Six Million Dollar Man now," she always said to me, laughing toothlessly. "Remember Six Million Dollar Man, Amir?" Then Mr. Nguyen would scowl like Lee Majors, pretend he was running in slow motion.

I was flipping through a worn copy of a Mike Hammer mystery when I heard screaming and glass breaking. I dropped the book and hurried across the street. I found the Nguyens behind the counter, all the way against the wall, faces ashen, Mr. Nguyen's arms wrapped around his wife. On the floor: oranges, an overturned magazine rack, a broken jar of beef jerky, and shards of glass at Baba's feet.

It turned out that Baba had had no cash on him for the oranges. He'd written Mr. Nguyen a check and Mr. Nguyen had asked for an ID. "He wants to see my license," Baba bellowed in Farsi. "Almost two years we've bought his damn fruits and put money in his pocket and the son of a dog wants to see my license!"

"Baba, it's not personal," I said, smiling at the Nguyens. "They're supposed to ask for an ID."

"I don't want you here," Mr. Nguyen said, stepping in front of his wife. He was pointing at Baba with his cane. He turned to me. "You're nice young man but your father, he's crazy. Not welcome anymore."

"Does he think I'm a thief?" Baba said, his voice rising. People had gathered outside. They were staring. "What kind of a country is this? No one trusts anybody!"

"I call police," Mrs. Nguyen said, poking out her face. "You get out or I call police."

"Please, Mrs. Nguyen, don't call the police. I'll take him home. Just don't call the police, okay? Please?"

"Yes, you take him home. Good idea," Mr. Nguyen said. His eyes, behind his wire-rimmed bifocals, never left Baba. I led Baba through the doors. He kicked a magazine on his way out. After I'd made him promise he wouldn't go back in, I returned to the store and apologized to the Nguyens. Told them my father was going through a difficult time. I gave Mrs. Nguyen our telephone number and address, and told her to get an estimate for the damages. "Please call me as soon as you know. I'll pay for everything, Mrs. Nguyen. I'm so sorry." Mrs. Nguyen took the sheet of paper from me and nodded. I saw her hands were shaking more than usual, and that made me angry at Baba, his causing an old woman to shake like that.

"My father is still adjusting to life in America," I said, by way of explanation.

I wanted to tell them that, in Kabul, we snapped a tree branch and used it as a credit card. Hassan and I would take the wooden stick to the bread maker. He'd carve notches on our stick with his knife, one notch for each loaf of *naan* he'd pull for us from the *tandoor*'s roaring flames. At the end of the month, my father paid him for the number of notches on the stick. That was it. No questions. No ID.

But I didn't tell them. I thanked Mr. Nguyen for not calling the cops. Took Baba home. He sulked and smoked on the balcony while I made rice with chicken neck stew. A year and a half since we'd stepped off the Boeing from Peshawar, and Baba was still adjusting.

We ate in silence that night. After two bites, Baba pushed away his plate.

I glanced at him across the table, his nails chipped and black with engine oil, his knuckles scraped, the smells of the gas station—dust, sweat, and gasoline—on his clothes. Baba was like the widower who remarries but can't let go of his dead wife. He missed the sugarcane fields of Jalalabad and the gardens of Paghman. He missed people milling in and out of his house, missed walking down the bustling aisles of Shor Bazaar and greeting people who knew him and his father, knew his grandfather, people who shared ancestors with him, whose pasts intertwined with his.

For me, America was a place to bury my memories.

For Baba, a place to mourn his.

"Maybe we should go back to Peshawar," I said, watching the ice float in my glass of water. We'd spent six months in Peshawar waiting for the INS to issue our visas. Our grimy one-bedroom apartment smelled like dirty socks and cat droppings, but we were surrounded by people we knew—at least people Baba knew. He'd invite the entire corridor of neighbors for dinner, most of them Afghans waiting for visas. Inevitably, someone would bring a set of tabla and someone else a harmonium. Tea would brew, and whoever had a passing singing voice would sing until the sun rose, the mosquitoes stopped buzzing, and clapping hands grew sore.

"You were happier there, Baba. It was more like home," I said.

"Peshawar was good for me. Not good for you."

"You work so hard here."

"It's not so bad now," he said, meaning since he had become the day manager at the gas station. But I'd seen the way he winced and rubbed his wrists on damp days. The way sweat erupted on his forehead as he reached for his bottle of antacids after meals. "Besides, I didn't bring us here for me, did I?"

I reached across the table and put my hand on his. My student hand, clean and soft, on his laborer's hand, grubby and calloused. I thought of all the trucks, train sets, and bikes he'd bought me in Kabul. Now America. One last gift for Amir.

Just one month after we arrived in the U.S., Baba found a job off Washington Boulevard as an assistant at a gas station owned by an Afghan acquaintance—he'd started looking for work the same week we arrived. Six days a week, Baba pulled twelve-hour shifts pumping gas, running the register, changing oil, and washing windshields. I'd bring him lunch sometimes and find him looking for a pack of cigarettes on the shelves, a customer waiting on the other side of the oil-stained counter, Baba's face drawn and pale under the bright fluorescent lights. The electronic bell over the door would *ding-dong* when I walked in, and Baba would look over his shoulder, wave, and smile, his eyes watering from fatigue.

The same day he was hired, Baba and I went to our eligibility officer in San Jose, Mrs. Dobbins. She was an overweight black woman with twinkling eyes and a dimpled smile. She'd told me once that she sang in church, and I believed her—she had a voice that made me think of warm milk and honey. Baba dropped the stack of food stamps on her desk. "Thank you but I don't want," Baba said. "I work always. In Afghanistan I work, in America I work. Thank you very much, Mrs. Dobbins, but I don't like it free money."

Mrs. Dobbins blinked. Picked up the food stamps, looked from me to Baba like we were pulling a prank, or "slipping her a trick" as Hassan used to say. "Fifteen years I been doin' this job and nobody's ever done this," she said. And that was how Baba ended those humiliating food stamp moments at the cash register and alleviated one of his greatest fears: that an Afghan would see him buying food with charity money. Baba walked out of the welfare office like a man cured of a tumor.

That summer of 1983, I graduated from high school at the age of twenty, by far the oldest senior tossing his mortarboard on the football field that day. I remember losing Baba in the swarm of families, flashing cameras, and blue gowns. I found him near the twenty-yard line, hands shoved in his pockets, camera dangling on his chest. He disappeared and reappeared behind the people moving between us: squealing blue-clad girls hugging, crying, boys high-fiving their fathers, each other. Baba's beard was graying, his hair thinning at the temples, and hadn't he been taller in Kabul? He was wearing his brown suit—his only suit, the same one he wore to Afghan weddings and funerals—and the red tie I had bought for his fiftieth birthday that year. Then he saw me and waved. Smiled. He motioned for me to wear my mortarboard, and took a picture of me with the school's clock tower in the background. I smiled for him—in a way, this was his day more than mine. He walked to me, curled his arm around my neck, and gave my brow a single kiss. "I am *moftakhir*, Amir," he said. Proud. His eyes gleamed when he said that and I liked being on the receiving end of that look.

He took me to an Afghan kabob house in Hayward that night and ordered far too much food. He told the owner that his son was going to college in the fall. I had debated him briefly about that just before graduation, and told him I wanted to get a job. Help out, save some money, maybe go to college the following year. But he had shot me one of his smoldering Baba looks, and the words had vaporized on my tongue.

After dinner, Baba took me to a bar across the street from the restaurant. The place was dim, and the acrid smell of beer I'd always disliked permeated the walls. Men in baseball caps and tank tops played pool, clouds of cigarette smoke hovering over the green tables, swirling in the fluorescent light. We drew looks, Baba in his brown suit and me in pleated slacks and sports jacket. We took a seat at the bar, next to an old man, his leathery face sickly in the blue glow of the Michelob sign overhead. Baba lit a cigarette and ordered us beers. "Tonight I am too much happy," he announced to no one and everyone. "Tonight I drinking with my son. And one, please, for my friend," he said, patting the old man on the back. The old fellow tipped his hat and smiled. He had no upper teeth.

Baba finished his beer in three gulps and ordered another. He had three before I forced myself to drink a quarter of mine. By then he had bought the old man a scotch and treated a foursome of pool players to a pitcher of Budweiser. Men shook his hand and clapped him on the back. They drank to him. Someone lit his cigarette. Baba loosened his tie and gave the old man a handful of quarters. He pointed to the jukebox. "Tell him to play his favorite songs," he said to me. The old man nodded and gave Baba a salute. Soon, country music was blaring, and, just like that, Baba had started a party.

At one point, Baba stood, raised his beer, spilling it on the sawdust floor, and yelled, "Fuck the Russia!" The bar's laughter, then its full-throated echo followed. Baba bought another round of pitchers for everyone.

When we left, everyone was sad to see him go. Kabul, Peshawar, Hayward. Same old Baba, I thought, smiling.

I drove us home in Baba's old, ochre yellow Buick Century. Baba dozed off on the way, snoring like a jackhammer. I smelled tobacco on him and alcohol, sweet and pungent. But he sat up when I stopped the car and said in a hoarse voice, "Keep driving to the end of the block."

236 · KHALED HOSSEINI

"Why, Baba?"

"Just go." He had me park at the south end of the street. He reached in his coat pocket and handed me a set of keys. "There," he said, pointing to the car in front of us. It was an old model Ford, long and wide, a dark color I couldn't discern in the moonlight. "It needs painting, and I'll have one of the guys at the station put in new shocks, but it runs."

I took the keys, stunned. I looked from him to the car.

"You'll need it to go to college," he said. I took his hand in mine. Squeezed it. My eyes were tearing over and I was glad for the shadows that hid our faces. "Thank you, Baba."

We got out and sat inside the Ford. It was a Grand Torino. Navy blue, Baba said. I drove it around the block, testing the brakes, the radio, the turn signals. I parked it in the lot of our apartment building and shut off the engine. "*Tashakor*, Baba jan," I said. I wanted to say more, tell him how touched I was by his act of kindness, how much I appreciated all that he had done for me, all that he was still doing. But I knew I'd embarrass him. "*Tashakor*," I repeated instead.

He smiled and leaned back against the headrest, his forehead almost touching the ceiling. We didn't say anything. Just sat in the dark, listened to the *tink-tink* of the engine cooling, the wail of a siren in the distance. Then Baba rolled his head toward me. "I wish Hassan had been with us today," he said.

A pair of steel hands closed around my windpipe at the sound of Hassan's name. I rolled down the window. Waited for the steel hands to loosen their grip.

I would enroll in junior college classes in the fall, I told Baba the day after graduation. He was drinking cold black tea and chewing cardamom seeds, his personal trusted antidote for hangover headaches.

"I think I'll major in English," I said. I winced inside, waiting for his reply.

"English?"

"Creative writing."

He considered this. Sipped his tea, "Stories, you mean. You'll make up stories." I looked down at my feet.

"They pay for that, making up stories?"

"If you're good," I said. "And if you get discovered."

"How likely is that, getting discovered?"

"It happens," I said.

He nodded. "And what will you do while you wait to get good and get discovered? How will you earn money? If you marry, how will you support your *khanum*?"

I couldn't lift my eyes to meet his. "I'll...find a job."

"Oh," he said. "*Wah wah*! So, if I understand, you'll study several years to earn a degree, then you'll get a *chatti* job like mine, one you could just as easily land today, on the small chance that your degree might someday help you get...discovered." He took a deep breath and sipped his tea. Grunted something about medical school, law school, and "real work."

My cheeks burned and guilt coursed through me, the guilt of indulging myself at the expense of his ulcer, his black fingernails and aching wrists. But I would stand my ground, I decided. I didn't want to sacrifice for Baba anymore. The last time I had done that, I had damned myself.

Baba sighed and, this time, tossed a whole handful of cardamom seeds in his mouth.

Sometimes, I got behind the wheel of my Ford, rolled down the windows, and drove for hours, from the East Bay to the South Bay, up the Peninsula and back. I drove through the grids of cottonwood-lined streets in our Fremont neighborhood, where people who'd never shaken hands with kings lived in shabby, flat one-story houses with barred windows, where old cars like mine dripped oil on blacktop driveways. Pencil gray chain-link fences closed off the backyards in our neighborhood.

Toys, bald tires, and beer bottles with peeling labels littered unkempt front lawns. I drove past tree-shaded parks that smelled like bark, past strip malls big enough to hold five simultaneous *Buzkashi* tournaments. I drove the Torino up the hills of Los Altos, idling past estates with picture windows and silver lions guarding the wrought-iron gates, homes with cherub fountains lining the manicured walkways and no Ford Torinos in the driveways. Homes that made Baba's house in Wazir Akbar Khan look like a servant's hut.

I'd get up early some Saturday mornings and drive south on Highway 17, push the Ford up the winding road through the mountains to Santa Cruz. I would park by the old lighthouse and wait for sunrise, sit in my car and watch the fog rolling in from the sea. In Afghanistan, I had only seen the ocean at the cinema. Sitting in the dark next to Hassan, I had always wondered if it was true what I'd read, that sea air smelled like salt. I used to tell Hassan that someday we'd walk on a strip of seaweed-strewn beach, sink our feet in the sand, and watch the water recede from our toes. The first time I saw the Pacific, I almost cried. It was as vast and blue as the oceans on the movie screens of my childhood.

Sometimes in the early evening, I parked the car and walked up a freeway overpass. My face pressed against the fence, I'd try to count the blinking red taillights inching along, stretching as far as my eyes could see. BMWs. Saabs. Porsches. Cars I'd never seen in Kabul, where most people drove Russian Volgas, old Opels, or Iranian Paikans.

Almost two years had passed since we had arrived in the U.S., and I was still marveling at the size of this country, its vastness. Beyond every freeway lay another freeway, beyond every city another city, hills beyond mountains and mountains beyond hills, and, beyond those, more cities and more people.

Long before the *Roussi* army marched into Afghanistan, long before villages were burned and schools destroyed, long before mines were planted like seeds of death and children buried in rock-piled graves, Kabul had become a city of ghosts for me. A city of harelipped ghosts.

America was different. America was a river, roaring along, unmindful of the past. I could wade into this river, let my sins drown to the bottom, let the waters carry me someplace far. Someplace with no ghosts, no memories, and no sins.

If for nothing else, for that, I embraced America.

The following summer, the summer of 1984—the summer I turned twenty-one—Baba sold his Buick and bought a dilapidated '71 Volkswagen bus for $550 from an old Afghan acquaintance who'd been a high-school science teacher in Kabul. The neighbors' heads turned the afternoon the bus sputtered up the street and farted its way across our lot. Baba killed the engine and let the bus roll silently into our designated spot. We sank in our seats, laughed until tears rolled down our cheeks, and, more important, until we were sure the neighbors weren't watching anymore. The bus was a sad carcass of rusted metal, shattered windows replaced with black garbage bags, balding tires, and upholstery shredded down to the springs. But the old teacher had reassured Baba that the engine and transmission were sound and, on that account, the man hadn't lied.

On Saturdays, Baba woke me up at dawn. As he dressed, I scanned the classifieds in the local papers and circled the garage sale ads. We mapped our route—Fremont, Union City, Newark, and Hayward first, then San Jose, Milpitas, Sunnyvale, and Campbell if time permitted. Baba drove the bus, sipping hot tea from the thermos, and I navigated. We stopped at garage sales and bought knickknacks that people no longer wanted. We haggled over old sewing machines, one-eyed Barbie dolls, wooden tennis rackets, guitars with missing strings, and old Electrolux vacuum cleaners. By midafternoon, we'd filled the back of the VW bus with used goods. Then early Sunday mornings, we drove to the San Jose flea market off Berryessa, rented a spot, and sold the junk for a small profit: a Chicago record that we'd bought for a quarter the day before might go for $1, or $4 for a set of five; a ramshackle Singer sewing machine purchased for $10 might, after some bargaining, bring in $25.

By that summer, Afghan families were working an entire section of the San Jose flea market. Afghan music played in the aisles of the Used Goods section. There was an unspoken code of behavior among Afghans at the flea market: You greeted the guy across the aisle, you invited him for a bite of potato *bolani* or a little *qabuli*, and you chatted. You offered *tassali*, condolences, for the death of a parent, congratulated the birth of children, and shook your head mournfully when the conversation turned to Afghanistan and the *Roussis*—which it inevitably did. But you avoided the topic of Saturday. Because it might turn out that the fellow across the aisle was the guy you'd nearly blindsided at the freeway exit yesterday in order to beat him to a promising garage sale.

The only thing that flowed more than tea in those aisles was Afghan gossip. The flea market was where you sipped green tea with almond *kolchas*, and learned whose daughter had broken off an engagement and run off with her American boyfriend, who used to be *Parchami*—a communist—in Kabul, and who had bought a house with under-the-table money while still on welfare. Tea, Politics, and Scandal, the ingredients of an Afghan Sunday at the flea market.

I ran the stand sometimes as Baba sauntered down the aisle, hands respectfully pressed to his chest, greeting people he knew from Kabul: mechanics and tailors selling hand-me-down wool coats and scraped bicycle helmets, alongside former ambassadors, out-of-work surgeons, and university professors.

One early Sunday morning in July 1984, while Baba set up, I bought two cups of coffee from the concession stand and returned to find Baba talking to an older, distinguished-looking man. I put the cups on the rear bumper of the bus, next to the REAGAN/BUSH '84 sticker.

"Amir," Baba said, motioning me over, "this is General Sahib, Mr. Iqbal Taheri. He was a decorated general in Kabul. He worked for the Ministry of Defense."

Taheri. Why did the name sound familiar?

The general laughed like a man used to attending formal parties where he'd laughed on cue at the minor jokes of important people. He had wispy silver-gray hair combed back from his smooth, tanned forehead, and tufts of white in his bushy eyebrows. He smelled like cologne and wore an iron-gray three-piece suit, shiny from too many pressings; the gold chain of a pocket watch dangled from his vest.

"Such a lofty introduction," he said, his voice deep and cultured. "*Salaam, bachem.*" Hello, my child.

"*Salaam*, General Sahib," I said, shaking his hand. His thin hands belied a firm grip, as if steel hid beneath the moisturized skin.

"Amir is going to be a great writer," Baba said. I did a double take at this. "He has finished his first year of college and earned A's in all of his courses."

"Junior college," I corrected him.

"*Mashallah*," General Taheri said. "Will you be writing about our country, history perhaps? Economics?"

"I write fiction," I said, thinking of the dozen or so short stories I had written in the leather-bound notebook Rahim Khan had given me, wondering why I was suddenly embarrassed by them in this man's presence.

"Ah, a storyteller," the general said. "Well, people need stories to divert them at difficult times like this." He put his hand on Baba's shoulder and turned to me. "Speaking of stories, your father and I hunted pheasant together one summer day in Jalalabad," he said. "It was a marvelous time. If I recall correctly, your father's eye proved as keen in the hunt as it had in business."

Baba kicked a wooden tennis racket on our tarpaulin spread with the toe of his boot. "Some business."

General Taheri managed a simultaneously sad and polite smile, heaved a sigh, and gently patted Baba's shoulder. "*Zendagi migzara*," he said. Life goes on. He turned his eyes to me. "We Afghans are prone to a considerable degree of exaggeration, *bachem*, and I have heard many men foolishly labeled great. But your father has the distinction of belonging to the minority who truly deserves the label." This little speech sounded to me the way his suit looked: often used and unnaturally shiny.

"You're flattering me," Baba said.

"I am not," the general said, tilting his head sideways and pressing his hand to his chest to convey humility. "Boys and girls must know the legacy of their fathers." He turned to me. "Do you appreciate your father, *bachem*? Do you really appreciate him?"

"*Balay*, General Sahib, I do," I said, wishing he'd not call me "my child."

"Then congratulations, you are already halfway to being a man," he said with no trace of humor, no irony, the compliment of the casually arrogant.

"Padar jan, you forgot your tea." A young woman's voice. She was standing behind us, a slim-hipped beauty with velvety coal black hair, an open thermos and Styrofoam cup in her hand. I blinked, my heart quickening. She had thick black eyebrows that touched in the middle like the arched wings of a flying bird, and the gracefully hooked nose of a princess from old Persia— maybe that of Tahmineh, Rostam's wife and Sohrab's mother from the *Shahnamah*. Her eyes, walnut brown and shaded by fanned lashes, met mine. Held for a moment. Flew away.

"You are so kind, my dear," General Taheri said. He took the cup from her. Before she turned to go, I saw she had a brown, sickle-shaped birthmark on the smooth skin just above her left jawline. She walked to a dull gray van two aisles away and put the thermos inside. Her hair spilled to one side when she kneeled amid boxes of old records and paperbacks.

"My daughter, Soraya jan," General Taheri said. He took a deep breath like a man eager to change the subject and checked his gold pocket watch. "Well, time to go and set up." He and Baba kissed on the cheek and he shook my hand with both of his. "Best of luck with the writing, " he said, looking me in the eye. His pale blue eyes revealed nothing of the thoughts behind them.

For the rest of that day, I fought the urge to look toward the gray van.

It came to me on our way home. Taheri. I knew I'd heard that name before.

"Wasn't there some story floating around about Taheri's daughter?" I said to Baba, trying to sound casual.

"You know me," Baba said, inching the bus along the queue exiting the flea market. "Talk turns to gossip and I walk away."

"But there was, wasn't there?" I said.

"Why do you ask?" He was looking at me coyly.

I shrugged and fought back a smile. "Just curious, Baba."

"Really? Is that all?" he said, his eyes playful, lingering on mine. "Has she made an impression on you?"

I rolled my eyes. "Please, Baba."

He smiled, and swung the bus out of the flea market. We headed for Highway 680. We drove in silence for a while. "All I've heard is that there was a man once and things...didn't go well." He said this gravely, like he'd disclosed to me that she had breast cancer.

"Oh."

"I hear she is a decent girl, hardworking and kind. But no *khastegars*, no suitors, have knocked on the general's door since." Baba sighed. "It may be unfair, but what happens in a few days, sometimes even a single day, can change the course of a whole lifetime, Amir," he said.

Lying awake in bed that night, I thought of Soraya Taheri's sickle-shaped birthmark, her gently hooked nose, and the way her luminous eyes had fleetingly held mine. My heart stuttered at the thought of her. Soraya Taheri. My Swap Meet Princess.

Dana Johnson

"Melvin in the Sixth Grade"
from *Break Any Woman Down*

Dana Johnson was born in 1967 and is a Los Angeles native. She worked as a magazine editor before completing her M.F.A. at Indiana University, where she now teaches creative writing and literature. Her debut collection of short stories, *Break Any Woman Down*, won the Flannery O'Connor Award for short fiction in 2001.

"Melvin in the Sixth Grade" is the opening story in *Break Any Woman Down*. Loosely connected, the stories explore the intersecting realms of identity and love in a world shaped by race.

Maybe it was around the time that the Crips sliced up my brother's arm for refusing to join their gang. Or it could have been around the time that the Crips *and* the Bloods shot up the neighborhood one Halloween so we couldn't go trick-or-treating. It could have even been the time that my brother's friend, Anthony, got shot for being at the wrong place at the wrong time. But my father decided it was time to take advantage of a veteran's loan, get out of L.A., and move to the suburbs. Even if I can't quite nail the events that spurred the move, I know that one and a half months after I climbed into my father's rusted-out Buick Wildcat and said good-bye to 80th Street and hello to Vermillion Street with its lawns and streets without sidewalks, I fell for my first man.

From the day Mrs. Campbell introduced him to the class, reprimanded us for laughing at his name, and sat him down next to me, I was struck by Melvin Bukeford with his stiff jeans, white creases ironed down the middle, huge bell-bottoms that rang, the kids claimed, every time the bells knocked against each other. Shiny jeans because he *starched* them. Melvin sporting a crew cut in 1981 when everybody else had long scraggly hair like the guys in Judas Priest or Journey. Pointed ears that stuck out like Halloween fake ones. The way he dragged out every single last word on account of being from Oklahoma. The long pointed nose and the freckles splattered all over his permanently pink face. Taller than everybody else because he was thirteen.

All that and a new kid is why nobody liked him. Plus he had to be named Melvin. All us kids, we'd never seen anything like him before, not in school, not for real, not in California. And for me he was even more of a wonder because I was just getting used to the white folks in West Covina, the way they spoke, the clothes they wore. Melvin was even weirder to me than the rest of them. It was almost like he wasn't white. He was an alien of some kind. My beautiful alien from Planet Cowboy.

I was writing *Melvin Melvin Melvin Melvin, Mrs. Avery Arlington Bukeford* on my Pee Chee folder by Melvin's second week of school. We walked the same way home every single school day. I fell in love with the drawl of his voice, the way he forgot the "e" in Avery; "Av'ry," he said it soft, or "AV'ry" when he thought I'd said the funniest thing, squinting at me sideways and giving me that dimple in his left cheek. All that made me feel like, well, just like I wanted to kiss my pillow at night and call it Melvin. So I did. "Ohhh, Mellllvin," I said, making out with my pillow every night. "Ohhh yeahh, Melvin."

I was keeping all that a secret until my eighteen-year-old brother saw my folder one day and asked me who Melvin was. "None ya," I said, and he said he knew it had to be some crazy-looking white boy—or a Mexican, because that's all West Covina had.

"Avery's done gone white boy crazy!" he called out. "I'ma tell Daddy!"

I ran into my room and slammed the door to stare at my four bare walls because Daddy had made me take down the posters I'd had up, all centerfolds from *Teen Beat* and *Tiger Beat* magazines. For one glamorous week I had Andy Gibb, Shaun Cassidy, and Leif Garret looking down on me while I slept. But one day Daddy passed my door, took one look at Leif Garret all blonde and golden tan in his tight white jeans that showed off a *very* big bulge, and asked me, "Avery, who in the *hell* are all these white boys?"

"Oh, Daddy, that's just Andy—"

"Get that shit down off those walls right now," Daddy said. He glared at Leif Garret.

I couldn't figure out why he was yelling at me. "But why—"

"What did I say?" he demanded.

"Take the posters down," I mumbled. And that's why I was staring at four blank walls.

But that was OK, because Melvin was my world. I didn't need him up on the wall. I had him in my head. I turned on the radio to listen to Ozzy Osbourne, who'd just bitten the head off a dove a few days before, singing about going off the rails on a crazy train.

Two months since being the new girl myself, Melvin was the only one who called me by my name; otherwise the other kids usually named me after my hairstyle. Like Minnie Mouse or

Cocoa Puffs if I wore my hair in Afro puffs. Or Afro Sheen if my mother had greased my hair and pressed it into submission the night before. Or Electric Socket if I was wearing a plain old Afro. Avery. To hear that coming out of someone else's mouth at school was like hearing "Hey, Superstar."

They were warming up to me, though. Lisa White, who always smelled like pee, had invited me to her Disneyland party. Why, I don't know, but I was going, grateful to be going. For no reason, one day, she said, "Hey, you," when she saw me standing by the monkey bars watching her and a bunch of friends jumping rope. "Come to my party if you want to." What I heard was something like, "Hey you, you just won a trillion, bizillion, cabillion dollars."

But everything had become even more tricky than usual. Lisa didn't like Melvin. Nobody did.

One day when the smog wasn't so bad in the San Gabriel Valley (the air was only orange, not brown, and you could sort of see the mountains if you squeezed your eyes some), Melvin and I stopped at the same place we did every day after school: by the ivy in front of Loretta Morales's house on the corner, fat Loretta with feathered hair and green eyes, in high school now, even though we used to play Barbies together, who got down with boys now, who had a mother in a wheelchair for no reason I could figure out. She could walk, Mrs. Morales.

Melvin stuck his hand in the ivy, pulling at this and that, not finding what he was looking for. "Hmm," he said. "Av'ry girl, I b'lieve you done took my cigarettes for yourself, ain't you?"

"Nuh uh!" I grinned at him and hugged my folders and books to my chest. "You just ain't looking good."

"Well, then, help me out some." He brushed his hands through the ivy like he was running them through bathwater to test it.

"There's rats in there." I wasn't going to put my hands in the ivy because it was dark and I couldn't see. If I couldn't see, there was no need to just stick my hands into all that dark space like a crazy person, I didn't think.

Melvin took off his jean jacket and handed it to me. It had MEL spelled out on the back with silver studs you pressed into the fabric. He was getting serious about looking for those Winstons. I put my face in his jacket and smelled it, since he wasn't watching me. It smelled like smoke and sweat and general boy. From then on forever, I decided, I would love the smell of boy.

"Here we go," he said in a minute. He stood up, tapped the package on his palm, pulled out the cigarette, popped it in his mouth, took the match that always seemed to be tucked behind his ear, struck it on his boot, and cupped the match while he lit his smoke, so the fire wouldn't go out. He drew a deep suck on his cigarette and then threw his head back and blew the smoke up toward the sky. Then he rolled the packet of cigarettes in the sleeve of his white T-shirt. I watched all this like a miracle.

"I been dying for that cigarette all day long. You don't know," he said, letting it dangle between his lips. He winked at me. "Whoo weee!" he hollered.

But I did know. How it felt to want something so bad. Whoo weee, Melvin. How could *you* not know?

Melvin tried to take his jacket back. "I got it," I said.

He shrugged. "If you wont to."

But five steps later we were at my street. Verdugo. So I had to give the jacket back anyway.

"Hey, Melvin," I started, trying to kill time and keep him with me a little longer, "you going to Lisa White's Disneyland party?" But the second the words were out of my mouth, I knew it was the dumbest question I could have asked. Like Lisa would have asked Melvin to her party, like Lisa even *thought* about Melvin. That was just stupid to even think. How dumb *are* you? I asked myself.

Melvin took his cigarette out of his mouth and offered me a puff, he knew I wouldn't. We had that little joke going on between us. He got a kick out of me being a Goody Two-shoes and not taking a puff, even though I nearly died at the thought of my lips touching something that Melvin's lips touched. He grinned. "There's your brother," he said, trying to scare me about the cigarette, but I knew Owen was already at work.

"You ain't funny, Melvin Bukeford," I said, and punched him in the shoulder.

He rubbed it like it hurt. I guess I punched him harder than I thought. "Dang, Killer, you tough when you wont to be, ain't you?" He took another puff before he said, "Lisa ast me to go to her party, but I said I didn't b'lieve I could cause of the money, but shoot, I can steal me enough money to go to Disneyland, I just ain't too impressed with her or no Disneyland neither."

I could not believe what I was hearing. Lisa asked Melvin *and* he said no? I thought I was asked because I was liked—or on my way to be liked.

Melvin said, "She just askin everybody to say that everybody came to her little party. So what about her little pissy party." He stubbed out his cigarette. "Later, Miss Av'ry," he said, pulling on his jacket. "And don't be reaching into my stash of cigs else a big rat'll chew off your fingers."

"Nuh uh, Melvin!" I sang. I still stung from Lisa not really warming up to me that much after all, but Melvin's teasing and winking and dimples and smoke drifting hazy over his watery blue eyes made me happier. I would never need anything else in a man as long as I walked the planet earth. I watched him walk downhill in that odd slopey way he did, knees bending a little too deep at every step, like a flamingo. A flamingo smoking a cigarette wearing a studded denim jacket.

By the time I was walking through the door, home from school, Mama was running out the door to catch the bus to her first job at the sprinkler factory and later, her room-cleaning job, like always. I was only eleven but already taller than she was—and bigger all the way around. She was a little woman with a tiny neat Afro, but you didn't mess around and confuse the little and the tiny with the way she ran things. And with Daddy, when you saw big and tall, you didn't mess around with that either.

She didn't wait for me to speak before she started telling me what all I had to do. "...And the dishes, and put that pot of beans on. I already seasoned them. Don't put no more salt in them beans and mess em up, do and you know what you gone be in for. And your Aunt Rochelle sent you some more clothes. They in the living room. Be sweet." She patted me on the shoulders, hard, heavy so you could hear it even. Then she was out the door.

I was afraid to even look in the living room to see what kind of clothes were waiting for me. Aunt Rochelle's hand-me-downs from somebody's friend's cousin's daughter used to be cool, but now that I was living in this new house in this new city far enough from L.A. that we were grateful when we saw other black people around town, I didn't like the hand-me-downs so much anymore because they were one more thing the kids could pick on me about. The fancy pants were Dittos or Chemin de Fers or Sergio Valentes or jackets that were Members Only. When they weren't calling me Afro Sheen they were calling me Polyester or Kmart, where I got my good clothes. Or they called me Welfare for getting in the "county" line when I lined up for my lunch from the free lunch program for people who needed it.

When I told my mother and father that I wanted different clothes, my mother said, "Chemin de Who for how much? You must be out your mind."

And of course I was. All eleven-year-olds were. I was out of my mind, especially for Melvin. Couldn't anybody understand that if I had just one cool outfit, like Melvin, I'd be on my way to the kids liking me for reals? Cool outfits may not have worked for Melvin, but he was an alien. I wasn't. If I tried hard enough,

I'd be *in*. I found these lime-green polyester slacks that I really liked and put the rest of the clothes in the bottom of my bedroom closet. I imagined him saying, "Whoo wee, Av'ry! Check you out!"

Melvin was going to get his ass kicked after school. I heard it from Terri Stovendorf, the tomboy with the protruding forehead and sharp teeth on the side like a dog. She got drunk behind the portables, cheap mobile add-ons to the rest of the elementary school. She was always pushing me around, making fun of the way I spoke. I didn't know there was anything wrong with the way I spoke. I said "prolly" when it was "probably." I said "fort" when they said "fart." I said I was "finna" go home and not "getting ready" to go home. That's how we'd always spoken and it was good enough until the suburbs. I started studying the kids and editing myself. *Mama, I practiced in the mirror at home. I'm go-eng to do my homework. Go-eng. Who farted? Somebody farted?*

"Groovy Jan and Cindy and Bobby and Marcia," Owen said, whenever he heard me. "Grue-vee."

When Terri told me the news, I was at the water fountain at recess taking a break from tetherball, trying to get some water from the warm trickle coming out. I had to put my lips right up against the spout and tried not to look at the gum somebody had stuck down by the drain. When I picked my head up and wiped the water from my mouth, Terri called me. "Hey, Burnt Toast."

I turned around.

"Nice pants."

"Really? Thanks." I smiled at her shyly.

"I was kidding, dumb-ass."

I scratched my scalp because I didn't know what else to do. I had eight neat cornrows that ran from my hairline to the base of my neck.

"Listen," Terri said, suddenly doing business. "You and that country cowboy guy are always going around." We said "going around" to mean dating. I smiled at the thought that people thought Melvin and I were together, even though I was still trying to keep my distance from him in front of other people. I was scared of having more wrath heaped on me.

"What are you smiling at, stupid?"

"We're not going together," I mumbled. I started kicking around a rock with my imitation Vans, which were cooler than cool sneakers. Mine were knockoffs from Kmart.

"No duh," Terri said. "Like Country Cowboy would even go around with a nigger. I meant, like, walking around and stuff."

I had been called so many names that even "nigger" didn't faze me anymore. Not so much anymore. There were Mexicans and Filipinos and Chinese kids sprinkled throughout the class, but they blended better than me. There was more than one of each of them, and when they were called "taco" when they were from Portugal or "chink," even when they happened to be Filipino or Korean, that was the best kids like Terri could do with them. With me, there seemed to be endless creativity. So all I said to Terri was "Melvin and me don't go around, walk around together. His house is on *my* way home."

"Whatever. He's going to get his ass kicked after school today, and you better not tell him."

"Why?"

"Because I'll kick your ass, too."

"No, I mean…" I started cracking my knuckles. A bad habit I still have. I finally left the rock alone. "I mean, why are y'all going to beat up Melvin?"

Terri looked at me with disgust and wonder, like I was eating my own boogers, like Casey McLaughlin did. He modeled kid underwear because he was good looking; long eyelashes like a deer, and lips that always looked like there was lipstick on them. You could see him in those color junk ads that were always shoved in every mailbox in the neighborhoods, and he was as stupid as a stick.

"Are you a total moron?" Terri ran her hands through her stringy brown hair and left before I could answer.

I went looking for Melvin to tell, but I couldn't be *seen* telling him. I saw him sitting on a swing, all alone. Spinning in one direction real fast to tighten the swing chains and then spinning the other way as fast as he could to get that dizzy rush. The playground was full: a bunch of kids were playing touch football in the field, all the tetherballs were taken, two dodgeball games were going on, and both of the handball courts were taken. I couldn't see Terri, or cross-eyed Eddie Chambers, or nasty Hector Hernandez, who was always grabbing himself and lapping his tongue in and out like a snake at the girls. They would all be the ringleaders after school. The coast seemed clear enough to warn Melvin, but before I could make my way over to him, somebody called me.

"Hey, Turd Head," Harry Collins called out to me, my name whenever I wore cornrows. "We need one more person for butt ball." He walked over toward me with the red rubber ball while I tried to figure out how to say no. Butt ball hurt. You and one other person had to volunteer to get on your hands and knees facing the handball wall while two people threw the ball at you and tried to nail you in the behind. It hurt, for one, and for another, I never seemed to get my chance to try to nail somebody in the behind. Plus, that day there were my lime-green pants to think about. I didn't want to get dirt smudges on them. "Well?" Harry bounced the ball as though each bounce was a second ticking away. I stared at his stomach, which was always, no matter what, poking out from a shirt that was too small for him.

"I don't want to, Harry."

"Tough titty. We need another person."

"Well, I don't want to get my pants dirty." I kept looking over at Melvin to make sure he was still on the swings across the playground. If recess ended before I got a chance to tell him, he wouldn't have a warning.

"C'mon, man," Harry said, "Quit wasting time." He grabbed the front of my 94.7 KMET T-shirt that I'd gotten from somewhere and wore in hopes I'd have at least one cool piece of clothing. It was one of the radio stations that played Def Leppard and AC/DC, though in secret I still liked my Chi Lites 45, "Have You Seen Her?" better. Harry started pulling me toward the handball court, and when I resisted, he pulled so hard I fell down. I looked over at the swings. Melvin wasn't there. My slacks had a tear where I fell on my knees. I got mad because I told him to leave me alone and he didn't. I started to cry because I was mad and couldn't kick Harry's ass, couldn't do anything.

"You all right, Av'ry?" Melvin drawled, and suddenly he was standing beside me. I was happy he was there and scared to talk to him, to be caught with Melvin, be a combo with Melvin, permanently paired so nobody would ever accept me because of my connection to Country Cowboy. But I was still in love with his pointy costume ears, and when he spoke my name, it was the first time I'd heard it all day. Not even our teacher, old powdery Mrs. Campbell, had called on me that day. So I mumbled a thanks, I'm OK, and Harry sneered at the both of us just when the freeze bell rang.

It was the bell that told us recess was over and we were to stop whatever it was we were doing, whatever games we were playing, and come back inside. We always took the bell literally. Until the bell stopped ringing, we froze right on the spot, like statues, like mannequins. There were me, Harry, and Melvin, frozen, along with everybody else on the playground, while tetherballs kept twirling and balls kept bouncing.

This is how kids start fights: "Hey, so and so. I'ma kick your ass." For no reason, out of the blue. So when Melvin was trying to leave school with his jean jacket slung over his shoulder, that's what cross-eyed Eddie said to him. Everybody else just agreed. I had warned Melvin, but all he did was frown and offer me half his piece of Juicy Fruit.

There was, then, the usually core group of fighters and the spectators when Eddie shoved Melvin. "C'mon, Country Cowboy. Fuckin Elvis." Eddie wasn't as tall as Melvin, but he was big and sloppy. Melvin didn't seem concerned, though. He ran his right hand over his crew cut and took his jacket off his shoulder. Melvin didn't want it to get dirty. He handed it to the person closest to him without thinking, gapped-tooth John Thompson, who said, "I'm not holding your stupid jacket, Country Ass," and dropped it on the ground. Just for that instant, Melvin looked dumb and awkward, as though he honestly didn't expect such rudeness from anybody. He picked up his jacket and dusted it off. I was behind him and panicked when I thought he might know this, turn around, and ask me to hold his jacket while he fought. What would I do? It had taken me weeks to get to where I was, which wasn't very far, but I was grateful for that slight break in the torture. The tiny thaw in the frost. I was going to Disneyland with Lisa White, and even if she didn't like me so much now, maybe at the party she would see who I really was and then like me.

"Av'ry, hold my jacket, will you?" Melvin held it out and his nostrils flared a little bit when I hesitated. I glanced at Terri, who was looking straight at me with a psychotic grin on her face. Melvin thrust the jacket at me. I took it. And then, well, it slipped from my fingers and fell to the ground. Melvin looked at his jacket and then at me, those pale blue eyes looking at me brand new and different from any time before. We both left the jacket there, and then he beat the shit out of Harry, then Hector, then Eddie. Not Terri, because she was a girl, but she chased me home for two weeks straight, even though I didn't hold the jacket, and even though Melvin didn't care when I told him that they were going to kick his ass after school.

Walking home after the fight, Melvin didn't say more than five words to me. I can't even say that he walked home *with* me, because he was walking fast and I couldn't keep up. His legs were so long, and for every stride he took I had to take two. I was looking forward to him searching for his cigarettes in the ivy, but he said he wasn't going to go the way we usually went. He was going home another way. I couldn't blame him for being disappointed in me, I'd let him down after he'd come to my rescue during recess. But couldn't he understand that, really and truly, it wasn't a personal thing. Couldn't he understand that I could be completely in love with him, but just not want to make waves? And anyway, it wasn't like I *threw* the jacket down or anything. It slipped.

"But, Melvin," I said, trying to get him to go my way. "This is the quickest way to get home. Your house is straight ahead. Plus, what about your cigarettes? Aren't you dying for a cigarette?"

"Darlin…" He pulled a cigarette from his jacket pocket and put it behind his ear. "I can get by with what I got right here until later."

Darlin. I'd never heard that from him, calling me that before. I didn't like the way it felt, like a pat on the head. Not like when he said my name, which felt like a kiss.

"See ya round," Melvin said and turned, walking uphill. I watched him for as long as I could see him, and I still didn't know that he was never going to walk my way again, but I was thinking, *You probably should have picked up his jacket. Pro-ba-bly.*

Too late. Melvin got farther and farther away, MEL on the back of his jacket, shimmering like diamonds, like he was some superstar. And me, I was feeling as though I wished somebody fighting had slugged me, too.

I walked up the hill to my house and replayed Melvin's fight. Only in my mind, it wasn't Melvin's fight. It became my fight. I imagined I had on a bad outfit, windowpane pants and a leather jacket, new—not used—and a large, perfectly round Afro like the one Foxy Brown had when she pulled a gun from it and blew away some white man who was messing with her. Owen was obsessed with Pam Grier and her big breasts, and I was awed by her ability to whup ass. People who messed with Foxy were sorry, all right. Just when they thought she was all brown sugar in a halter top, she had a gun or a karate kick to set them straight.

Listen, I said. I was talking to myself. *All y'all mothafuckas better leave Melvin alone. That's right, I cussed. And I did say, muthafucka, not mo-ther fuck-er. It's the way I speak, dumb-asses, and unless you want your butt kicked, you best to leave me and my man alone. Who you calling a nigga?* I swung around and pointed a gun at the nearest palm tree. *That's what I thought.*

I kept replaying my and Melvin's fight. When I got in the house, I was surprised to see Owen at the refrigerator, home from work early, drinking milk from a carton.

"You not supposed to be doing that. Mama said."

"Mama said," he mimicked me. "You always got to do everything everybody say, goody-goody. Who were you talking to, anyway?"

I put my books down on the dining room table, round and glass. I didn't want to stop my daydream. Melvin was holding my hand. *Darlin, I guess you told them what side of the sidewalk they can spit on, didn't you?*

I went to the cabinet for a glass and poured myself a glass of milk dramatically, to show Owen how it was supposed to be done. He thumped me on the head.

"You still ain't told me who you was talking to all loud."

I drank my milk down in two gulps, washed my glass out then and there because Mama liked her kitchen kept neat, and then I picked up my books so I could go to my room and get out of my torn green pants. "Nobody. OK? I wasn't saying anything to anybody. I was just talking to myself."

"Trippin," he said, making his way to his room. He hardly seemed fazed by anything, not even moving to the suburbs.

"Hey," I said. "Owen."

"What?"

"Isn't it weird going to school with all these white people sometime? Don't it make you feel..." My voice trailed off. I was looking for the word. "Bad? *Doesn't* it make you feel bad?"

"What?" Owen rolled his eyes. "I'm graduating this year, Ave. I ain't stuttin these white folks." He went into his room and closed the door and soon I could hear Peabo Bryson blaring from his stereo, *I'm so into you, I don't know what I'm going to do.*

Stuttin, Owen said. Stuttin meant "studying." I repeated the word in my head. I'd heard that word my whole life from my grandmamas, Mama, Daddy, everybody. But when Owen said it then, "stuttin" sounded like a word he'd just made up. For the first time I really heard what the kids in school heard when I spoke. Owen sounded strange to me, from someplace else, using that word. Part of a language I knew but was already beginning to forget.

John Steinbeck

from *Travels with Charley*

John Steinbeck was born in Salinas in 1902 and was of German-Irish ancestry. His father was county treasurer and his mother was a teacher. Steinbeck attended Salinas High School and studied marine biology at Stanford University, although he never took his degree. His novels—including *Of Mice and Men* (1937) and Pulitzer Prize–winner *The Grapes of Wrath* (1939)—showcase his journalist's grasp of significant detail. In the early 1960s, Steinbeck toured forty states with his poodle, turning the experience into *Travels with Charley: In Search of America* (1962). That same year he was awarded the Nobel Prize in literature. He died in 1968.

This excerpt from *Travels with Charley* records Steinbeck's brief homecoming, where the changing face of America, as seen throughout the book, takes on a fierce and bitter personal meaning.

I find it difficult to write about my native place, northern California. It should be the easiest, because I knew that strip angled against the Pacific better than any place in the world. But

I find it not one thing but many—one printed over another until the whole thing blurs. What it is is warped with memory of what it was and that with what happened there to me, the whole bundle wracked until objectiveness is nigh impossible. This four-lane concrete highway slashed with speeding cars I remember as a narrow, twisting mountain road where the wood teams moved, drawn by steady mules. They signaled their coming with the high, sweet jangle of hame bells. This was a little little town, a general store under a tree and a blacksmith shop and a bench in front on which to sit and listen to the clang of hammer on anvil. Now little houses, each one like the next, particularly since they try to be different, spread for a mile in all directions. That was a woody hill with live oaks dark green against the parched grass where the coyotes sang on moonlit nights. The top is shaved off and a television relay station lunges at the sky and feeds a nervous picture to thousands of tiny houses clustered like aphids beside the roads.

And isn't this the typical complaint? I have never resisted change, even when it has been called progress, and yet I felt resentment toward the strangers swamping what I thought of as my country with noise and clutter and the inevitable rings of junk. And of course these new people will resent the newer people. I remember how when I was a child we responded to the natural dislike of the stranger. We who were born here and our parents also felt a strange superiority over newcomers, barbarians, *forestieri,* and they, the foreigners, resented us and even made a rude poem about us:

> The miner came in forty-nine,
> The whores in fifty-one.
> And when they got together,
> They made a Native Son.

And we were an outrage to the Spanish-Mexicans and they in their turn on the Indians. Could that be why the sequoias make folks nervous? Those natives were grown trees when a political execution took place on Golgotha. They were well toward middle age when Caesar destroyed the Roman republic in the process of saving it. To the sequoias everyone is a stranger, a barbarian.

Sometimes the view of change is distorted by a change in oneself. The room which seemed so large is shrunk, the mountain has become a hill. But this is no illusion in this case. I remember Salinas, the town of my birth, when it proudly announced four thousand citizens. Now it is eighty thousand and leaping pell mell on in a mathematical progression—a hundred thousand in three years and perhaps two hundred thousand in ten, with no end in sight. Even those people who joy in numbers and are impressed with bigness are beginning to worry, gradually becoming aware that there must be a saturation point and the progress may be a progression toward strangulation. And no solution has been found. You can't forbid people to be born—at least not yet.

I spoke earlier of the emergence of the trailer home, the mobile unit, and of certain advantages to their owners. I had thought there were many of them in the East and the Middle West, but California spawns them like herrings. The trailer courts are everywhere, lapping up the sides of hills, spilling into river beds. And they bring with them a new problem. These people partake of all the local facilities, the hospitals, the schools, police protection, welfare programs, and so far they do not pay taxes. Local facilities are supported by real-estate taxes, from which the mobile home is immune. It is true that the state imposes a license fee, but that fee does not come to the counties or the towns except for road maintenance and extension. Thus the owners of immovable property find themselves supporting swarms of guests, and they are getting pretty angry about it. But our tax laws and the way we think about them were long developing. The mind shies away from a head tax, a facility tax. The concept of real property is deeply implanted in us as the source and symbol of wealth. And now a vast number of people have found a way to bypass it. This might be applauded, since we generally admire those who can escape taxes, were it not that the burden of this freedom falls with increasing weight on others. It is obvious that within a very short time a whole new method of taxation will have to be devised, else the burden on real estate will be so great that no one will be able to afford it; far from being a source of profit, ownership will be a penalty, and this will be the apex of a pyramid of paradoxes. We have in the past been forced into reluctant change by weather, calamity, and plague. Now the pressure comes from our biologic success as a species. We have overcome all enemies but ourselves.

When I was a child growing up in Salinas we called San Francisco "the City." Of course it was the only city we knew, but I still think of it as the City, and so does everyone else who has ever associated with it. A strange and exclusive word is "city." Besides San Francisco, only small sections of London and Rome stay in the mind as the City. New Yorkers say they are going to town. Paris has no title but Paris. Mexico City is the Capital.

Once I knew the City very well, spent my attic days there, while others were being a lost generation in Paris. I fledged in San Francisco, climbed its hills, slept in its parks, worked on its docks, marched and shouted in its revolts. In a way I felt I owned the City as much as it owned me.

San Francisco put on a show for me. I saw her across the bay, from the great road that bypasses Sausalito and enters the Golden Gate Bridge. The afternoon sun painted her white and gold—rising on her hills like a noble city in a happy dream. A city on hills has it over flat-land places. New York makes its own hills with craning buildings, but this gold and white acropolis rising wave on wave against the blue of the Pacific sky was a stunning thing, a painted thing like a picture of a medieval Italian city which can never have existed. I stopped in a parking place to look

at her and the necklace bridge over the entrance from the sea
that led to her. Over the green higher hills to the south, the
evening fog rolled like herds of sheep coming to cote in the
golden city. I've never seen her more lovely. When I was a child
and we were going to the City, I couldn't sleep for several nights
before, out of bursting excitement. She leaves a mark.

Then I crossed the great arch hung from filaments and I was
in the city I knew so well.

It remained the City I remembered, so confident of its great-
ness that it can afford to be kind. It had been kind to me in the
days of my poverty and it did not resent my temporary solvency.
I might have stayed indefinitely, but I had to go to Monterey to
send off my absentee ballot.

In my young days in Monterey County, a hundred miles south
of San Francisco, everyone was a Republican. My family was
Republican. I might still be one if I had stayed there. President
Harding stirred me toward the Democratic party and President
Hoover cemented me there. If I indulge in personal political his-
tory, it is because I think my experience may not be unique.

I arrived in Monterey and the fight began. My sisters are still
Republicans. Civil war is supposed to be the bitterest of wars,
and surely family politics are the most vehement and venomous.
I can discuss politics coldly and analytically with strangers. That
was not possible with my sisters. We ended each session panting
and spent with rage. On no point was there any compromise. No
quarter was asked or given.

Each evening we promised, "Let's just be friendly and loving.
No politics tonight." And ten minutes later we would be screaming at each other. "John Kennedy was a so-and-so—"

"Well, if that's your attitude, how can you reconcile Dick Nixon?"

"Now let's be calm. We're reasonable people. Let's explore this."

"I have explored it. How about the scotch whiskey?"

"Oh, if you take that line, how about the grocery in Santa
Ana? How about Checkers, my beauty?"

"Father would turn in his grave if he heard you."

"No, don't bring him in, because he would be a Democrat today."

"Listen to you. Bobby Kennedy is out buying sacks full of votes."

"You mean no Republican ever bought a vote? Don't make me laugh."

It was bitter and it was endless. We dug up obsolete convention weapons and insults to hurl back and forth.

"You talk like a Communist."

"Well, you sound suspiciously like Genghis Khan."

It was awful. A stranger hearing us would have called the police to prevent bloodshed. And I don't think we were the only ones. I believe this was going on all over the country in private. It must have been only publicly that the nation was tongue-tied.

The main purpose of this homecoming seemed to be fighting over politics, but in between I visited old places. There was a touching reunion in Johnny Garcia's bar in Monterey, with tears and embraces, speeches and endearments in the *poco* Spanish of my youth. There were Jolón Indians I remembered as shirttail *chamacos*. The years rolled away. We danced formally, hands locked behind us. And we sang the southern county anthem, "There wass a jung guy from Jolón—got seek from leeving halone. He want to Keeng Ceety to gat sometheeng pretty— *Puta chingada cabrón.*" I hadn't heard it in years. It was old home week. The years crawled back in their holes. It was the Monterey where they used to put a wild bull and a grizzly bear in the ring together, a place of sweet and sentimental violence, and a wise innocence as yet unknown and therefore undirtied by undiapered minds.

We sat at the bar, and Johnny Garcia regarded us with his tear-blown Gallego eyes. His shirt was open and a gold medal on a chain hung at his throat. He leaned close over the bar and said to the nearest man, "Look at it! Juanito here gave it to me years ago, brought it from Mexico—la Morena, La Virgincita de Guadalupe, and look!" He turned the gold oval. "My name and his."

I said, "Scratched with a pin."

"I have never taken it off," said Johnny.

A big dark *paisano* I didn't know stood on the rail and leaned over the bar. *"Favor?"* he asked, and without looking Johnny extended the medal. The man kissed it, said *"Gracias,"* and went quickly out through the swinging doors.

Johnny's chest swelled with emotion and his eyes were wet. "Juanito," he said. "Come home! Come back to your friends. We love you. We need you. This is your seat, *compadre,* do not leave it vacant."

I must admit I felt the old surge of love and oratory and I haven't a drop of Galician blood. *"Cuñado mio,"* I said sadly, "I live in New York now."

"I don't like New York," Johnny said.

"You've never been there."

"I know. That's why I don't like it. You have to come back. You belong here."

I drank deeply, and darned if I didn't find myself making a speech. The old words unused for so long came rattling back to me. "Let your heart have ears, my uncle, my friend. We are not baby skunks, you and I. Time has settled some of our problems."

"Silence," he said. "I will not hear it. It is not true. You still love wine, you still love girls. What has changed? I know you. *No me cagas, niño."*

"Te cago nunca. There was a great man named Thomas Wolfe and he wrote a book called *You Can't Go Home Again.* And that is true."

"Liar," said Johnny. "This is your cradle, your home." Suddenly he hit the bar with the oaken indoor ball bat he used in arguments to keep the peace. "In the fullness of time—maybe a hundred years—this should be your grave." The bat fell from his hand and he wept at the prospect of my future demise. I puddled up at the prospect myself.

I gazed at my empty glass. "These Gallegos have no manners."

"Oh, for God's sake," Johnny said. "Oh, forgive me!" and he filled us up.

The line-up at the bar was silent now, dark faces with a courteous lack of expression.

"To your home-coming, *compadre*," Johnny said. "John the Baptist, get the hell out of those potato chips."

"*Conejo de mi alma,*" I said. "Rabbit of my soul, hear me out."

The big dark one came in from the street, leaned over the bar and kissed Johnny's medal, and went out again.

I said irritably, "There was a time when a man could be listened to. Must I buy a ticket? Must I make a reservation to tell a story?"

Johnny turned to the silent bar. "Silence!" he said fiercely, and took up his indoor ball bat.

"I will now tell you true things, brother-in-law. Step into the street—strangers, foreigners, thousands of them. Look to the hills, a pigeon loft. Today I walked the length of Alvarado Street and back by the Calle Principál and I saw nothing but strangers. This afternoon I got lost in Peter's Gate. I went to the Field of Love back of Joe Duckworth's house by the Ball Park. It's a used-car lot. My nerves are jangled by traffic lights. Even the police are strangers, foreigners. I went to the Carmel Valley where once we could shoot a thirty-thirty in any direction. Now you couldn't shoot a marble knuckles down without wounding a foreigner. And Johnny, I don't mind people, you know that. But these are rich people. They plant geraniums in big pots. Swimming pools where frogs and crayfish used to wait for us. No, my goatly friend. If this were my home, would I get lost in it? If this were my home could I walk the street and hear no blessing?"

Johnny was slumped casually over the bar. "But here, Juanito, it's the same. We don't let them in."

I looked down the line of faces. "Yes, here it is better. But can I live on a bar stool? Let us not fool ourselves. What we knew is dead, and maybe the greatest part of what we were is dead. What's out here is new and perhaps good, but it's nothing we know."

Johnny held his temples between his cupped hands and his eyes were bloodshot.

"Where are the great ones? Tell me, where's Willie Trip?"

"Dead," Johnny said hollowly.

"Where is Pilon, Johnny, Pom Pom, Miz Gragg, Stevie Field?"

"Dead, dead, dead," he echoed.

"Ed Ricketts, Whitey's Number One and Two, where's Sonny Boy, Ankle Varney, Jesús María Corcoran, Joe Portagee, Shorty Lee, Flora Wood, and that girl who kept spiders in her hat?"

"Dead—all dead," Johnny moaned.

"It's like we was in a bucket of ghosts," said Johnny.

"No. They're not true ghosts. We're the ghosts."

The big dark one came in and Johnny held out his medal for the kissing without being asked.

Johnny turned and walked with widespread legs back to the bar mirror. He studied his face for a moment, picked up a bottle, took out the cork, smelled it, tasted it. Then he looked at his fingernails. There was a stir of restlessness along the bar, shoulders hunched, legs were uncrossed.

There's going to be trouble, I said to myself.

Johnny came back and delicately set the bottle on the bar between us. His eyes were wide and dreamy.

Johnny shook his head. "I guess you don't like us any more. I guess maybe you're too good for us." His fingertips played slow chords on an invisible keyboard on the bar.

For just a moment I was tempted. I heard the wail of trumpets and the clash of arms. But hell, I'm too old for it. I made the door in two steps. I turned. "Why does he kiss your medal?"

"He's placing bets."

"Okay. See you tomorrow, Johnny."

The double door swung to behind me. I was on Alvarado Street, slashed with neon light—and around me it was nothing but strangers.

In my flurry of nostalgic spite, I have done the Monterey Peninsula a disservice. It is a beautiful place, clean, well run, and progressive. The beaches are clean where once they festered with fish guts and flies. The canneries which once put up a sickening stench are gone, their places filled with restaurants, antique shops, and the like. They fish for tourists now, not pilchards, and that species they are not likely to wipe out. And Carmel, begun by starveling writers and unwanted painters, is now a community of the well-to-do and the retired. If Carmel's founders should return, they could not afford to live there, but it wouldn't go that far. They would be instantly picked up as suspicious characters and deported over the city line.

The place of my origin had changed, and having gone away I had not changed with it. In my memory it stood as it once did and its outward appearance confused and angered me.

What I am about to tell must be the experience of very many in this nation where so many wander and come back. I called on old and valued friends. I thought their hair had receded a little more than mine. The greetings were enthusiastic. The memories flooded up. Old crimes and old triumphs were brought out and dusted. And suddenly my attention wandered, and looking at my ancient friend, I saw that his wandered also. And it was true what I had said to Johnny Garcia—I was the ghost. My town had grown and changed and my friend along with it. Now returning, as changed to my friend as my town was to me, I distorted his picture, muddied his memory. When I went away I had died, and so became fixed and unchangeable. My return caused only confusion and uneasiness. Although they could not say it, my old friends wanted me gone so that I could take my proper place in the pattern of remembrance—and I wanted to go for the same reason. Tom Wolfe was right. You can't go home again because home has ceased to exist except in the mothballs of memory.

My departure was flight. But I did do one formal and sentimental thing before I turned my back. I drove up to Fremont's Peak, the highest point for many miles around. I climbed the last spiky rocks to the top. Here among these blackened granite out-crops General Frémont made his stand against a Mexican army, and defeated it. When I was a boy we occasionally found cannon balls and rusted bayonets in the area. This solitary stone peak overlooks the whole of my childhood and youth, the great Salinas Valley stretching south for nearly a hundred miles, the town of Salinas where I was born now spreading like crab grass toward the foothills. Mount Toro, on the brother range to the west, was a rounded benign mountain, and to the north Monterey Bay shone like a blue platter. I felt and smelled and heard the wind blow up from the long valley. It smelled of the brown hills of wild oats.

I remembered how once, in that part of youth that is deeply concerned with death, I wanted to be buried on this peak where without eyes I could see everything I knew and loved, for in those days there was no world beyond the mountains. And I remembered how intensely I felt about my interment. It is strange and perhaps fortunate that when one's time grows nearer one's interest in it flags as death becomes fact rather than a pageantry. Here on these high rocks my memory myth repaired itself. Charley, having explored the area, sat at my feet, his fringed ears blowing like laundry on a line. His nose, moist with curiosity, sniffed the wind-borne pattern of a hundred miles.

"You wouldn't know, my Charley, that right down there, in that little valley, I fished for trout with your namesake, my Uncle Charley. And over there—see where I'm pointing—my mother shot a wildcat. Straight down there, forty miles away, our family ranch was—old starvation ranch. Can you see that darker place there? Well, that's a tiny canyon with a clear and lovely stream bordered with wild azaleas and fringed with big oaks. And on one of those oaks my father burned his name with a hot iron together with the name of the girl he loved. In the long years the bark grew over the burn and covered it. And just a little while ago, a man cut that oak for firewood and his splitting wedge uncovered my father's name and the man sent it to me. In the spring, Charley, when the valley is carpeted with blue lupines like a flowery sea, there's the smell of heaven up here, the smell of heaven."

I printed it once more on my eyes, south, west, and north, and then we hurried away from the permanent and changeless past where my mother is always shooting a wildcat and my father is always burning his name with his love.

James D. Houston

"The Light Takes Its Color from the Sea"
from *One Can Think About Life After the Fish Is in the Canoe*

James D. Houston was born in 1933 in San Francisco. He is the author of seven novels, including the trilogy *Continental Drift*, *Love Life*, and *The Last Paradise*, which received a 1999 American Book Award. He is also the recipient of a Wallace Stegner Writing Fellowship at Stanford, and a Joseph Henry Jackson Award for fiction. Among his several nonfiction works is *Farewell to Manzanar*, a memoir of life in the Japanese internment camps of World War II, which he co-authored with his wife, Jeanne Wakatsuki Houston. They currently live in Santa Cruz.

"The Light Takes Its Color from the Sea" is a lesser known essay by Houston written shortly after his return home to

California after many years abroad. The love of California that informs the rest of his career is here presented with sensitivity and passion.

From here I can see the candy store shaped like a Dutch windmill. Atop its red, peaked roof sits an eight-sided dome painted white, with windows too small, too toy-like and too curiously placed for anyone to look through. I used to imagine someone lurked in that stubby tower watching me. But this is impossible. It's a make-believe windmill, with make-believe windows. Last year in a storm its vanes blew down. Few people think of it as a windmill anymore. It's just a candy store, with a Dutch girl on its sign, and she is fading fast. All day she faces the sun. I doubt that many who pass by realize she is supposed to be Dutch.

The store is called *Buckhart's,* which might be a Dutch name, except that the long sign over its door features not a girl but an enormous heart, and gazing from within the heart is a well-antlered buck who looks pirated from some Yorkshire hunting lodge. The heart was red once. After the vanes blew down they painted it white. The buck is white. The girl is white. The eight-sided dome is white. Where the morning sun catches it, the dome gleams and leaves an angular flash on my retina when I look away.

It's a landmark, that candy store. If I want to tell someone how to find my house, I mention Buckhart's. Everyone knows where it is. "I live across the street from Buckhart's," I say. A strange identity.

A famous road passes between Buckhart's and me, an old road that curves along the coast and carries thousands of cars a day, tourist cars, visitors' cars, beach-bound and water-seeking cars. This is a seacoast town, spread along one edge of Monterey

Bay. It's winter now, the end of February, a leap-year day, in fact, the twenty-ninth, the rarest day. It's winter, and the stream of cars along this famous road is thicker now than it ever was in the summers when I first discovered the town, fourteen years ago.

And what about this year's summer? Who dares predict what that will bring? It isn't a wide road, two lanes laid perhaps thirty years ago. In this state, that is a long time for anything to last. It is already 1964, and this is Santa Cruz, resort town for that great megalopolis rapidly surrounding San Francisco Bay.

A range of mountains separates us from the megalopolis, and so far we only feel the explosive overflow on weekends. It is just a matter of time, of course. Everything in California is just a matter of time. But so far this town has been spared. That's one reason I came here, to taste it again. That is why I watch Buckhart's from my window. Who knows how old it is? Forty, maybe fifty years? This house I watch from is even older. Sixty, the owner tells me. Older than Buckhart's and higher by a cupola. If I sit up here in this cupola and watch the dome of Buckhart's hard enough, I don't see the traffic. For long moments it isn't there. I burn my eyes on his gleaming dome, and the stream dies.

Buckhart, it is said, lived here once himself, roamed these red-wood rooms, kept the little garden, and each morning crossed that small acre of apple trees to his store. He didn't live here long. No one has lived here long, not in the twenty years this house has been rented, not since the original candy man died and took his secret formula with him, and the deed to the land changed hands.

In the old days it was an estate, with the aura about it of a southern novel. The old Frazier-Lewis place, everybody called it. The lawn spread two hundred yards down to the sea. The grounds covered what has become several square blocks of bungalows. The lake that is now a State game preserve came with the land, a private vista from the wide front porch. In those days the candy man would go next door to his candy factory, lock himself in a small upstairs room, and mix his formula for the chocolate confection that made him famous. But the candy man died sometime before the Second World War. His daughters died without issue. The family died, and this immense house was gradually surrounded. The grandeur that depended so much on distance and perspective was lost. It became a rental property. They closed his little factory. Now its weathered wooden frame bulges next door with a hundred years of dusty, warping furniture.

The candy he made there made him a fortune, and I suspect that is why Buckhart lived here a while. He was searching for the formula that died with Frazier-Lewis. Imagine Buckhart scouring this creaking house for any scrap of yellowed paper. Sometimes late at night the wind rises from the sea in a sudden thrust that shivers the ceiling. Nails draw, floorboards settle. It is almost certain then that Buckhart is up in the attic again, creeping and tapping the walls for hollow spots that might hold the longlost recipe for the chocolate marvel that only Frazier-Lewis could concoct.

Buckhart's hunch was reasonable, if he ever thought to search, because this is a house of gothic secrets, of hidden nooks and dark stairways, sudden rooms and unpried window seats, a house to explore on a rainy afternoon. When it was built, two years after San Francisco's earthquake and fire, it was elegant, a Victorian climax. Everyone must have built such houses that season. This town is dotted with them. From here I can see their spires, turrets and domes, gables, newel posts and dormer windows. I can't help thinking, though, that this is, first of all, a boy's dream house. Tom Sawyer deserved it. Penrod Schofield should have planned adventures here. It is a house for Jack Armstrong to surround, for the Katzenjammer Kids to invade, for Huckleberry Finn to find floating down the Mississippi.

I have always coveted old houses, with a boy's fascination for the ancient and curious, similar to the way I once collected coins, and later old cars. Not vintage cars. Just old ones. I have sought old houses as one seeks an old man whose tales verify what sometimes seems never to have existed. Call it a yearning for continuity. In California I have watched mountains change their contour, seen orchards swallowed by bulldozers, known whole towns to sprout in a summer, watched familiar roads inflate like inner tubes to thrice their size, and felt square miles of asphalt raise a valley's temperature until seasons lose their shape. Such transformations are, of course, the experience of the western world, in one form or another, for the past couple of hundred years. And it is nothing new to seek permanencies in a shifting environment. But in California things change faster than in most other places. And I happened to fasten on old houses, like hoary boulders in the inexorable flood.

We first saw this one from several blocks away, actually saw its cupola first, which rises higher than any building in sight. It rests atop a black roof so sloped it's almost a house-long steeple. The cupola is square, with a pointed roof of its own, and windows on all sides. The top panes are stained maroon. The house overlooks a lake surrounded by eucalyptus trees. But between the house and lake runs that road with its stream of Jaguars and Impalas and Thunderbirds. So one enters from the rear, up a narrow alleyway.

From the ground it is a fortress of flaking gray-green. Along one side a wide staircase rises to the second-floor porch. Around the porch is the original front door. When we first approached, the house had been two years empty. The foot of the entry stair-case was lush with high grass, untrimmed rose bushes, and a choir of wild, white-mouthed lilies. Blackberry vines had crept across the stairs. Most of the bannisters' latticed siding had fallen away, so they sagged and leaned. At the head of the stairs, beneath the porch's vast overhang, a ragged wicker rocker nod-ded in the breeze that blew up from the beach and across the lake.

Peering through the heavy windows and through dust that lay like gauze over everything, we saw panelled walls of heart redwood, twelve-foot redwood ceilings, cherrywood sideboards, and walnut chests, dark Boston rockers, chandeliers of brass, with yellow bulbs as big as streetlights.

No one had lived upstairs for two years. No one had lived downstairs for twenty. The lower floor was a warehouse for the relics of two families—the family of the candy man whose forebearers had survived the Donner Party disaster of 1846, and the present owner's family, who arrived in this region soon after the Civil War and acquired the house when the candy man passed away.

In that downstairs repository we found a delicately carved chest of shelves holding hundreds of birds eggs, a room full of elderly sewing machines, another room filled with carved bedsteads, a four-foot engraving of Queen Victoria that had never been uncrated, a moth-eaten Union Army sergeant's jacket, a certificate of merit for that sergeant signed by Abraham Lincoln, a first edition of the first proceedings of the California State Legislature (1850), turn-of-the-century sepia-tones of the descendants of the Donner Party survivors, framed photos of long-gone redwood giants, back issues of the *San Francisco Chronicle* announcing the First World War through a split in the linoleum, other issues lauding Calvin Coolidge, Ramon Navarro, Rin Tin Tin.

Blending with the dust and the fumes, a spirit hung in the air above those old clothes and furnishings and documents. I knew it had drifted up to permeate the whole building. At sixty years of age, this house with its store-rooms of neglected history reached that far again into the nation's past. Twice sixty years still isn't long, by eastern or European standards, but in California it is about as far back as a non-hispanic caucasian can expect to reach. Unless of course you count the walls themselves, the ceiling and the door frames cut from nearby forests that grew a thousand years before the Spanish came, walls whose very touch can send one's nerve-ends probing fern layers of primeval loam.

And so I rented it, at a bargain, agreeing to help the owners restore its livability, having found, it seemed, a great deal more than a roof over our heads. Even with this wealth of continuity, however, it must be pointed out that such a house located somewhere else, say farther inland, in the Sacramento Valley or in the Mother Lode, would have held far less fascination. What appealed so is that it overlooks this stretch of coastline. It belongs to this particular beach, this curve of bay, to a fall of northern light I have spent fourteen years running to.

A lot depends on the light here. It shapes the mountains and draws a mossy green from those high meadow patches that never turn brown. Down along the river that runs through town, the light swells up under a cloud of seagulls as they rise in a swirl, between the concrete bridges. They turn, soar, dive like a shower of white sparks and descend again to their marshy, lowtide, inland island. In late afternoon the light turns the bay white. It catches eucalyptus leaves with their undersides up, like a thousand new moons.

The sea, as much as the light, gives this curve of coast its flavor. The light takes its color from the sea, sometimes seems to be emerging from it. And the sea here is ever-present. On clear days it coats the air with a transparent tinge of palest blue that salts and sharpens every detail.

It's not a placid sea. This is a bend of the Pacific. Swells roll in from storm centers north and south of the equator and steadily wear away the cliffs that edge these towns. Every winter, somewhere, a wall of sandstone finally lets go and slides out from under the topsoil to be dissolved and strewn along the beaches. A few years back a block-long section of a scenic cliff-drive highway fell into the surf that had torn out its underpinnings.

So far the sea's intrusion has produced more beauty than havoc. This is the northern curve of Monterey Bay. A wooded arm of the Coast Range curves with it, embracing these lowlands. The Pacific is softened here. The worst winds are softened. The slow process of erosion has left many-colored cliffs—yellow, buff, brown and ochre. Each striated layer reveals the pressed sand of beaches eons old. Sometimes in the low sun of an autumn afternoon they turn orange and glow like the horizon itself. Miles of these cliffs are notched with sandy coves, whose eroded walls give the beaches a wildness, a remoteness. The coves are hot and protected, yet far enough below the cliff edges that one can forget a town lies just above. Tree roots hang through the walls. Tenacious cedars and eucalyptus, like sprung umbrellas, frame the sky. Sometimes slick brown seals glide past offshore. Pelicans swoop, searching for fish. Low tides bare pocked reefs and mossy primordial worlds of anemones and chitons and hermit crabs. From any of these coves, on most days, Monterey Peninsula, twenty miles south across the bay, seems to rise from the sea like a longlost, velvet island.

From the water's edge one can look west toward the main part of town. There, the sand that draws its half-moon around the bay, lays a final broad hot stripe along The Boardwalk, below the high-looped roller coaster, past a long row of arches that leads to a turn-of-the-century pleasure palace called *The Casino,* red-domed, and of a style with the spires and turrets that cap the knolls behind it. Farther along the main beach, bearded pilings grow from the sand, anchoring a crusty pier that probes the bay for half a mile. The long beach ends at last, beyond the pier, as a final row of cliffs bend south.

From here, two miles away and seen from the east, those cliffs are a straight line reaching out from town, a brown palisade fending off the open sea. An islet sits just beyond the palisade, thick with seals who bark and sun themselves. Atop the cliff there is a jagged stand of eucalyptus trees that never move. They have not moved in fourteen years. At sunset they are tall and black against a flaming sky. Then the seal rock is the town's last outpost. The water across the bay turns silver-white, with only the long dark pier to cut the whiteness.

I call myself a Californian. I am fascinated by everything about this state. But when it becomes an image in my mind, it is most often this town, this coast, this view. During three years in Europe not long ago (when we lived, by the way, in a 400-year-old Tudor cottage), I spent two and a half of those years glad to be free of America. I actually toyed with the idea of never coming back. When I finally began to long again for the homeland, I saw nothing but a mile of orange cliffs, a slate-blue bay catching sea winds, a crusty pier. This curve of coast has been among the few constants in my life, and that is curious, in a way, because this coast is not, strictly speaking, home. I was born in San Francisco, started high school there. I came of age over the mountains in Santa Clara Valley.

The town of Santa Cruz (Holy Cross) was first a mission colony founded by Franciscans soon after the time of the American Revolution. The mission's adobe walls have long since eroded away. Now a white-washed and timbered replica stands on the site. Later it was a port town, and lumber town, surrounded by superb farm and ranching country. Part of it still is a fishing town. Every day a stubby fleet chugs out before dawn in search of salmon, snapper, albacore. But for as long as I have known it, this has been a beach town, first of all, a resort town and a retirement haven, with trailer courts on the outskirts, Victorian manors at the core, and interlaced with rows of summer bungalows. Around and beyond Buckhart's bleached windmill I can see them—cottages and bungalows with brick-red roofs, shingle-gray roofs, checkered roofs, shake and composition roofs, a field of roofs broken with clumps of pine and cedar and lines of eucalyptus that crisscross the town.

From here, a block back from the beach, I can see quaint streets whose houses are trellised and filigreed, slightly weathered from winter gales and salt air, painted pink or white or forest green, bedecked with driftwood or with an occasional pink plaster flamingo on the lawn, and labeled with plaques of redwood lettering: *Port-o-Call, Vista del Mar, Pair-o-Dice, The Darlingtons—Mary and Frank, This is IT, Bide-a-Wee, My Blue Haven.*

I first saw these houses and the beach and the pier and the lines of eucalyptus during my initial escape to Santa Cruz, at age sixteen, a high school junior in San Jose. It was Easter vacation, and "everybody" was renting motel rooms for the week, as they still do here, to drink beer and misbehave and hopefully get arrested.

I kept returning because I liked to swim and lie in the sun and play volleyball and ride the waves, and it was easy enough to get here, thirty miles in less than an hour through wooded mountains, over good roads. One year the summer came and went and I kept coming, spending long hours alone hiking empty beaches in the fall and through the winter. I had found an unexpected fulfillment by this wide bay. The light, the sand, the glinting sea seemed to explain almost everything well enough.

In California the beach, like wine tasting, can become a way of life. My time invested served as a kind of initiation fee, admitting me to a loose fraternity of beachrats, surfers and selfappointed exiles who found some common bond in the a-social and irresponsible womb-warmth along the coast. This was an important first, an identity not pressed upon me by family, church or school. There followed then a series of memorable firsts that linked me to this region. I first got unmanageably drunk here, on several quarts of Lucky Lager, and vomited into that marvelous sand. I pursued my first serious love affair here, in a sleeping bag, in and out of all those wild and lovely coves. I learned what my Scoutmaster had tried in vain to teach me, how to start a fire with one match. Maybe it was the salt in the driftwood, or the extra dryness of newsprint that has baked all day in the sun. Finally, I experienced, in the presence of this sky and this reach of windworn cliff, that short-lived but overwhelming sense of unity with nature that at once dissolves and expands and defines the human soul.

U ntil recently I never stayed here more than a week at a time, rarely more than two or three days. Yet whenever I made that trip through the mountains I knew what to expect. Like old houses, this town with its turrets and cupolas and bungalows and fleet of fishing boats has been a refuge from change itself. And like old houses, the town is ever more archaic and out of step with the times. For many, it is becoming something of a nuisance in America's fastest growing state. And so its face, its style must soon be altered. Every weekend now the megalopolis gets closer. Between the mountains and the sea, fields vibrate, waiting for the bulldozers. Foresighted realtors have already mapped out the program of growth. Some envision a white city, agleam and curving right around the bay to connect this northern edge with Monterey. In their vision, beehive hotels will line the beaches, like Acapulco and Miami.

Evenings now I watch my favorite view, one I have come to love more than any in the world—that long arm, the palisade, capped with upright eucalyptus, the dark pier probing a silver bay—and think of the man who has promised to build a convention center there, at the edge of the farthest cliff, overlooking seal rock. He wants to tear down the trees and install a hotel in the shape of a pyramid and next to it an auditorium in the shape of a perfect sphere, where Lions and Oddfellows can assemble every year.

Part of me takes it for granted that this will happen because I have grown up in a state where such things happen every day. As a Californian I have learned that fourteen years is a fairly long moment to enjoy one view. Perhaps I am luckier than I care to admit. Who am I, after all? At best, a fourteen-year man in a fourteen-decade town, a thirty-year man in a two-century state. Have I any claim on a view? It is only a lucky chance that my father decided to leave Texas when he did, to settle in San Francisco before I came along. If he had not moved out in the early 30s, among the thousands in search of better jobs and better weather, I would not have been born a Native Son of The Golden West, might never have seen these cliffs and beaches. Can I begrudge the multitudes who continue pushing west, for the same reasons? Can I even begrudge the weekend quests which so clog the roads to this seaside town, little pilgrimages I myself so often made? Who do you challenge? Where do you draw the line?

Well, there is another part of me that knows you have to challenge the pyramid. That goes without saying. And you have to fight the perfect sphere. Schemes like that just have to be resisted, though you may not be able to resist the flood itself.

Each time I look out and find my view still there, intact, I feel twice-blessed, reprieved. From here, from this decaying boy's dream of a manor house I can watch it, or walk to the beach for a swim or a hike over lowtide reefs. I watch gulls soar, the seals sunning, slender leaves that turn in the wind, along the curve of coast that is the country I know and which I realize now I have always expected California to be. The knowledge that it is all a matter of time doesn't diminish the pleasure of living here. If anything, I suppose this sharpens it, like the tang of apples stolen from the yard of the mean old man. Sometimes I ask myself, If those pyramids ever began to rise, where would you go? I don't know.

It is a strange identity, to live across the street from Buckhart's bleached and vaneless windmill, to be rooted in the land of the rootless, committed to a country that seems committed to unbridled change, all the while clutching at Walt Whitman and Johnny Appleseed and Huckleberry Finn as they grab for handholds on the last lip of the western precipice. One has little choice in such matters, of course. I have no place else to be from, but here.

Luis J. Rodriguez

"My Ride, My Revolution"
from *The Republic of East L.A.*

Luis J. Rodriguez was born in 1954 and is an accomplished activist, poet, and author of many books, including the acclaimed memoir *Always Running: La Vida Loca, Gang Days in East L.A.* and a collection of short stories titled *The Republic of East L.A.* He currently lives in Los Angeles.

"My Ride, My Revolution" is a story from *The Republic of East L.A.*, published in 2002. The collection provides a realistic yet surprising glimpse into the lives of the Latino community in the San Fernando Valley.

The long sleek limousine lays into the curved street as kids of all sizes, of many coughs and giggles, skirmish around it, climb its blinding chrome and white armor, smearing dirt and fingerprints on its tinted windows. The unshaven men gather around to put words together about this wonder on the roadway, to excavate a new vocabulary for this intrusion that seems to smirk at their poverty, to lay like a diamond on a garbage-strewn lot. But still, it's kind of their hostage. Here in a run-down section of East Los where limos don't belong—although here it is, laughing at fate, at "everything in its place," at a segmented society of "who has" and "who hasn't" and practically telling the world, "see...here I am, in the barrio—how about that!"

I'm awake sitting at the edge of my bed with my hands on my head, startled by the wedges of daylight through torn curtains, by the voices and inflections, their wild abandon, and by the men's search for living poignancy from the polished enormity in their midst.

We're all neighbors of small cottages near Prospect Park in Boyle Heights. The cottages face each other and onto a dry courtyard as *vecindades* are wont to do wherever old Los Angeles still rises out of gray ground, which I know something about because I read, because I spend many hours in libraries, because I care to know most everything about most nothing. One of the cottages, I swear, has twenty people in it: children, grandparents, wives, husbands, uncles, aunts, and probably a stranger who nobody knows, but they make him breakfast anyway.

I'm the limo driver. It's hard to believe that me, a long-haired, chiseled-faced, brown-red man, can be the chauffeur of a luxury vehicle that we mostly only see in movies or magazines. But this is just the latest gig in a lengthy row of short-term and sometimes bizarre jobs I've had in my twenty-nine years—mostly because I won't do any work that demands commitment or an emotional investment. Like I won't clean the windows of downtown highrises or dig ditches—which only the undocumented would do anyway—or kill rats in sewage tunnels, or sit in an office cell, surrounded by half walls, bulletin boards, and phones.

Man, I hate phones.

I've been an extra in obscure movies, though I have to say I'm like an extra extra—you'd never spot me in a crowd of nobodies. I've played acoustic guitar at the Metro station downtown when it first opened—and before the cops started pushing the musicians out. And I've sat for people's apartments with their flea-bitten cats—one time I had to bomb a place with Raid to clear out the annoying blood-sucking vermin that practically ate me alive. Those cats were probably the most grateful co-workers I ever had.

What I like are jobs where I can think, listen to music, maybe read a book, and check out every mole and pimple of the city.

Like a limo driver.

I've just started. Only the other day, I first brought the limo home. It's not your basic paint-peeling Chevy or rusty pickup like the rest of the junk heaps around here. It is an extra seventy-one inches of curved metal-and-glass epiphany—creamy white, tinted windows, and dark gray leather interior. And apparently it's a big hit. I don't normally score big points with my cottage neighbors as it is.

My name is Cruz Blancarte. I'm Mexican, but I'm Indian. That's what everyone around here always brings to my attention—like they're not. Only I happen to look like I come out of the reservation. That's because I'm what you call a Purépecha. It's good to be clear about these things, especially for those who don't have an inkling about these matters. Some people call us Tarascans. We're known for taking on the Aztecs—the Mexikas—back before the *conquista*. We even made the Spaniards wish they'd never crossed our paths. We're a tough people from the hardiest parts of Michoacán. Many Purépechas still speak their original tongues and don't have anything to do with the mestizos—who are mostly Indians who've forgotten they're Indians. But the Purépechas are getting close to their last stand as poverty and neglect piles up against them. They're now too hungry, too drunk, and too despised most of the time to do anything substantial about it.

The thing is I don't wear my hair long because I'm Indian. I wear it long because I'm in a rap-and-rock band. The group is called La Cruz Negra—the Black Cross. It's a play on my name but also on darkness, Christ, and not being Christ. Somebody may consider us a rockero band—you know the Spanish-language rock groups that have streamed out of Mexico and other Latin countries. But except for our name, we only throw in Spanish words here and there. We sing mostly unintelligible English. But nobody cares. It's yells and hiccups. It's gravelly throats, guitar feedback, and ass-kicking drums. It's heart jumper cables—this is what we are.

There are four of us—four like most garage bands, like Metallica, like Rage Against the Machine, like Limp Bizkit. There's Lilo, Dante, Patrick, and myself. The other guys in the band don't know how to play that good—I'm the only one who's actually studied some music: guitar, a little piano, and bass. But they're the shits, man. They rock.

My mom, Ruby, is a Chicana activist from back in the day— you know, the sixties and seventies: the Chicano Moratorium, *el movimiento*, Aztlán Libre. Ruby taught me many things, including being proud of what I am, which is why I know so much about my heritage. Ruby never married after having me, though. She's a community organizer—holds a master's in social work, too—helping families around the Flats neighborhood with a not-for-profit agency.

Ruby's had boyfriends, sure, but she's put almost everything behind me—behind my eccentricities, my dumb ideas, my music. I know she doesn't like some of the decisions I've made— and that at times I'm wasting my time with frivolous pursuits— but she never discourages me. I love Ruby.

I think she's raised me okay. Single moms aren't bad. Sometimes they make miracles happen with little to work with. But love is love, man. I'm not into drugs, for example. I don't drink much—it messes me up so that I can't think, can't create, can't do anything worth a shit. I pride myself in having my wits about me, so I stay away from anything that deadens the senses.

I also don't get into trouble with the law, except sometimes for the noise we make when we play in my cottage room.

As you can imagine, I'm not like most people. I spend most of my life trying to be different. In the neighborhood, whenever the cliques break off into their own worlds, I stand aside, listening to my own rhythms. I don't want to be one of the cholos, the gang-bangers. They have their own problems, I'm sure, their own identity issues. I can't relate to them. Like I *want* to live. I don't care about the dance crews too much. I don't want to end up a working stiff, stuck in some sweatshop, waiting to retire, only to sit in the backyard with beer in hand, bored to death. I don't want to be like those *ranchera*-loving *mejicanos* in bars drowning in their losses. I don't enjoy wearing a suit either—like the sales-men on First Street that try to sell covered-over worn-out furni-ture for more than they're worth. Or the fast-talking swindlers at the used car lots on Atlantic Boulevard. Like I said, I hate work-ing in a bank or a store.

But I also don't want to float in the world. I consider myself a philosopher—and I don't mean like they say that everyone is. Sure, we all got opinions. We all have our beliefs and ideas that we stake our lives on. But, to repeat, I love to read—Buddha, the Bible, Marx, Jung, Black Elk, Stephen King. I mean if you're going to put everything behind anything, you might as well know as much as you can about everything. I have a spiritual curiosity that isn't just to fill in the voids. It's also not about hooking onto any one belief—it's the satisfaction one gets from learning about the vibrant universe of arts, words, images, and ideas that human beings have created over time.

I have Ruby to thank for this. In her heart stirs a revolution-ary. And I'm not talking about a malcontent or a party pooper. For Ruby, a true revolutionary believes in the best in people, in their courage and brains.

"You want change—you have to study," Ruby would always say. "And you have to impact the people and world around you."

Not just theory. Not just practice. Truth is both. Although at first I thought Ruby was half off her *mecedora*.

Eventually, I came around. This isn't hard if—like Jesus or Zapata—you care about those at the bottom. It isn't hard if you don't fit in. If you feel and taste the daily injustices and hypocrisies—and it makes you gag. If it seems that the churches, the schools, the politicians, and corporations are all in collusion against you. That's the way I see it—it's good to be about something *they* hate.

So I play bass for the La Cruz Negra—thumping out a bloody rage and calling for a worldwide uprising. *Claro que* hell yes!

For now, I also have to drive this shiny slick white limo.

There's a certain advantage in being a limo driver. It's being able to see the world through a lens that few ever get a chance to do. Not just the "lives of the rich and famous." But about *our* lives, the rest of us—the fool-hearted talented whose glories never leave a garage; the hip-hop rebels and the dream-starved street women; the urban vaqueros in their tightly woven molded hats and ornate leather boots and the assembly-line kings and queens waiting for the week's shift to end so they can reign on a dance floor.

I'm talking about all those who get convinced that watching TV, shopping on weekends, or drinking tequila and singing tear-drenched ballads at the *compadres'* house is all that matters.

In my limo I see the world beneath the world, the under-carriage of the glass-and-marble city—every pothole and man-hole along our greased byways, every piece of dust and mold on brick, slate, or stucco edifices.

The limo service allows me on rare occasions to take the "beast" home when I've been out all night. My boss trusts me, if you can believe that—but he should. Despite my weirdness at times, I won't ever burn anyone. That's not my nature—that's not the way Ruby raised me.

So I bring the limo to the block—and pay for the extra car washes because of the kids—and I'm special here. A local hero. But, you know what? This won't last long. Because life goes on. The streets don't stop being crummy. The cottages are still sullen matchboxes.

The fact is no limo is going to make things better in the long run. Even for the factory-slaving men who have been standing around this royal carriage discerning the mysteries of life. Even for the little bit of magic that I pull from the only bona fide symbol of power and wealth ever to grace our little spot of God's funky, rooster-infested, weed-filled backyard. Nope. No limo's going to change that.

The airport is always holy hell. Especially for limo drivers. You have to pull up to tiny spots that a long limo won't fit into. There's always a cop telling you to keep moving. There're the long waits for your pickup to show. There's the chance you have to take running into the baggage area with a crudely made sign with your pickup's name so they can spot you—and the skycap you have to bribe so he can watch your ride.

Then there are the people who just hate anyone in a limo. I can see why—you get the impression that people in limos think they're better than anyone else is because they see the world through dark glass. I try not to let this get to me—it's a job, one that I like for now.

I can tell you stories about these streets, about the partially lit office buildings outlined by night, and the angular houses on tired lawns. I can tell you about the nagging billboards—smoke this, eat that, buy this, look at that—flashing by like unwanted memories. I can tell you about the limo and the people who've graced its meticulously polished interior. I can tell you about the worlds that some of them spit on—and the world of spit where most of them have landed. How a silent laughter seems to emanate from the asphalt as I pass.

I can tell you about the Taiwanese businessmen that I take to fancy hotels in Alhambra—down Valley Boulevard's Asia Heights with that beautiful oriental lettering on all the stores. The hotels look like any other—with the best service and smiling patrons—only these have gambling, booze, and women in a back room that's set aside just for these businessmen.

Or I can tell you about the California state senator with a hand in some young woman's blouse—not his wife—who I chauffeured to a gala political ball on Santa Monica Boulevard.

Or about the Beverly Hills High School—*90210*—prom dates who leave fluids of all colors and shapes on the floor and seats…well, you get the picture.

The limo is my doorway to a world of glitz, power, and corruption inside the canopied palaces of Los Angeles that I would never have otherwise known.

But soon all this gets old. Where I'm from, people get scared, desperate, mean, stupid, and downright ugly. East L.A. has its share of murderers, rapists, abusers, drunks, and psychos. What I realize, though, is that it's practically the same all over Los Angeles—only some of *those* people get their names on the marquees, the bank accounts, and the stock options.

After a while, the sheen on that white limo doesn't seem so bright. The leather seats don't look so sharp. After a while—like most things—the excitement wears thin. The celebrities, the bankers, the high school jocks, the white-hair society ladies, the airport call girls—they all start looking and sounding alike.

One day, I come to the airport to get some famous author. I read a lot of books, but I never read any of his. A best-seller, they say. But I had heard his name. Thaddeus Rosewood Turner. A Southerner, if you ask me. And he is—one of those Texas noir writers who ruminates about real murders, real places, with a real Texas accent.

There's something about some outsiders' view of L.A., though—they already hate the place before they even get here. Turner is no exception.

"Son, can you please pull up the air some—I'm dryin' up like a junebug in winter," Mr. Turner says while maneuvering his hefty body into the leather seats. "Man, this town ain't got no feel to it. I don't know how anybody can rightly stand it."

Famous or not, Mr. Turner turns out to be a real pain in the ass. First off, he has these weird gray eyes, like clouds in a darkening sky, an orange tan, and a pointy chin with globs of flesh pushed around it. His hands are pink hairy tarantulas with diamond-laden gold rings.

Unfortunately, we limo drivers belong to the pickup for the time a publisher or company pays for our service. So I am literally at Mr. Turner's beck and call. Most of the time, people are nice and don't demand too much. Most of them are just happy to be inside a limo, seeing the world through dark glass (maybe, for a moment, believing they're better than anybody else). But Mr. Turner has been in many limos. This doesn't stop him from whining about everything and everybody.

"Now this fruit bowl looks like a withered hat come out of a rain," he starts about the basket of fruit the limo service likes to have in the backseat. "Get me some real fruit, son—apples and peaches—not these California shits. These bananers, kiawas, and goddamned grapes."

So we make stops at fruit markets, tie stores, cigar stores, porno shops (I know, but what the hey), between the fancy-ass hotel Mr. Turner complains about, and the barbershop. All within a few turns of the Westside. All the famous people I pick up never ever go deep into downtown L.A.—or near East L.A. for that matter. It's all Westside with them—Beverly Hills, Santa Monica, Hollywood. They think *that's* L.A. They got no idea about L.A.!

And sometimes they pay attention to me, sometimes they don't. Mr. Turner did.

"Hey, are you one of them injuns?" he asks, staring at my thick long hair and my sharp dark features. "You look just like an injun...has anyone ever tol' you that?"

"Once or twice."

"I got some injun in me, too," Turner replies smartly. "Cherokee. Got it on my mother's side, God rest her soul."

Many Southerners claim this, I find out, and usually it's Cherokee.

I also find out that it's no good telling them I'm Mexican. When I do, all of a sudden I'm no stoic heroic Indian (that some of their ancestors killed, robbed, and left to starve in funky reservations in the first place). But I tell Turner anyway.

"God dang, Meskins—they're everywhere," Mr. Turner obliges. "Now they're drivin' limos—hell horse, I've seen everythin' now."

The limo service sends me to this colossal hotel on Wilshire Boulevard—a castlelike structure that you have to pull in almost a mile from the street to get to the front steps. I have a CD of Pavement in the limo's CD player—I mean, this beast is loaded with all the electronic conveniences. I wait for my pickup, bopping my head along to wailing guitars.

When I see her, I can't believe my eyes. She's one of those dream honeys—pretty with tight silk pants, see-through blouse, and a lacy black bra underneath. She has dark shiny hair to her shoulders and a made-up face that accentuates her checks and lips. Rouge and gloss galore. I get out to open the back door.

"Hey, hon, I'm set, how about you?" she says.

I don't know what she means, but I say, "Like always."

"You know, I don't feel like getting anywhere just now—how about we just drive around for a while?"

"Whatever you want," I say, a little nervous. "'I'm yours, for the night."

"Whoa there, tiger, let's just cruise, and we'll see about *that* night."

"I...I didn't mean nothing by it, ma'am. I just mean the service is at your disposal for as long as it's paid for."

"Yeah, I know what you…just drive will you."

She's bad-tempered beneath her bubble of beauty. That's okay. It's my job to be as nice as I can, regardless. At least she's a looker.

We end up in Hollywood, which for those who haven't been here is really nothing to write home about. I think of Hollywood as having unexpected ordinariness. I suppose it's had its glory days—they try to recapture this even now with new specialty bars, sparkling theater marquees, and tourist buses. But Hollywood to me is more about lost middle-class teens hooked on smack; about bikers sitting around their hogs at tattoo shops with their pierced girlfriends; or Saturday-night cruising with hydraulic-hopping lowriders and sporadic gunfire. It's more about the lonely white-shirted men entering X-rated bookstores and peepshows.

There's the Salvadoran and Armenian street gangs, the home-less on crack, and the hourly rate motels where once in a while some prostitute is found murdered in a bathtub. Most people with stars in their eyes don't make it to the movie lots or the good-paying modeling studios. You've heard this before, I know, but it's true. I'm not sure many of them even want to make it, really. They get stuck on motel row, on the next dope high, on the street life with its yelling, violence, and fast sex—and that's it. They're gone.

Beneath the bright lights and glamour of movies there's this Hollywood—one is connected to the other.

So Miss I'm-Gorgeous-And-You're-A-Stupid-Limo-Driver starts talking again.

"This sure is a long way from Nebraska."

I think she's making a reference to Dorothy and Kansas and Oz.

She grabs a bottle of Chivas Regal from the bar in front of her. She turns on the TV set, mutes the sound, and with tiny manicured fingers takes out a thin brown cigarette from a silver case. *She's all that,* I think.

"You got a light, hon?" she asks. I push in the lighter on the dashboard and wait for it to pop out. She starts pouring a drink into a glass. One thing about these limos is that they're smooth. So we're gliding down Hollywood Boulevard. Gliding through dreamland and bright lights, and somehow from behind the windshield of this vehicle, Hollywood starts looking like it's supposed to—carefree, inviting, and safe.

"I got lots of plans, hon," she says as I hand her the lighter. "I'm going to make my money—you better believe that! And I'm going to put it away. I ain't going down like some of those whores and bastard pimps who don't got nothing to show for their fuckin' efforts."

She keeps drinking. She keeps talking. I keep driving. And pretty soon my vision of loveliness is drunker than shit.

"I was just visiting with this really rich guy—you know, where you picked me up."

I nod while getting glimpses of her in the rearview mirror. After a while, another face comes through from below the make-up—a lived-in face, a street-sculpted face, a slash-and-burn kind of face.

"I party with the best of them, hon, and they pay me real good, too. And you know what—I'm worth every cent."

I understand now what she is—one of those high-priced escorts. I calm down. Nervousness gone, I guess, because I know she's not going to give up anything for me. So I listen—the biggest part of my job is to drive, listen, and hope nobody goes off on my ass.

"Only his money can't make his shit smell sweet," she says, dropping ashes on the floor rug. "Trying to tell me what to do. I make *him* look good! I'm not his slave or piece of ass. But he starts in on me, yelling, pushing me around. Hello!"

I turn into a side street, make a couple of left-handed turns, and glide down the Boulevard again.

296 · LUIS J. RODRIGUEZ

"Sometimes, though, I wish I were in Nebraska—you ever been there, hon?"

"No, ma'am, only to Arizona...Mexico."

"Oh, Mex-i-co. I just love Mex-i-co. Cancoon. Alcapoolco. Porto Valarda. I love margaridas—you don't got any margaridas, do you?"

"No, just what's there in the bar."

"Yeasss, Chivas—the best!" she exclaims, wiping the hair that has fallen across her face. "I'm from Nebraska. Small town called Brewster. Real small. Knew everybody. Everybody knows you. I was homecoming queen, if you can believe that! That's why I'm no street 'ho—I'm high class, all the way. I always was, always will be."

I can see she's a sad lonely person, despite her job. Somewhere she's made some wrong turns, met some wrong people, and now she can't see her way out of this except in a dream of money— what everybody tends to do. Money, though, is an illusion with green faces. I think this is so money has personality—like the way our deities end up with traits like the rest of us. People create money and then they let money create them. Money is a facade but it has a force greater than nature. Sure, we've all gone to the woods, to the most mellow of beaches, or a serene desert, and praised the Creator for the handiwork. But as soon as money becomes an issue, *olvídate!*

My lovely friend here is like many of the people I drive around in this glimmering city. They are so removed from whatever fire they were born with that all their dreams become mud. She's no different—wounded and truly beautiful.

"Brewster's got some pretty fields—ripe green and yellow corn ones. I loved those stalks, straight up into the sky, like a sea more alive to me than any ocean," she says softly. "Tall stalks with leafy arms to hold you. We lived in town; we didn't do any farming or anything. But I just loved to go out into those fields.

Just wading through the stalks. And there're bugs, but I don't worry about bugs. Something about the corn, the smell, the late afternoons with the sun hanging low in the sky and then later as the lightnin' bugs flash here and there like Christmas lights. I don't know—I guess I miss it about now. I miss not seeing my sisters, my ma and pa, those green fields, and that sun. I guess I miss not being who I was. But I tell you one thing—I'm doing better now. Got me more money than I would ever have with a lifetime in Brewster. Got money to put away, invest; get me a nice big mansion in Hancock Park. Yeah, better than Brewster, I tell you….But there are days, hon, days like around midsummer with that orange light over the horizon, small birds crying out, and them crows fluttering like black hands across that sky— umm, umm, sometimes there are days."

Driving around most of the night, I finally drop off my Homecoming Queen from Brewster, Nebraska, at a secured apartment complex of low buildings in Hollow-wood. I open the door for her. She hands me a twenty-dollar bill, which is mighty nice of her—or anybody for that matter. She also gently places a card in my hand. The card is glossy black with words in embossed gold lettering: "She-La's Premier Escort Service." There's a beeper number below the letters.

"Just in case you get lonely, hon," she says.

I smile and thank her. When she's not looking, I crush the card in my hand and put it in my coat pocket to toss later.

"Hey," She-la asks as she walks away, "has anyone ever said you look like an Indian?"

When I'm not with the limo, I'm with the band. As usual, we crowd into my cottage room. Lilo tears into the lead guitar, slashing the strings with callused fingers; Dante pours the sticks down on top of his drums like ceaseless rain; and Patrick shouts incoherent hate into the mike. I'm bopping my head, pulling on the bass strings like I'm pulling weeds out of a cactus garden—something I've done in my spotted work record, by the way.

> *Lies, betrayals, this system smells—*
> *My brain is crammed with rusted nails,*
> *Time to blow it all down—got to fight it—*
> *Tear it all down—*
> *Can't be cruel to the Brown—*

These are the words that Patrick mouths into a handheld mike while the rest of us envelop him with backbeats, feedback, and screeching guitars. As for the song…well, let's just say I drive a limo better than we write lyrics, okay? But we're learning, as Ruby points out. We're La Cruz Negra—there's mean intention there. Besides, the few people who come to hear us at the downtown bar where we sometimes practice don't seem to give a shit. Raw is better. Raw is power.

Raw means we're never gonna get a record deal.

I know this. Right now, it's just about being there—losing oneself in the venomous three-chord assaults, in the blood-boiling guitars, heart-stopping bass, and the drums with mayhem on their mind. It's being in that unnameable space between voice and microphone, flesh and metal alloy; between what screams I pull from my bass-plucking hands and the suicide eyes of the people listening to us.

Patrick's girl Luz, the bleached-hair metal chick, likes it. She sits lazily on a beanbag with a thin halter top and worn jeans as we hammer the walls with deafening noise. It's a good ten minutes before I realize there's knocking at the door.

"Hold it…hold it—someone's here."

I step over the amp in the middle of the room to unlatch the bolt. Ruby comes in, grimacing, as she usually does when she visits. She's bearing a bucket of Pollo Loco chicken for us to munch on.

"Darn, *m'ijos,* you could peel paint with that noise," she offers.

"Hey, Ruby, how does it sound today?" Lilo asks.

"Better, really—a lot better. I could almost hear a melody."

"Damn, we messin' up bad then," I add.

As it turns out, most people in the cottages can't stand our playing. But even after the initial death threats and cursing, they eventually get used to hearing us. Like the way we've all gotten used to the incessant roar of traffic on the San Bernardino Freeway. We just can't play at night or during the weekdays when the night workers rest—people like me, actually. But on Saturdays, we're allowed to jam during the day with a slight downturn of the volume so as not to tax our neighbors' immense generosity (by rights, they should have lynched us).

I walk out into the noontime sun with a piece of chicken in my hand. Our neighbors are out on this warm summer day. The kids are playing everywhere; one ten-year-old girl is pushing around a toddler in a dirt-encrusted wobbly carriage in the courtyard.

Across the way, a cholo and his robust girlfriend relax on two lawn chairs in front of their doorway, brews in hand, next to a three-week-old baby in a bassinet. The six undocumented guys who share a room at the far end are working on a Dodge sedan that sits on top of cinder blocks in the alley behind the cottages.

My prized limo is parked on the street, now watched over by almost everyone whenever I leave it there in case some fool thinks about ripping it off.

And then there's Bernarda.

On that bright and immaculate day, Bernarda is standing at her doorway with a bikini top and tight black shorts around her ample hips.

"So when are you going to take me for a ride, Cruz? You promised."

"Oh, hi, Bernarda...how are you doing today?"

"Don't change the subject. You told me the first time you brought that thing that we'd go cruising—well?"

"It's not that easy. I could get in trouble if something happens to the limo when I'm not on the job."

"So why did you bring it down here—to tease?"

This exchange between Bernarda and me is of recent vintage. Before the limo, Bernarda had nothing but bad things to say about La Cruz Negra and me. But the limo has become like a bargaining chip—I believe it's why people now tolerate our playing once a week.

So let me tell you a little bit about Girlfriend. Bernarda lives alone in that cottage of hers. She also works at night in a downtown dancing joint where men—mostly Spanish-speaking—pay for tickets that allow them to dance and drink with the women for a set amount of time. Supposedly no hanky-panky accompanies those ticket purchases, but you hear stories about guys paying a little extra to get a little extra.

I'm not sure where Bernarda stands on this issue. I consider it degrading to work in a place like that, but I don't blame the women. It's kind of something they fall into—and sometimes they're unable to get out.

Bernarda is unusually tall—for a Mexican. She's five feet eight inches, without heels. A real giant. I'm only five six. She's also dark-skinned with thick curly short hair and an oval face. For all her supposed dancing and partying, she's got a complexion like silk and a to-die-for figure.

"Well, Cruz, I'm not letting you off the hook. You owe me a night out in that thing."

Bernarda is in a long flamingo pink skirt and a tight white silk blouse. She's looking as nice as she ever does when she goes to her dancing jobs. Only this time she's going out with me. Finally, after months of prodding, I decide to take her and that beast out for a spin.

Things slow down in winter—even in L.A., where you better believe it gets cold. It may not be Minneapolis or Buffalo, but I hear that as many homeless people die of hypothermia in the streets here as they do in Chicago. I don't have stats, it's just what I hear.

Bernarda has a friend—real nice, sweet almost—who works at the same dance establishment. Her name is Suyapa, and she's Honduran. They're quite a pair—Bernarda and Suyapa—especially before they leave for work, wearing the slickest dresses, tallest high heels, and hair curled and brushed back with the most delicate of strokes.

"Cruzito, we better get going so we can get Suyapa before it gets dark," Bernarda says while putting on a leather coat and taking one last peek at herself through a mirror hanging on her bathroom door.

Yes, her Honduran friend is joining us this evening. You didn't think I'd get an actual one-on-one date with Bernarda, did you? I know the score. She's in for the ride, nothing more. That's okay. Ruby taught me to be realistic—even with dreams.

I got on my finest beige jacket and slacks with my favorite white-striped blue shirt—the few decent clothes I own. Needless to say, when you're in a rock band you don't need fancy duds. And I didn't think it was right to put on my black suit and white shirt that I wear for working. Even if it's not an official date, I'm going to hang loose and have me one hell of a good time.

There's a fast-breaking wind coming through the trees, hitting the city at intense speeds and at strange angles. Dark clouds menace the sky. I hope there's no rain with those winds. The problem is that in winter, drastic weather changes can occur in any given hour.

Suyapa lives in Echo Park. From our block, we turn west on Chavez Avenue and go straight—past small homes, taco joints, darkened bars, and dollar stores toward downtown's lit skyline as the sun begins to set. We pass the twin towers of the county jail,

Union Station, and Olvera Street's open stalls of Mexican and old California trinkets and wares with Japanese and Anglo tourists crowded into the alley-like thoroughfare. Then over across Chinatown with its banners, pagodas, and restaurants, and onto Sunset Boulevard and the E.P. barrio.

When we hit Alvarado Street, we turn north, then left on another street. After a few blocks, we hang a right where I promptly double park in front of a set of small family homes.

Suyapa emerges from a beige duplex in a dark red satin dress that swerves around her every curve. Man, these are some beautiful womens, I think. But my plan is to be a gentleman—a real caballero—and try to enjoy myself without imposing any base desires. I really want Bernarda to think the best of me—although in the back of my mind is the issue of a possible future one-on-one date with her.

You should see the people that surround the limo, which I had buffed to a perfect luster. Most of the residents on Suyapa's block are Central American. A limo for one of their own—now there's something to recall for days to come. I feel a tinge of manly pride, I must say, to open the doors and let in songs of nature like Bernarda and Suyapa into my castle on wheels.

Men in front of tireless car frames smile at me, then chatter among themselves. Others, including a pregnant woman, circle the limo as if they're evaluating its worth. Then the kids start to run up, and I decide it's time to leave.

"So Cruzito, where do we start?" Bernarda asks from the backseats that face each other as we transition onto Sunset Boulevard and Suyapa waves from the opened sunroof to anybody on the street. I drive toward the much more famous and ritzier sections of Sunset Boulevard on the Westside.

"Wherever your little hearts desire," I say. "See me as your personal chauffeur."

The evening starts out nice: The girls snicker, enjoy the imbibements, tell jokes, make fun of my hair. We go from club to club—not so much to spend time in them, it seems, but to see the people's faces as the statuesque Bernarda and sumptuous Suyapa get in and out of the vehicle.

I only drink sporadically—since this is not my thing. But the girls are going buck wild with the booze. As the night wears on, Bernarda eventually pulls herself in next to me while Suyapa crashes in the backseat. I put on an old AC/DC cassette tape, *Highway to Hell*—and Bernarda just about back flips.

"No, no, no, *querido*—we're not going to listen to that monstrosity," Bernarda insists. "Don't you got nothing nice and soulful?"

"No, I'm sorry, I don't," I say, crossed. "But you can put on whatever you want from the radio."

Then Bernarda dares to ask me the big limo no-no question— she has enough nerve to ask if she can drive the beast.

"No, I can't do that," I explain. "I'm the only one qualified to drive. Besides, I'm not drinking that much."

"Oh, Cruzito," Bernarda purrs. "We don't have to go into traffic. A parking lot is okay. How about at the beach? Then we can get out and sit on the sand for a while."

I'm weak. I know, I know. I figure it won't harm anything if Bernarda drives the limo around a parking lot. So we cruise on over to Malibu Beach on Pacific Coast Highway. It's three a.m. The ocean view is nice and tranquil—nary a soul lingers. I pull over into a lot next to a beach condo. Suyapa is snoring big time. It seems the lot is large enough for Bernarda to get a feel for driving this thing.

Meanwhile, I'm fantasizing about kissing her full wet lips later on a blanket near the waves.

Bernarda runs over to the driver's side. I jump over to the passenger's. I know she knows how to drive because she's got a Nova or something. She sits there for a while—taking in the extraordinary number of lights on the dashboard and the sensation of the steering wheel under her fingers.

"You ready?" I ask. "Now put it in drive and go up a ways, then stop, make a turn, and come back. Got it?"

Easy enough. But that's when you know that Tatadios has other plans. That's when you know that there's a reason you shouldn't give in to purring stoned women against your better judgment. It's times like these when the word *"pendejo"* has salient significance. I think Bernarda has everything in place—wheels straight, lights on, hand brake off, gears on drive. That's what I think anyway.

She punches the accelerator—which is bad enough—but she had inadvertently put the stick shift in reverse. The Limo thrusts backward and rams into a row of squat bushes and into the condo behind us; an explosion of glass and wood soon follows as we smash through the plate glass wall that separates the living room from the bushes. We shatter antique china cabinets, ceramic-topped coffee tables, and Tiffany lamps before Bernarda gets the presence of mind to brake.

Yes, two couples are relaxing on a sofa watching TV as we fly past them. Yes, Bernarda screams and Suyapa sleeps through it all. And yes, of course, a windy rain begins to fall as we wait for the police and tow truck to arrive while our reluctant hosts yell the most exquisite obscenities into our ears.

I suppose I don't have to tell you about the deep-ass trouble I get from this. I don't have to tell you that I lose my job (although the limo's insured for stunts like these). And that I'll never have another date with Bernarda again.

The last words Bernarda screeches from the driver's side are: "Why did you let me do that?"

Back on the Eastside, sans limo, my stock among my neighbors greatly diminished, I practice on my bass with the power off. The smell of menudo and freshly toasted tortillas wafts through the open window. It's Sunday morning. The cottages stir beneath the brown haze. The twenty or so people next door start making their morning racket—cupboards slamming, balls bouncing, a Spanish-language evangelist shouting *aleluyas* on TV. I contemplate my next move, my next job adventure, the next possible gig for La Cruz Negra. I contemplate last weekend's events—and I know I'm gonna miss that limo for what time it lasted. I also think about the shame I brought to Purépechas everywhere. But I realize I have to get over it—and soon. The big three-O is around the corner for me. Where am I going in life? Who am I going to be? I think about this for about two minutes before I decide to ask my neighbors for a bowl of menudo—maybe as a charity case. As bad as I feel, I also know there's always another thing past the last thing. Maybe, someday, I'll get really serious about that revolution.

Chitra Banerjee Divakaruni

"Mrs. Dutta Writes a Letter"
from *The Unknown Errors of Our Lives*

Chitra Banerjee Divakaruni is a widely known author and poet. Born in 1957 in India, she lived there until she was nineteen, at which point she left Calcutta and moved to the United States. She continued her education in the field of English by receiving an M.A. from Wright State University in Dayton, Ohio, and a Ph.D. from the University of California, Berkeley. She has been published in more than fifty magazines, including the *Atlantic Monthly* and the *New Yorker,* and her writing has been included in over thirty anthologies. Her major works include the novels *The Mistress of Spices* and *Sister of My Heart* and an award-winning collection of short stories, *Arranged Marriage.* She currently splits her time between San Jose and Houston, where she teaches English literature at the University of Texas.

"Mrs. Dutta Writes a Letter" is taken from the collection of short stories *The Unknown Errors of Our Lives,* published in 2001.

When the alarm goes off at 5:00 a.m., buzzing like a trapped wasp, Mrs. Dutta has been lying awake for quite a while. Though it has now been two months, she still has difficulty sleeping on the Perma Rest mattress Sagar and Shyamoli, her son and daughter-in-law, have bought specially for her. It is too American-soft, unlike the reassuringly solid copra ticking she is used to at home. *Except this is home now*, she reminds herself. She reaches hurriedly to turn off the alarm, but in the dark her fingers get confused among the knobs, and the electric clock falls with a thud to the floor. Its insistent metallic call vibrates out through the walls of her room until she is sure it will wake everyone. She yanks frantically at the wire until she feels it give, and in the abrupt silence that follows she hears herself breathing, a sound harsh and uneven and full of guilt.

Mrs. Dutta knows, of course, that this turmoil is her own fault. She should just not set the alarm. There is no need for her to get up early here in Sunnyvale, in her son's house. But the habit, taught to her by her mother-in-law when she was a bride of seventeen, *a good wife wakes before the rest of the household,* is one she finds impossible to break. How hard it was then to pull her unwilling body away from her husband's sleep-warm clasp, Sagar's father whom she had just learned to love. To stumble to the kitchen that smelled of stale garam masala and light the coal unoon so she could make morning tea for them all—her parents-in-law, her husband, his two younger brothers, the widow aunt who lived with them.

After dinner, when the family sits in front of the TV, she attempts to tell her grandchildren about those days. "I was never good at starting that unoon—the smoke stung my eyes, making me cough and cough. Breakfast was never ready on time, and my mother-in-law—oh, how she scolded me until I was in tears. Every night I would pray to Goddess Durga, please let me sleep late, just one morning!"

"Mmmm," Pradeep says, bent over a model plane.

"Oooh, how awful," says Mrinalini, wrinkling her nose politely before she turns back to a show filled with jokes that Mrs. Dutta does not understand.

"That's why you should sleep in now, Mother," says Shyamoli, smiling from the recliner where she sits looking through the *Wall Street Journal*. With her legs crossed so elegantly under the shimmery blue skirt she has changed into after work, and her unusually fair skin, she could pass for an American, thinks Mrs. Dutta, whose own skin is brown as roasted cumin. The thought fills her with an uneasy pride.

From the floor where he leans against Shyamoli's knee, Sagar adds, "We want you to be comfortable, Ma. To rest. That's why we brought you to America."

In spite of his thinning hair and the gold-rimmed glasses which he has recently taken to wearing, Sagar's face seems to Mrs. Dutta still that of the boy she used to send off to primary school with his metal tiffin box. She remembers how he crawled into her bed on stormy monsoon nights, how when he was ill no one else could make him drink his barley water. Her heart balloons in sudden gladness because she is really here, with him and his children in America. "Oh, Sagar"—she smiles—"now you're talking like this! But did you give me a moment's rest while you were growing up?" And she launches into a description of childhood pranks that has him shaking his head indulgently while disembodied TV laughter echoes through the room.

But later he comes into her bedroom and says, a little shame-faced, "Mother, please, don't get up so early in the morning. All that noise in the bathroom, it wakes us up, and Molli has such a long day at work…"

And she, turning a little so he shouldn't see her foolish eyes filling with tears as though she were a teenage bride again and not a woman well over sixty, nods her head, *yes, yes.*

Waiting for the sounds of the stirring household to release her from the embrace of her Perma Rest mattress, Mrs.

Dutta repeats the 108 holy names of God. *Om Keshavaya Namah, Om Narayanaya Namah, Om Madhavaya Namah.* But underneath she is thinking of the bleached-blue aerogram from Mrs. Basu that has been waiting unanswered on her bedside table all week, filled with news from home. There was a robbery at Sandhya Jewelry Store, the bandits had guns but luckily no one was hurt. Mr. Joshi's daughter, that sweet-faced child, has run away with her singing teacher, who would've thought it. Mrs. Barucha's daughter-in-law had one more baby girl, yes, their fourth, you'd think they'd know better than to keep trying for a boy. Last Tuesday was Bangla Bandh, another labor strike, everything closed down, even the buses not running, but you can't really blame them, can you, after all factory workers have to eat, too. Mrs. Basu's tenants, whom she'd been trying to evict forever, had finally moved out, good riddance, but you should see the state of the flat.

At the very bottom Mrs. Basu wrote, *Are you happy in America?*

Mrs. Dutta knows that Mrs. Basu, who has been her closest friend since they both came to Ghoshpara Lane as young brides, cannot be fobbed off with descriptions of Fisherman's Wharf and the Golden Gate Bridge, or even anecdotes involving grandchildren. And so she has been putting off her reply while in her heart family loyalty battles with insidious feelings of—but she turns from them quickly and will not name them even to herself.

Now Sagar is knocking on the children's doors—a curious custom, this, children being allowed to close their doors against their parents—and with relief Mrs. Dutta gathers up her bathroom things. She has plenty of time. It will take a second rapping from their mother before Pradeep and Mrinalini open their doors and stumble out. Still, she is not one to waste the precious morning. She splashes cold water on her face and neck (she does not believe in pampering herself), scrapes the night's gumminess from her tongue with her metal tongue cleaner, and brushes vigorously, though the minty toothpaste does not leave her mouth feeling as clean as did the bittersweet neem stick she'd been using all her life. She combs the knots out of her hair. Even at her age, it is thicker and silkier than her daughter-in-law's permed curls. *Such vanity,* she scolds her reflection, *and you a grandmother and a widow besides.* Still, as she deftly fashions her hair into a neat coil, she remembers how her husband would always compare it to night rain.

She hears a commotion outside.

"Pat! Minnie! What d'you mean you still haven't washed up? I'm late every morning to work nowadays because of you kids."

"But, Mom, *she's* in there. She's been there forever..." says Mrinalini.

Pause. Then, "So go to the downstairs bathroom."

"But all our stuff is here," says Pradeep, and Mrinalini adds, "It's not fair. Why can't *she* go downstairs?"

A longer pause. Inside the bathroom Mrs. Dutta hopes Shyamoli will not be too harsh on the girl. But a child who refers to elders in that disrespectful way ought to be punished. How many times had she slapped Sagar for something far less, though he was her only one, the jewel of her eye, come to her after she had been married for seven years and everyone had given up hope already? Whenever she lifted her hand to him it was as though her heart was being put through a masala grinder. Such is a mother's duty.

But Shyamoli only says, in a tired voice, "That's enough! Go put on your clothes, hurry."

The grumblings recede. Footsteps clatter down the stairs. Inside the bathroom Mrs. Dutta bends over the sink, gripping the folds of her sari. Hard to think through the pounding in her head to what it is she feels most—anger at the children for their rudeness, or at Shyamoli for letting them go unrebuked. Or is it shame that clogs her throat, stinging, sulfuric, indigestible?

It is 9:00 a.m. and the house, after the flurry of departures, of frantic "I can't find my socks," and "Mom, he took my lunch money," and "I swear I'll leave you kids behind if you're not in the car in exactly one minute," has settled into its placid daytime rhythms.

Busy in the kitchen, Mrs. Dutta has recovered her spirits. It is too exhausting to hold on to grudges, and, besides, the kitchen— sunlight sliding across its countertops while the refrigerator hums reassuringly—is her favorite place.

Mrs. Dutta hums too as she fries potatoes for alu dum. Her voice is rusty and slightly off-key. In India she would never have ventured to sing, but with everyone gone, the house is too quiet, all that silence pressing down on her like the heel of a giant hand, and the TV voices, with their unreal accents, are no help at all. As the potatoes turn golden-brown, she permits herself a moment of nostalgia for her Calcutta kitchen—the new gas stove bought with the birthday money Sagar sent, the scoured brass pots stacked by the meat safe, the window with the lotus-pattern grille through which she could look down on children playing cricket after school. The mouth-watering smell of ginger and chili paste, ground fresh by Reba the maid, and, in the evening, strong black Assam cha brewing in the kettle when Mrs. Basu came by to visit. In her mind she writes to Mrs. Basu, *Oh, Roma, I miss it all so much, sometimes I feel that someone has reached in and torn out a handful of my chest.*

But only fools indulge in nostalgia, so Mrs. Dutta shakes her head clear of images and straightens up the kitchen. She pours the half-drunk glasses of milk down the sink, though Shyamoli has told her to save them in the refrigerator. But surely Shyamoli, a girl from a good Hindu family, doesn't expect her to put contaminated jutha things in with the rest of the food? She washes the breakfast dishes by hand instead of letting them wait inside the dishwater till night, breeding germs. With practiced fingers she throws an assortment of spices into the blender: coriander, cumin, cloves, black pepper, a few red chilies for vigor. No stale bottled curry powder for *her! At least the family's eating well since I arrived,* she writes in her mind, *proper Indian food, rutis that puff up the way they should, fish curry in mustard sauce, and real pulao with raisins and cashews and ghee—the way you taught me, Roma—instead of Rice-a-roni.* She would like to add, *They love it,* but thinking of Shyamoli she hesitates.

At first Shyamoli had been happy enough to have someone take over the cooking. It's wonderful to come home to a hot dinner, she'd say, or, Mother, what crispy papads, and your fish gravy is out of this world. But recently she's taken to picking at her food, and once or twice from the kitchen Mrs. Dutta has caught wisps of words, intensely whispered: *cholesterol, all putting on weight, she's spoiling you.* And though Shyamoli always refuses when the children ask if they can have burritos from the freezer instead, Mrs. Dutta suspects that she would really like to say yes.

The children. A heaviness pulls at Mrs. Dutta's entire body when she thinks of them. Like so much in this country they have turned out to be—yes, she might as well admit it—a disappointment.

For this she blames, in part, the Olan Mills portrait. Perhaps it had been impractical of her to set so much store on a photograph, especially one taken years ago. But it was such a charming scene—Mrinalini in a ruffled white dress with her arm around her brother, Pradeep chubby and dimpled in a suit and bow tie, a glorious autumn forest blazing red and yellow behind them. (Later Mrs. Dutta would learn, with a sense of having been betrayed, that the forest was merely a backdrop in a studio in California, where real trees did not turn such colors.)

The picture had arrived, silver-framed and wrapped in a plastic sheet filled with bubbles, with a note from Shyamoli explaining that it was a Mother's Day gift. (A strange concept, a day set aside to honor mothers. Did the sahebs not honor their mothers the rest of the year, then?) For a week Mrs. Dutta could not decide where it should be hung. If she put it in the drawing room, visitors would be able to admire her grandchildren, but if she put it on the bedroom wall, she would be able to see the photo, last thing, before she fell asleep. She had finally opted for the bedroom, and later, when she was too ill with pneumonia to leave her bed for a month, she'd been glad of it.

Mrs. Dutta was not unused to living on her own. She had done it for the last three years, since Sagar's father died, politely but stubbornly declining the offers of various relatives, well-meaning and otherwise, to come and stay with her. In this she had surprised herself as well as others, who thought of her as a shy, sheltered woman, one who would surely fall apart without her husband to handle things for her. But she managed quite well. She missed Sagar's father, of course, especially in the evenings, when it had been his habit to read to her the more amusing parts of the newspaper while she rolled out rutis. But once the grief receded, she found it rather pleasant to be mistress of her own life, as she confided to Mrs. Basu. She liked being able, for the first time ever, to lie in bed all evening and read a new novel of Shankar's straight through if she wanted, or to send out for hot brinjal pakoras on a rainy day without feeling guilty that she wasn't serving up a balanced meal.

When the pneumonia hit, everything changed.

Mrs. Dutta had been ill before, but those illnesses had been different. Even in bed she'd been at the center of the household, with Reba coming to find out what should be cooked, Sagar's father bringing her shirts with missing buttons, her mother-in-law, now old and tamed, complaining that the cook didn't brew her tea strong enough, and Sagar running in crying because he'd had a fight with the neighbor boy. But now there was no one to ask her, querulously, *Just how long do you plan to remain sick*, no one waiting in impatient exasperation for her to take on her duties again, no one whose life was inconvenienced the least bit by her illness.

There was, therefore, no reason for her to get well.

When this thought occurred to Mrs. Dutta, she was so frightened that her body grew numb. The walls of the room spun into blackness, the bed on which she lay, a vast four-poster she had shared with Sagar's father since her marriage, rocked like a mastless dinghy caught in a storm, and a great, muted roar reverberated in the cavities of her skull. For a moment, unable to move or see, she thought, *I'm dead.* Then her vision, desperate and blurry, caught on the portrait. *My grandchildren.* She focused, with some difficulty, on the bright, oblivious sheen of their child faces, the eyes so like Sagar's that for a moment she could feel heartsickness cramping her joints like arthritis. She drew in a shuddering breath; the roaring seemed to recede. When the afternoon post brought another letter from Sagar, *Mother, you really should come and live with us, we worry about you all alone in India, especially when you're sick like this,* she wrote back the same day, with fingers that still shook a little, *You're right, my place is with you, with my grandchildren.*

But now that she is here on the other side of the world, she is wrenched by doubt. She knows the grandchildren love her—how can it be otherwise among family? And she loves them, she reminds herself, though they have put away, somewhere in the back of a closet, the vellum-bound *Ramayana for Young Readers* that she carried all the way from India in her hand luggage. Though their bodies twitch with impatience when she tries to tell them stories of her girlhood. Though they offer the most transparent excuses when she asks them to sit with her while she chants the evening arati. *They're flesh of my flesh, blood of my blood,* she reminds herself. But sometimes when she listens, from the other room, to them speaking on the phone, their American voices rising in excitement as they discuss a glittering alien world of Power Rangers, Spice Girls, and Spirit Week at school, she almost cannot believe it.

Stepping into the backyard with a bucket of newly washed clothes, Mrs. Dutta views the sky with some anxiety. The butter-gold sunlight is gone, black-bellied clouds have taken over the horizon, and the air feels still and heavy on her face, as before a Bengal storm. What if her clothes don't dry by the time the others return home?

Washing clothes has been a problem for Mrs. Dutta ever since she arrived in California.

"We can't, Mother," Shyamoli had said with a sigh when Mrs. Dutta asked Sagar to put up a clothesline for her in the backyard. (Shyamoli sighed often nowadays. Perhaps it was an American habit? Mrs. Dutta did not remember the Indian Shyamoli, the docile bride she'd mothered for a month before putting her on a Pan Am flight to join her husband, pursing her lips in quite this way to let out a breath at once patient and vexed.) "It's just not *done,* not in a nice neighborhood like this one. And being the only Indian family on the street, we have to be extra careful. People here, sometimes—." She'd broken off with a shake of her head. "Why don't you just keep your dirty clothes in the hamper I've put in your room, and I'll wash them on Sunday along with everyone else's."

Afraid of causing another sigh, Mrs. Dutta had agreed reluctantly. But she knew she should not store unclean clothes in the same room where she kept the pictures of her gods. That brought bad luck. And the odor. Lying in bed at night she could smell it distinctly, even though Shyamoli claimed the hamper was airtight. The sour, starchy old-woman smell embarrassed her.

What embarrassed her more was when, Sunday afternoons, Shyamoli brought the laundry into the family room to fold. Mrs. Dutta would bend intensely over her knitting, face tingling with shame, as her daughter-in-law nonchalantly shook out the wisps of lace, magenta and sea-green and black, that were her panties, laying them next to a stack of Sagar's briefs. And when, right in front of everyone, Shyamoli pulled out Mrs. Dutta's own crumpled, baggy bras from the clothes heap, she wished the ground would open up and swallow her, like the Sita of mythology.

Then one day Shyamoli set the clothes basket down in front of Sagar.

"Can you do them today, Sagar?" (Mrs. Dutta, who had never, through the forty-two years of her marriage, addressed Sagar's father by name, tried not to wince.) "I've got to get that sales report into the computer by tonight."

Before Sagar could respond, Mrs. Dutta was out of her chair, knitting needles dropping to the floor.

"No no no, clothes and all is no work for the man of the house. I'll do it." The thought of her son's hands searching through the basket and lifting up his wife's—and her own—underclothes filled her with horror.

"Mother!" Shyamoli said. "This is why Indian men are so useless around the house. Here in America we don't believe in men's work and women's work. Don't I work outside all day, just like Sagar? How'll I manage if he doesn't help me at home?"

"I'll help you instead," Mrs. Dutta ventured.

"You don't understand, do you, Mother?" Shyamoli said with a shaky smile. Then she went into the study.

Mrs. Dutta sat down in her chair and tried to understand. But after a while she gave up and whispered to Sagar that she wanted him to teach her how to run the washer and dryer.

"Why, Mother? Molli's quite happy to…"

"I've got to learn it.…" Her voice warped with distress as she rummaged through the tangled heap for her clothes.

Her son began to object, then shrugged. "Oh very well. If that's what you really want."

But later, when she faced them alone, the machines with their cryptic symbols and rows of gleaming knobs terrified her. What if she pressed the wrong button and flooded the entire floor with soapsuds? What if she couldn't turn the machines off and they kept going, whirring maniacally, until they exploded? (This had happened to a woman on a TV show just the other day, and she had jumped up and down, screaming. Everyone else found it hilarious, but Mrs. Dutta sat stiff-spined, gripping the armrest of her chair.) So she took to washing her clothes in the bathtub when she was alone. She had never done such a chore before, but she remembered how the village washerwomen of her childhood would beat their saris clean against river rocks. And a curious satisfaction filled her as her clothes hit the porcelain with the same solid wet *thunk.*

My small victory, my secret.

This is why everything must be dried and put safely away before Shyamoli returns. Ignorance, as Mrs. Dutta knows well from years of managing a household, is a great promoter of harmony. So she keeps an eye on the menacing advance of the clouds as she hangs up her blouse and underwear. As she drapes her sari along the redwood fence that separates her son's property from the neighbor's, first wiping it clean with a dish towel she has secretly taken from the bottom drawer of the kitchen. But she isn't too worried. Hasn't she managed every time, even after that freak hailstorm last month when she had to use the iron from the laundry closet to press everything dry? The memory pleases her. In her mind she writes to Mrs. Basu, *I'm fitting in so well here, you'd never guess I came only two months back. I've found new ways of doing things, of solving problems creatively. You would be most proud if you saw me.*

When Mrs. Dutta decided to give up her home of forty-five years, her relatives showed far less surprise than she had expected.

"Oh, we all knew you'd end up in America sooner or later," they said. "It was a foolishness to stay on alone so long after Sagar's father, may he find eternal peace, passed away. Good thing that boy of yours came to his senses and called you to join him. Everyone knows a wife's place is with her husband, and a widow's with her son."

318 · CHITRA BANERJEE DIVAKARUNI

Mrs. Dutta had nodded meek agreement, ashamed to let anyone know that the night before she had awakened weeping.

"Well, now that you're going, what'll happen to all your things?"

Mrs. Dutta, still troubled over those treacherous tears, had offered up her household effects in propitiation. "Here, Didi, you take this cutwork bedspread. Mashima, for a long time I meant for you to have these Corning Ware dishes, I know how much you admire them. And, Boudi, this tape recorder that Sagar sent a year back is for you. Yes yes, I'm quite sure. I can always tell Sagar to buy me another one when I get there."

Mrs. Basu, coming in just as a cousin made off triumphantly with a bone china tea set, had protested. "Prameela, have you gone crazy? That tea set used to belong to your mother-in-law."

"But what'll I do with it in America? Shyamoli has her own set—"

A look that Mrs. Dutta couldn't read flitted across Mrs. Basu's face. "But do you want to drink from it for the rest of your life?"

"What do you mean?"

Mrs. Basu hesitated. Then she said, "What if you don't like it there?"

"How can I not like it, Roma?" Mrs. Dutta's voice was strident, even to her own ears. With an effort she controlled it and continued, "I'll miss my friends, I know—and you most of all. The things we do together—evening tea, our walk around Rabindra Sarobar Lake, Thursday night Bhagavat Geeta class. But Sagar—they're my only family. And blood is blood after all."

"I wonder," Mrs. Basu said dryly, and Mrs. Dutta recalled that though both of Mrs. Basu's children lived just a day's journey away, they came to see her only on occasions when common decency demanded their presence. Perhaps they were tightfisted in money matters too. Perhaps that was why Mrs. Basu had started renting out her downstairs a few years ago, even though, as anyone in Calcutta knew, tenants were more trouble than they

were worth. Such filial neglect must be hard to take, though
Mrs. Basu, loyal to her children as indeed a mother should be,
never complained. In a way Mrs. Dutta had been better off, with
Sagar too far away for her to put his love to the test.

"At least don't give up the house," Mrs. Basu was saying. "It'll
be impossible to find another place in case—"

"In case what?" Mrs. Dutta asked, her words like stone chips.
She was surprised to find that she was angrier with Mrs. Basu
than she'd ever been. Or was it fear? *My son isn't like yours,* she'd
been on the verge of spitting out. She took a deep breath and
made herself smile, made herself remember that she might
never see her friend again.

"Ah, Roma," she said, putting her arm around Mrs. Basu, "you
think I'm such an old witch that my Sagar and my Shyamoli will
be unable to live with me?"

Mrs. Dutta hums a popular Rabindra Sangeet as she pulls
her sari from the fence. It's been a good day, as good as it
can be in a country where you might stare out the window for
hours and not see one living soul. No vegetable vendors with
wicker baskets balanced on their heads, no knife-sharpeners calling *scissors-knives-choppers, scissors-knives-choppers* to bring the
children running. No dehati women with tattoos on their arms
to sell you cookware in exchange for your old silk saris. Why,
even the animals that frequented Ghoshpara Lane had personality. Stray dogs that knew to line up outside the kitchen door just
when leftovers were likely to be thrown out, the goat who
maneuvered its head through the garden grille hoping to get at
her dahlias, cows who planted themselves majestically in the
center of the road, ignoring honking drivers. And right across
the street was Mrs. Basu's two-story house, which Mrs. Dutta
knew as well as her own. How many times had she walked up
the stairs to that airy room painted sea-green and filled with
plants where her friend would be waiting for her.

What took you so long today, Prameela? Your tea is cold already.

Wait till you hear what happened, Roma. Then you won't scold me for being late....

Stop it, you silly woman, Mrs. Dutta tells herself severely. Every single one of your relatives would give an arm and a leg to be in your place, you know that. After lunch you're going to write a nice, long letter to Roma, telling her exactly how delighted you are to be here.

From where Mrs. Dutta stands, gathering up petticoats and blouses, she can look into the next yard. Not that there's much to see, just tidy grass and a few pale-blue flowers whose name she doesn't know. There are two wooden chairs under a tree, but Mrs. Dutta has never seen anyone using them. What's the point of having such a big yard if you're not even going to sit in it? she thinks. Calcutta pushes itself into her mind again, Calcutta with its narrow, blackened flats where families of six and eight and ten squeeze themselves into two tiny rooms, and her heart fills with a sense of loss she knows to be illogical.

When she first arrived in Sagar's home, Mrs. Dutta wanted to go over and meet her next-door neighbors, maybe take them some of her special rose-water rasogollahs, as she'd often done with Mrs. Basu. But Shyamoli said she shouldn't. Such things were not the custom in California, she explained earnestly. You didn't just drop in on people without calling ahead. Here everyone was busy, they didn't sit around chatting, drinking endless cups of sugar tea. Why, they might even say something unpleasant to her.

"For what?" Mrs. Dutta had asked disbelievingly, and Shyamoli had said, "Because Americans don't like neighbors to"—here she used an English phrase—"invade their privacy." Mrs. Dutta, who didn't fully understand the word *privacy* because there was no such term in Bengali, had gazed at her daughter-in-law in some bewilderment. But she understood enough to not ask again. In the following months, though, she often looked over the fence, hoping to make contact. People were people, whether in India or America, and everyone appreciated a friendly face. When Shyamoli was as old as Mrs. Dutta, she would know that, too.

Today, just as she is about to turn away, out of the corner of her eye Mrs. Dutta notices a movement. At one of the windows a woman is standing, her hair a sleek gold like that of the TV heroines whose exploits baffle Mrs. Dutta when sometimes she tunes in to an afternoon serial. She is smoking a cigarette, and a curl of gray rises lazily, elegantly from her fingers. Mrs. Dutta is so happy to see another human being in the middle of her solitary day that she forgets how much she disapproves of smoking, especially in women. She lifts her hand in the gesture she has seen her grandchildren use to wave an eager hello.

The woman stares back at Mrs. Dutta. Her lips are a perfect-painted red, and when she raises her cigarette to her mouth, its tip glows like an animal's eye. She does not wave back or smile. Perhaps she is not well? Mrs. Dutta feels sorry for her, alone in her illness in a silent house with only cigarettes for solace, and she wishes the etiquette of America had not prevented her from walking over with a word of cheer and a bowl of her fresh-cooked alu dum.

Mrs. Dutta rarely gets a chance to be alone with her son. In the morning he is in too much of a hurry even to drink the fragrant cardamom tea which she (remembering how as a child he would always beg for a sip from her cup) offers to make him. He doesn't return until dinnertime, and afterward he must help the children with their homework, read the paper, hear the details of Shyamoli's day, watch his favorite TV crime show in order to unwind, and take out the garbage. In between, for he is a solicitous son, he converses with Mrs. Dutta. In response to his questions she assures him that her arthritis is much better now; no, no, she's not growing bored being at home all the time; she has everything she needs—Shyamoli has been so kind—but perhaps he could pick up a few aerograms on his way back tomorrow? She recites obediently for him an edited list of her day's activities and smiles when he praises her cooking. But when he says, "Oh, well, time to turn in, another working day tomorrow," she is racked by a vague pain, like hunger, in the region of her heart.

So it is with the delighted air of a child who has been offered an unexpected gift that she leaves her half-written letter to greet Sagar at the door today, a good hour before Shyamoli is due back. The children are busy in the family room doing homework and watching cartoons (mostly the latter, Mrs. Dutta suspects). But for once she doesn't mind because they race in to give their father hurried hugs and then race back again. And she has him, her son, all to herself in a kitchen filled with the familiar, pungent odors of tamarind sauce and chopped coriander leaves.

"Khoka," she says, calling him by the childhood name she hasn't used in years, "I could fry you two-three hot-hot luchis, if you like." As she waits for his reply she can feel, in the hollow of her throat, the rapid beat of her blood. And when he says yes, that would be very nice, she shuts her eyes and takes a deep breath, and it is as though merciful time has given her back her youth, that sweet, aching urgency of being needed again.

Mrs. Dutta is telling Sagar a story."When you were a child, how scared you were of injections! One time, when the government doctor came to give us compulsory typhoid shots, you locked yourself in the bathroom and refused to come out. Do you remember what your father finally did? He went into the garden and caught a lizard and threw it in the bathroom window, because you were even more scared of lizards than of shots. And in exactly one second you ran out screaming—right into the waiting doctor's arms."

Sagar laughs so hard that he almost upsets his tea (made with real sugar, because Mrs. Dutta knows it is better for her son than that chemical powder Shyamoli likes to use). There are tears in his eyes, and Mrs. Dutta, who had not dared to hope he would find her story so amusing, feels gratified. When he takes off his glasses to wipe them, his face is oddly young, not like a father's at all, or even a husband's, and she has to suppress an impulse to put out her hand and rub away the indentations the glasses have left on his nose.

"I'd totally forgotten," says Sagar. "How can you keep track of those old, old things?"

Because it is the lot of mothers to remember what no one else cares to, Mrs. Dutta thinks. To tell them over and over until they are lodged, perforce, in family lore. We are the keepers of the heart's dusty corners.

But as she starts to say this, the front door creaks open, and she hears the faint click of Shyamoli's high heels. Mrs. Dutta rises, collecting the dirty dishes.

"Call me fifteen minutes before you're ready to eat so I can fry fresh luchis for everyone," she tells Sagar.

"You don't have to leave, Mother," he says.

Mrs. Dutta smiles her pleasure but doesn't stop. She knows Shyamoli likes to be alone with her husband at this time, and today in her happiness she does not grudge her this.

"You think I've nothing to do, only sit and gossip with you?" she mock-scolds. "I want you to know I have a very important letter to finish."

Somewhere behind her she hears a thud, a briefcase falling over. This surprises her. Shyamoli is always so careful with her case because it was a gift from Sagar when she was finally made a manager in her company.

"Hi!" Sagar calls, and when there's no answer, "Hey, Molli, you okay?"

Shyamoli comes into the room slowly, her hair disheveled as though she's been running her fingers through it. A hectic color blotches her cheeks.

"What's the matter, Molli?" Sagar walks over to give her a kiss. "Bad day at work?" Mrs. Dutta, embarrassed as always by this display of marital affection, turns toward the window, but not before she sees Shyamoli move her face away.

"Leave me alone." Her voice is wobbly. "Just leave me alone."

"But what is it?" Sagar says in concern.

"I don't want to talk about it right now." Shyamoli lowers herself into a kitchen chair and puts her face in her hands. Sagar stands in the middle of the room, looking helpless. He raises his hand and lets it fall, as though he wants to comfort his wife but is afraid of what she might do.

A protective anger for her son surges inside Mrs. Dutta, but she leaves the room silently. In her mind-letter she writes, *Women need to be strong, not react to every little thing like this. You and I, Roma, we had far worse to cry about, but we shed our tears invisibly. We were good wives and daughters-in-law, good mothers. Dutiful, uncomplaining. Never putting ourselves first.*

A sudden memory comes to her, one she hasn't thought of in years, a day when she scorched a special kheer dessert. Her mother-in-law had shouted at her, "Didn't your mother teach you anything, you useless girl?" As punishment she refused to let Mrs. Dutta go with Mrs. Basu to the cinema, even though *Sahib, Bibi aur Ghulam*, which all Calcutta was crazy about, was playing, and their tickets were bought already. Mrs. Dutta had wept the entire afternoon, but before Sagar's father came home she washed her face carefully with cold water and applied kajal to her eyes so he wouldn't know.

But everything is getting mixed up, and her own young, trying-not-to-cry face blurs into another—why, it's Shyamoli's—and a thought hits her so sharply in the chest she has to hold on to the bedroom wall. *And what good did it do? The more we bent, the more people pushed us, until one day we'd forgotten that we could stand up straight. Maybe Shyamoli's doing the right thing, after all....*

Mrs. Dutta lowers herself heavily on to her bed, trying to erase such an insidious idea from her mind. Oh, this new country where all the rules are upside down, it's confusing her. Her mind feels muddy, like a pond in which too many water buffaloes have been wading. Maybe things will settle down if she can focus on the letter to Roma.

Then she remembers that she has left the half-written aerogram on the kitchen table. She knows she should wait until after dinner, after her son and his wife have sorted things out. But a restlessness—or is it defiance?—has taken hold of her. She's sorry Shyamoli's upset, but why should she have to waste her evening because of that? She'll go get her letter—it's no crime, is it? She'll march right in and pick it up, and even if Shyamoli stops in midsentence with another one of those sighs, she'll refuse to feel apologetic. Besides, by now they're probably in the family room, watching TV.

Really, Roma, she writes in her head as she feels her way along the unlighted corridor, *the amount of TV they watch here is quite scandalous. The children too, sitting for hours in front of that box like they've been turned into painted Kesto Nagar dolls, and then talking back when I tell them to turn it off.* Of course, she will never put such blasphemy into a real letter. Still, it makes her feel better to say it, if only to herself.

In the family room the TV is on, but for once no one is paying it any attention. Shyamoli and Sagar sit on the sofa, conversing. From where she stands in the corridor, Mrs. Dutta cannot see them, but their shadows—enormous against the wall where the table lamp has cast them—seem to flicker and leap at her.

She is about to slip unseen into the kitchen when Shyamoli's rising voice arrests her. In its raw, shaking unhappiness it is so unlike her daughter-in-law's assured tones that Mrs. Dutta is no more able to move away from it than if she had heard the call of the nishi, the lost souls of the dead on whose tales she grew up.

"It's easy for you to say 'Calm down.' I'd like to see how calm *you'd* be if she came up to you and said, 'Kindly tell the old lady not to hang her clothes over the fence into my yard.' She said it twice, like I didn't understand English, like I was an idiot. All these years I've been so careful not to give these Americans a chance to say something like this, and now—"

"Shhh, Shyamoli, I *said* I'd talk to Mother about it."

"You always say that, but you never *do* anything. You're too busy being the perfect son, tiptoeing around her feelings. But how about mine?"

"Hush, Molli, the children…"

"Let them hear. I don't care anymore. They're not stupid. They already know what a hard time I've been having with her. You're the only one who refuses to see it."

In the passage Mrs. Dutta shrinks against the wall. She wants to move away, to not hear anything else, but her feet are formed of cement, impossible to lift, and Shyamoli's words pour into her ears like smoking oil.

"I've explained over and over, and she still keeps on doing what I've asked her not to—throwing away perfectly good food, leaving dishes to drip all over the countertops. Ordering my children to stop doing things I've given them permission for. She's taken over the entire kitchen, cooking whatever she likes. You come in the door and the smell of grease is everywhere, in all our clothes. I feel like this isn't my house anymore."

"Be patient, Molli, she's an old woman, after all."

"I know. That's why I tried so hard. I know having her here is important to you. But I can't do it any longer. I just can't. Some days I feel like taking the kids and leaving." Shyamoli's voice disappears into a sob.

A shadow stumbles across the wall to her, and then another. Behind the weatherman's nasal tones announcing a week of sunny days, Mrs. Dutta can hear a high, frightened weeping. The children, she thinks. It's probably the first time they've seen their mother cry.

"Don't talk like that, sweetheart." Sagar leans forward, his voice, too, miserable. All the shadows on the wall shiver and merge into a single dark silhouette.

Mrs. Dutta stares at that silhouette, the solidarity of it. Sagar and Shyamoli's murmurs are lost beneath a noise—is it in her veins, this dry humming, the way the taps in Calcutta used to hum when the municipality turned the water off? After a while she discovers that she has reached her room. In darkness she lowers herself on to her bed very gently, as though her body is made of the thinnest glass. Or perhaps ice, she is so cold. She sits for a long time with her eyes closed, while inside her head thoughts whirl faster and faster until they disappear in a gray dust storm.

When Pradeep finally comes to call her for dinner, Mrs. Dutta follows him to the kitchen where she fries luchis for everyone, the perfect circles of dough puffing up crisp and golden as always. Sagar and Shyamoli have reached a truce of some kind: she gives him a small smile, and he puts out a casual hand, to massage the back of her neck. Mrs. Dutta demonstrates no embarrassment at this. She eats her dinner. She answers questions put to her. She smiles when someone makes a joke. If her face is stiff, as though she has been given a shot of Novocain, no one notices. When the table is cleared, she excuses herself, saying she has to finish her letter.

Now Mrs. Dutta sits on her bed, reading over what she wrote in the innocent afternoon.

Dear Roma,

Although I miss you, I know you will be pleased to hear how happy I am in America. There is much here that needs getting used to, but we are no strangers to adjusting, we old women. After all, haven't we been doing it all our lives?

Today I'm cooking one of Sagar's favorite dishes, alu-dum....It gives me such pleasure to see my family gathered around the table, eating my

*food. The children are still a little shy of me, but I am hopeful that we'll
soon be friends. And Shyamoli, so confident and successful—you
should see her when she's all dressed for work. I can't believe she's the
same timid bride I sent off to America just a few years ago. But, Sagar,
most of all, is the joy of my old age....*

With the edge of her sari Mrs. Dutta carefully wipes a tear that
has fallen on the aerogram. She blows on the damp spot until it
is completely dry, so the pen will not leave an incriminating
smudge. Even though Roma would not tell a soul, she cannot risk
it. She can already hear them, the avid relatives in India who have
been waiting for something just like this to happen. *That Dutta-
ginni, so set in her ways, we knew she'd never get along with her
daughter-in-law.* Or worse, *Did you hear about poor Prameela, how
her family treated her, yes, even her son, can you imagine?*

This much surely she owes to Sagar.

And what does she owe herself, Mrs. Dutta, falling through
black night with all the certainties she trusted in collapsed upon
themselves like imploded stars, and only an image inside her eye-
lids for company? A silhouette—man, wife, children—joined on
a wall, showing her how alone she is in this land of young
people. And how unnecessary.

She is not sure how long she sits under the glare of the overhead light, how long her hands clench themselves in her lap.
When she opens them, nail marks line the soft flesh of her palms,
red hieroglyphs—her body's language, telling her what to do.

Dear Roma, Mrs. Dutta writes,

*I cannot answer your question about whether I am happy, for I am
no longer sure I know what happiness is. All I know is that it isn't what
I thought it to be. It isn't about being needed. It isn't about being with
family either. It has something to do with love, I still think that, but in
a different way than I believed earlier, a way I don't have the words to*

explain. Perhaps we can figure it out together, two old women drinking cha in your downstairs flat (for I do hope you will rent it to me on my return), while around us gossip falls—but lightly, like summer rain, for that is all we will allow it to be. If I'm lucky—and perhaps, in spite of all that has happened, I am—the happiness will be in the figuring out.

Pausing to read over what she has written, Mrs. Dutta is surprised to discover this: Now that she no longer cares whether tears blotch her letter, she feels no need to weep.

Francisco Jiménez

"Moving Still"
from *The Circuit*

Francisco Jiménez was born in 1943 in Mexico and immigrated to the United States with his parents, migrant workers, when he was four years old. He is now a professor at Santa Clara University and the author of two books about his childhood, *The Circuit* and *Breaking Through*. He was named U.S. Professor of the Year in 2002.

What follows is the last chapter of *The Circuit*, a collection of autobiographical stories about the author's childhood experiences in California.

For days, when I got home from school, I found Papá lying flat and complaining about not being able to pick cotton because his back was killing him. He often talked about leaving Corcoran and going back to Santa Maria, but he kept changing his mind, hoping to get better. He constantly worried that we would not have enough money saved at the end of the cotton season to carry us over the winter months. It was already the end of December, and Roberto, my older brother, was the only one working. Mamá stayed home to take care of Papá, Rorra, and Rubén. My other two younger brothers, Torito and Trampita, went to school with me, and on weekends, when it did not rain, we went to work with Roberto. The only cotton left for us to harvest was *la bola*, the leftovers from the first picking, which paid one and a half cents a pound.

But one day when I got home, Papá did not complain about anything, not even his back. As soon as I entered the cabin, he strained to straighten up from the mattress that lay on the floor and exclaimed, *"Mi'jo, are you all right?"*

"Sí, Papá," I responded, wondering why he looked so worried.

"Gracias a Dios," he said. *"La migra* swept through the camp about an hour ago, and I didn't know if the immigration officers searched your school too."

Mamá must have noticed the fright in my eyes when I heard the word *"migra"* because she immediately came and hugged me.

That word evoked fear ever since the immigration raid in Tent City, a labor camp in Santa Maria where we sometimes lived. It was a Saturday, late afternoon. I was playing marbles with Trampita in front of our tent when I heard someone holler, *"¡La migra! ¡La migra!"* I looked over my shoulder and saw several vans screech to a halt, blocking the entrance to the camp. The vans' doors flew open. Out dashed armed men dressed in green uniforms. They invaded the camp, moving through tents, searching for undocumented workers who ran into the wilderness behind the camp, trying to escape. Many, like Doña María, *"la curandera,"* were caught, herded, and hauled away in the Border Patrol vehicles. A few managed to get away. We were lucky. Mamá and Roberto had gone to town to buy groceries. Papá showed the officers his "green card" that Ito had helped him get, and they did not ask about Trampita or me.

When Roberto came home from work that evening, Papá and Mamá were relieved to see him. "You didn't see *la migra?*" Papá asked.

"It came to our camp, but missed us," Mamá said, rubbing her hands together.

"It didn't come to the field," Roberto responded.

"So, you didn't go out with *la migra,*" Papá said jokingly, trying to ease the tension.

Roberto went along with Papá's joke. "No, Papá, she's not my type," he answered. We all laughed nervously.

When Papá stopped laughing and bit his lower lip, I knew what was coming. "You have to be careful," he warned us, waving his index finger at Roberto and me. "You can't tell a soul you were born in Mexico. You can't trust anyone, not even your best friends. If they know, they can turn you in." I had heard those words so many times, I had memorized them. "Now, where were you born, Panchito?" he asked in a firm tone, giving me a piercing look.

"Colton, California," I answered.

"Good, *mi'jo,*" he said.

Roberto then handed Papá the money he had earned that day. Papá clenched his fists, looked away toward the wall, and said, "I am useless; I can't work; I can't feed my family; I can't even protect you from *la migra.*"

"Don't say that, Papá," Roberto answered. "You know that's not so."

Papá glanced at Roberto, lowered his eyes, and asked me to bring him the small, silver metal box where he kept our savings. When I brought it, he sat up slightly, opened it, and counted the money inside. "If I work in Santa Maria, we might be able to get through this winter with what we've saved," he said worriedly. "But what if my back won't let me?"

"Don't worry, Papá," Roberto responded. "Panchito and I can find work in Santa Maria thinning lettuce and topping carrots."

Seeing this as a chance to persuade my father to leave Corcoran, and knowing I was anxious to return to Santa Maria, Mamá winked at me and said to Papá, "Roberto is right, *viejo*. Let's leave. Besides, the immigration may come around again. It's safer living in Santa Maria."

After a long pause, Papá finally said, "You're right. We'll go back to Bonetti Ranch, tomorrow morning."

Like swallows returning to Capistrano, we would return to our nest, Bonetti Ranch in Santa Maria, every year after the cotton season was over in Corcoran. The ranch became our temporary home. We had lived there in barracks eight months out of the year, from January through August, ever since Tent City, the farm labor camp, had been torn down. The ranch was located on East Main Street but had no address. Most of the residents were Mexican field laborers who were American citizens or had immigrant visas like Papá. This made the ranch relatively safe from Border Patrol raids.

I was so excited about going back to Bonetti Ranch that I was the first one up the following morning. After we packed our belongings and loaded them into the car, we headed south to Santa Maria. I could hardly contain myself. Roberto and Trampita were excited too. I imagined this was how kids felt when they talked about going away on vacation. Papá could not drive because of his back pain so Roberto drove. The trip took about five hours, but it seemed like five days to me. Sitting in the back seat, I opened the window and stuck my head out, looking for road signs saying Santa Maria. "Can't you go faster?" I asked impatiently, poking Roberto in the back.

"Sure, if you want us to get a ticket," he responded.

"That's all we need," Papá said, chuckling. "If that happens, we may just as well turn ourselves in to *la migra*."

I immediately closed the window and sat back without saying a word.

After traveling for a couple of hours, Mamá suggested we stop to have lunch, which she had prepared that morning. I was hungry but I did not want to waste time. "We can eat in the car," I said, hoping my little sister and brothers would go along with my idea.

"What about Roberto? He can't eat and drive," Papá responded.

We stopped by the side of the road to eat. Papá slowly got out of the car, holding on to Roberto's arm and mine. He lay on the ground and stretched his back. I gobbled my two-egg and chorizo tacos and, making sure Papá was not looking, signaled to Roberto to hurry. "*Ya pues*, Panchito," he said, a bit annoyed. "I am almost finished."

After lunch we continued our trip. The closer we got to Santa Maria, the more excited I became because I knew where we were going to live for the next several months. I especially looked forward to seeing some of my classmates in the eighth grade at El Camino Junior High. I had not seen them since last June when school ended. "I wonder if they'll remember me?" I thought to myself.

As we drove by Nipomo, the last town before Santa Maria, my heart started pounding. And as soon as I saw the Santa Maria bridge, which marked the entrance to the city limits, I yelled out, "We're here! We're here!" Trampita and Torito also began to cheer and woke up Rubén, who had fallen asleep. Mamá looked at us and laughed.

"*Se han vuelto locos*," Papá said, smiling and gesturing with his hand that we had gone crazy.

Once we crossed the cement bridge, which went over a dry river bed for a quarter of a mile, I stretched my neck and tried to pinpoint the location of Bonetti Ranch. I knew it was near where Tent City used to be, about a mile south of the city dump.

The highway became Broadway and went right through the center of the town. When we got to Main Street, Roberto turned left and drove east for about ten miles. Along the way, I kept pointing out places I recognized: Main Street School; KRESS, the Five and Dime Store; the Texaco gas station where we got our drinking water; and the hospital where Torito stayed when he got sick. We then crossed Suey Road, which marked the end of the city limits and the beginning of hundreds of acres of recently planted lettuce and carrots.

When we turned into Bonetti Ranch I noticed nothing had changed from the year before. We were greeted by dozens of stray dogs. Roberto had to slow down the *Carcachita* to a crawl to avoid hitting them, and to dodge the deep potholes in the dirt path that circled the front of the barracks. A few of the dogs belonged to the residents, but most of them had no owners. They slept underneath the dwellings and ate whatever they found in the garbage. But they were never alone. They were plagued by hundreds of bloodthirsty fleas. I felt sorry for them and wondered if the dogs were bothered by the fleas as much as I was when they invaded our bed at night.

The barracks were still the same. Mr. Bonetti, the owner, continued to ignore them. Looking like victims of a war, the dwellings had broken windows, parts of walls missing, and large holes in the roofs. Scattered throughout the ranch were old, rusty pieces of farm machinery. In the middle of the ranch was a large storehouse where Mr. Bonetti kept lumber, boxes of nails, and other building supplies that he planned to use someday.

We rented and moved into the same barrack we had lived in the previous year. We covered the gaps between wall boards with paper, painted the inside, and covered the kitchen floor using paint and pieces of linoleum we found at the city dump. We had electricity. And even though we could not drink the water because it was oily and smelled like sulphur, we used it for bathing. We heated it in a pot on the stove and poured it into the large aluminum container that we used for a bathtub. To get drinking water, we took our five-gallon bottle and filled it at the

Texaco gas station downtown. Along the front edge of our barrack, Roberto planted red, pink, and white geraniums. Around them, he built a fence and painted it, also using supplies from the city dump.

To the right of our house, a few yards away, stood three large empty oil barrels that served as garbage cans for the residents. Mr. Bonetti periodically burned the garbage and hauled the remains to the city dump in his truck. Behind our barrack was the outhouse that we shared with two other families. Sometimes, on rainy days, the earth underneath would shift and tilt the toilet to one side, making it difficult to balance inside. Mr. Bonetti nailed a rope to the side wall inside to give us something to hold on to.

The week after we arrived in Santa Maria, we enrolled in school. Roberto started the tenth grade at Santa Maria High School for the first time that year; Trampita and Torito resumed elementary school at Main Street School. At El Camino Junior High I continued the eighth grade, which I had started in Corcoran the first week of November after the grape season was over. Rubén and Rorra were still too young for school. Mamá stayed home to take care of them.

Even though this was my first time in the eighth grade at El Camino, I did not feel too nervous. I remembered a few of the kids in my class because they had been in my seventh-grade class the year before. Some I hardly recognized. They had grown taller, especially the boys. I had stayed the same, four feet eleven inches. I was one of the smallest kids in the school.

I liked my two teachers. I had Mr. Milo for math and science in the mornings and Miss Ehlis for English, history, and social studies in the afternoons. In history, we concentrated on U.S. Government and the Constitution. I enjoyed Mr. Milo's class the most because I did better in math than in English. Every Thursday Mr. Milo gave us a math quiz, and the following day he arranged our desks according to how well we did on the test.

The student with the highest score had the honor of sitting in the front seat, first row. Sharon Ito, the daughter of the Japanese sharecropper for whom we picked strawberries during the summer, and I alternated taking the first seat, although she sat in it more often than I did. I was glad we did not have the same seating arrangement for English!

As days went by, Papá's back did not get better and neither did his mood. Mamá, Roberto, and I took turns massaging him with Vick's Vaporub. When he was not complaining about not being able to work, he lay in bed, motionless, with an empty look in his eyes. He took a lot of aspirins, ate very little, and hardly slept during the night. During the day, when he was exhausted, he took short naps.

Early one evening, when Papá had dozed off, Mamá took Roberto and me aside. "I don't think your Papá can work in the fields any more," she said, rubbing her hands on her apron. "What are we going to do?"

After a long pause, Roberto answered, "I've been thinking about getting a job in town. I am tired of working in the fields."

"Yes, a job that is year-round," Mamá said.

"That's a good idea!" I said enthusiastically. "Then we won't have to move to Fresno again."

"Maybe Mr. Sims can help me," Roberto said.

"Who's Mr. Sims?" Mamá asked.

"He's the principal of Main Street School," I answered. "Remember? He gave me a green jacket."

Trying to help her memory, Roberto added, "He also bought me a pair of shoes when he saw mine were worn out. I was in the sixth grade."

"*Ah, sí. Es muy buena gente,*" Mamá said, finally recalling who he was.

Mr. Sims agreed to help Roberto find a part-time job in town. He told my brother he would let him know when he found something. Meanwhile, Roberto and I continued working, thinning lettuce and topping carrots, after school and on Saturdays and Sundays.

Several days later, Mr. Sims told Roberto that he had found a job for him. He set up an appointment for my brother to see the owner of the Buster Brown Shoe Store on Broadway that Saturday afternoon. Roberto, Mamá, and I were very excited.

Early Saturday morning, Roberto and I headed for work thinning lettuce. As he drove, Roberto could not stop talking about his new job at the shoe store. His appointment that afternoon seemed a long time away. To make the hours in the field go by faster, we decided to challenge ourselves. We marked a spot in our rows, about a third of the way in, to see if we could reach it without straightening up. "Ready? Go!" Roberto said.

I stooped over and began thinning with my six-inch hoe. After about twenty minutes without rest I could no longer stand the pain in my back. I dropped to my knees and continued thinning without stopping. As soon as I reached the marked spot, I fell over. Roberto did too. "We did it," I said out of breath. "But my back is killing me." To ease the pain, I lay flat on my stomach in the furrow and Roberto pressed down on my back with his hands. I felt relief as my spine cracked.

"You're getting old, Panchito. Let's rest," Roberto said, laughing. I chuckled between moans.

Roberto lay on his stomach next to me. I turned over on my back and looked up at the gray sky. The dark clouds threatened to rain.

"I am tired of moving every year," Roberto said, picking up small dirt clods and tossing them.

"Me too," I said. Then, following a moving cloud with my eyes, I asked, "Do you ever wonder what we'll be doing ten or twenty years from now? Or where we'll be living?"

Looking around to make sure no one was listening, Roberto whispered, "If we don't get deported..." Then he added confidently, "In Santa Maria, of course. I can't imagine living any-where else. What about you?"

Recalling the different labor camps we lived in, I answered, "I don't want to live in Selma, Visalia, Bakersfield, or Corcoran." After thinking about it for a while, I said, "I like Santa Maria. So if you decide to live here forever, I will too."

Right after lunch, Roberto left work to clean up and keep his appointment. I continued working and thinking about Roberto's new job. Every few minutes I straightened up to give my back a rest. "This is our chance to stay in Santa Maria all year and not move to Fresno to pick grapes and miss school," I said to myself. The more I thought about the idea, the more excited I became. "Perhaps Roberto will get me a job at the shoe store too." I thought. "How about that, Buster Brown!" I said out loud, flip-ping the hoe in the air and catching it by the handle. Just as I fin-ished my row, it started to rain. I ran for cover under a pepper tree and waited for Roberto.

When he returned to pick me up, his mood was darker than the sky. "What's the matter?" I asked. "You didn't get the job?"

Roberto shook his head, "No, I got the job," he said. "But not working at the store."

"Doing what then?" I asked impatiently.

"Cutting his lawn. Once a week," Roberto answered sadly. His lips quivered.

"Oh no!" I exclaimed, throwing my hoe on the ground in anger.

Roberto cleared his throat, wiped his eyes with his shirt sleeve, and said, "I am going to see Mr. Sims after school on Monday. Maybe he can suggest something else." He picked up my hoe, handed it to me. "Don't lose faith, Panchito," he said, putting his arm around me. "Things will work out."

Monday morning, my mind was not on school. I kept worrying about Papá and thinking about Roberto. "I hope he gets a job," I thought. "But what if he doesn't? No, he will," I said to myself.

To make things worse, that afternoon Miss Ehlis gave our class an assignment I was not expecting. "I am passing out an important part of the Declaration of Independence that I want you to memorize," she said, counting the number of sheets to hand out in each row. Her announcement evoked a series of moans and groans from the class. "Now, there is no need for that," she said smiling. "The part I want you to know by heart is very short." Once everyone had the sheet of paper, she read the first few lines to the class.

"'We hold these truths to be self-evident: that all men are created equal; that they are endowed by their creator with certain inalienable rights; that among these are life, liberty, and the pursuit of happiness; that to secure these rights, governments are instituted among men, deriving their just powers from the consent of the governed...' You see, it's not difficult. You can recite it to me independently or, for extra credit, in front of the class."

We were to let her know our preference the following week. For me there was only one choice: to recite it to her privately. I did not want to get in front of the class and risk being laughed at because of my Mexican pronunciation. I knew I had a thick accent, not because I heard it myself, but because kids sometimes made fun of me when I spoke English. I could not take a chance of this happening in front of the whole class, even though I wanted to get the extra credit.

That afternoon after school, I took the bus home. On the way, I tried to memorize the lines of the Declaration of Independence, but I had trouble concentrating. I kept wondering what Mr. Sims told Roberto. When I got home and saw the *Carcachita*, I knew Roberto was already there. I rushed in. Papá, Mamá and Roberto were sitting at the kitchen table. "What happened? Tell me!" I said excitedly.

"What do you think?" Roberto asked, trying to conceal his smile.

I glanced at Papá and Mamá. They were beaming. "You got a job!" I cried out.

"Yes. Mr. Sims offered me the janitorial job at Main Street School," he answered, grinning from ear to car.

"It's a year-round job," Mamá said, looking at Papá.

Being careful with his back, Papá stood up slowly and hugged her gently. He then turned to Roberto and said, "Education pays off, mi'jo. I am proud of you. Too bad your Mamá and I didn't have the opportunity to go to school."

"But you've taught us a lot, Papá," I answered. I had not seen Papá that happy for weeks.

After supper, I sat at the table to do my homework. I was so excited about Roberto's new job that it was difficult to focus. But I was determined to memorize the lines from the Declaration of Independence and recite them perfectly, without forgetting a single word. I took the text and broke it down, line by line. I looked up in the dictionary the words I did not know: "self-evident," "endowed," "inalienable," and "pursuit." I added them to the list of English words I kept in my new, black pocket note pad. I had gotten in the habit of writing down a different English word and its definition every day and memorizing it. After I looked up the meaning of the words, I wrote the entire text in my note pad in tiny letters: "We hold these truths to be self-evident: that all men are created equal…" I went over the first line many times until I memorized it. My plan was to memorize at least one line a day so that I could recite it on Friday of the following week.

On Wednesday after school, Roberto drove to El Camino Junior High to pick me up so that I could help him clean Main Street School. It was starting to rain. When we arrived at the school, we headed down to the basement to the janitor's room to get the cleaning cart. It held a large cloth trash bag, a dust broom, a sponge, and toilet supplies. As we entered the first classroom we were to clean, it brought back memories. It was the same room I had been in in the first grade when I had had Miss Scalapino. Everything looked the same except that the desks and chairs seemed a lot smaller. I sat down at the teacher's desk, took out my pocket note pad, and read the second and third lines I needed to memorize: "that they are endowed by their creator with certain inalienable rights; that among these are life, liberty, and the pursuit of happiness." I went over to the cart, picked up the wet sponge and began wiping the blackboard as I recited the lines in my head. Thunder and lightning interrupted my concentration. I looked out the window. It was pouring rain. Through the reflection on the window pane, I could see Roberto behind me dust mopping the floor.

By Friday, I had memorized the introductory lines to the Declaration of Independence and could recite them with relative ease. Only the word "inalienable" caused me problems. I had trouble saying it, so I broke it into syllables and repeated each sound slowly, followed by the whole word. On my way to school on the bus, I took out the black note pad from my shirt pocket, closed my eyes, and practiced saying "in-a-li-en-a-ble" silently to myself. The kid sitting next to me gave me a puzzled look and asked, "Are you trying to say something?"

His question took me by surprise. "No," I answered. "Why do you ask?"

"Well, you keep moving your lips."

A bit embarrassed, I told him what I was doing. I don't think he believed me because he stared at the note pad I was holding in my hand, mumbled, and changed seats.

The school day started out just right. In the morning, Mr. Milo returned the math exams to the class and asked us to rearrange our seats according to our scores. I sat in the first seat in the first row. This was definitely a good sign. I even looked forward to my recitation in Miss Ehlis's class that afternoon.

At one o'clock, right after lunch, I was the first one in Miss Ehlis's classroom. I sat at my desk and went over the recitation in my mind one last time: "We hold these truths to be self-evident: that all men are created equal; that they are endowed by their creator with certain inalienable rights; that among these are life, liberty and the pursuit of happiness..." I checked the text in my note pad to make sure I had not forgotten anything. It was perfect. Feeling confident, I placed the note pad inside the desk and waited for the class to start.

After the bell rang and everyone was seated, Miss Ehlis began to take roll. She was interrupted by a knock at the door. When she opened it, I could see Mr. Denevi, the principal, and a man standing behind him. The instant I saw the green uniform, I panicked. I wanted to run but my legs would not move. I began to tremble and could feel my heart pounding against my chest as though it wanted to escape too. Miss Ehlis and the immigration officer walked up to me. Putting her right hand on my shoulder, and looking up at the officer, she said sadly, "This is him." My eyes clouded. I stood up and followed the immigration officer out of the classroom and into his car marked "Border Patrol." I sat in the front seat as the officer drove down Broadway to Santa Maria High School to pick up Roberto.

Richard Rodriguez

"Where the Poppies Grow"
from *Made in California: Art, Image, and Identity 1900–2000*

Richard Rodriguez was born in 1944 in San Francisco. He has written three books: *Brown: The Last Discovery of America; Hunger of Memory: The Education of Richard Rodriguez;* and *Days of Obligation: An Argument with My Mexican Father.* Rodriguez is an editor at Pacific News Service and a contributing editor for *Harper's Magazine, U.S. News & World Report,* and the Sunday "Opinion" section of the *Los Angeles Times.* He lives in San Francisco.

    "Where the Poppies Grow" is part of the exhibition catalog *Made in California: Art, Image, and Identity in California, 1900–2000,* edited by Stephanie Barron.

The world met itself in California. Karl Marx, that cast-iron
oracle of the nineteenth century, saw the California Gold Rush
as an event unprecedented in history. In 1849, Chilean and Scot
and Chinese and Aussie and Mexican and Yankee—people of
every age and tongue and disused occupation—waded knee-
deep through the mud of Amador County.

All my life I have lived within the irony created by the many
Californians. Though, finally, there are only two: I mean
those who came here from elsewhere and the native born.

The first California natives, a laid-back tribe, watched the
approach, in the distance, of Junípero Serra—"the father of
California"—paternity thus stalking them with a limping gait. I
am so thoroughly Californian as to imagine the genesis cine-
matically; the camera shuttling back and forth between distance
and foreground—rather, between foreground and foreground
(two cameras, that's the point)—obliterating distance, bisecting
narrative, eventually making one of twain.

My own domestic comedy reflected that first splice: My parents from Mexico; their children born at the destination. My
Mexican parents' ambition was California. Mine was to join the
greater world.

I didn't get far. I live today in a San Francisco Victorian
subdivided by memory. Upstairs, Arizona. Across the hall,
Tennessee. Downstairs, Alabama—the sweetest landlord in the
world, Alabama. My neighbors seem at home in this city; it is
theirs. I am the uneasy tenant, for I was born at St. Joseph's
Hospital, less than a mile from where I write these words.
St. Joseph's Hospital no longer exists.

A common, early theme of America was the theme of leaving home; almost an imperative for writers and other misfits.
The subordinate theme was the impossibility of return—*you
can't go home again.* I always read the theme primarily as East
Coastal or Midwestern; I construed from it the gravity of tall

cities rather than the constriction of towns. There is a newer American refrain, a western refrain: *What happens when home leaves you?* I hear it now in places like Houston, where natives say they rarely meet one another because their city has filled, so quickly, with people from elsewhere. Or from Coloradans who remark that everyone they know seems to have arrived last year from California.

California's nativist chagrin is older and louder because California has, for so long, played America's America. The end of the road. Or a second shot at the future. California has served also as Asia's principal port of entry. Now, too, the busiest border crossing from Latin America.

California's native-born children—whatever our color or tongue—realize very early that California takes every impression. Our parents, on the other hand, are often surprised by how many Californias they find when they get here. Nothing at all like they expected. Nothing like the movie.

My early intuition as a native son was that California was dreamed into being elsewhere. I noticed that paradigmatic Californians weren't so by birth. Richard Diebenkorn came from Oregon. Cesar Chavez was born in Yuma. Willie Mays, Louis B. Mayer, Jack Kerouac, Richard Neutra, Lucy and Desi, Edward Teller—all of them from far away. All of them living forever in California on the same street.

Mickey Mouse was conceived aboard the Santa Fe, westward bound. Minnie was drawn from his rib, born here. As was John Steinbeck, born in Salinas; his house still stands. Steinbeck's generosity was to invent the Joad family's first view of orange groves, to believe that Oklahoma Joads were more important to the myth of California than their native-born grandchildren who live in suburban Bakersfield and complain about "the changes."

When I was a kid, the nationally advertised version of California was the GI version. Early in the forties, thousands of young men had seen California light from train windows—light receding as they shipped out toward tragedy. And in the midst of tragedy, they remembered, perhaps, some song in the air that promised to redeem them.

After the war, the survivors returned with narrowed eyes, with the GI Bill, with FHA loans, to build a pacific ever-after. They buried the shudder of death beneath hard sentimental weight; beneath lawns, green lawns, all-electric kitchens, three bedrooms, two kids, a boy and a girl, and an orderly succession of Christmas lights, tacked up with much goddammit.

Many of these veterans were middle-aged by the time I was their newspaper boy. Many had jobs in the defense industry, because they would forbid tragedy. Each afternoon, I folded and lobbed the world onto their porches. But I was otherwise complicitous in their cover-up. I willingly played the innocent—the native—as did their two towheaded children, a boy and a girl, whooping through the bushes with pheasant feathers tied onto our heads.

I played another role. I played the son of the Old Country, the tragedian. For I lived in "el norte," a memory of dread, which I took from my parents' eyes. I also put on Bombay eyes—my uncle came from India. My Mexican parents and my Indian uncle saw California as a refuge from chaos, but they understood that tragedy was preeminently natural.

My California was also imagined in the Azores, the wraith of some Atlantic storm. I grew up among Portuguese, Irish. My Catholic nuns came from Ireland and brought with them—as if it were ground into the glass of the spectacles they wore—a tragic vision. This despite the luxurious light of California opening over all. Can it have been a coincidence that my first allegiance to a writer was to William Saroyan, who had grown up in Fresno, under a cloudless sky, listening to Armenian grandmothers' tales of genocide?

Eureka! (I have found it.) California's official motto should be mistranslated: *I have brought it*. I folded California into my portmanteau and carried it over the sea, then across the Sierra. Or I invented California in my Kwangtung village, from the gaunt letters Hong-on Sam sent his long-dead wife. I sketched California on the steps of my parents' brownstone in Brooklyn, listening to my grandfather's stories of castles in Poland. What did he know from castles? We were peasants. Very few people do know castles. I'll prove it. What did I do when I got to Hollywood? I put his damn palaces into my movies and now the whole world takes my grandfather's version of how Greta Garbo should behave in a palace. All a barnyard dream.

I grew up in Sacramento, in a Prairie house decorated with Mexican statues with imprecisely painted sclera and stigmata. Outside my window were camellias, every winter, red and white globes.

Any sense I have of California is beholden to the importations of Iowa and Spain and New England and Oklahoma and the Philippines. Without the prompting of Midwestern artisans, I would never have noticed the austerity, the utility, the beauty of California Indian baskets. Without the cues of newcomers, I would not have noticed the austerity, the beauty of California: Nancy, describing in letters from Ohio—this was years after she had left Stanford—her yearning for the scent of eucalyptus and the smell of salt; her longing for brown hills and the chemical distance of the Santa Clara Valley, an ostensible autumn haze— *L'Amertume* (a poem she wrote, she admitted, having just learned the word).

My own naive first impression of Stanford was to wonder why no one watered it. Old brown hills. For my sense of pre-California, as of pre-Californians, was one of parchment, of absence—nakedness, leisure, freedom, pacificism.

Gertrude Stein's famous skepticism concerning Oakland sounds native to me, though she wasn't. No "there" there. Why not extend that to the entire state? If you list California's famous exports to the world, you come up with a volley of blanks. I mean spiceless tacos, accentless newscasters, birth control pills, strip malls, tract homes, hula hoops, cyberspace, Marilyn Monroe.

And yet, as a Californian, having taken so many impressions, I feel at home any place in the world.

And yet, California has invented so much of the postmodern world that most places in the world are packing away their idiosyncrasies in order to more closely resemble California.

Louis Kahn, the Philadelphia architect, gave California one of our best modernist buildings, the Salk Institute (named for Jonas Salk, a native New Yorker). Kahn's method, before starting any construction, was to brood over the landscape in several lights, several weathers. *What does this space want to become?* One imagines the soil of Bangladesh or Fort Worth responding more forthrightly to Kahn's question than the cloudless idiot, California.

California is never more recognizable than when it supports a completely incongruous construction. A giant orange or a giant donut or a statue of John Wayne. The landscape otherwise seems without an idea of itself.

I went to a party in a house by the sea. The house, a famous California house, was imagined into being by Midwesterners. The principal architect, Charles Greene (of the brothers Greene and Greene, Ohio-born), had been commissioned by a client from Kansas City. The house successfully reconciles England with Spain, Protestantism with Catholicism, Robert Louis Stevenson with Alfred Hitchcock, the nineteenth with the twentieth century, and, what's more, Northern with Southern California. The front yard is the Pacific Ocean—sometimes undulant, the color of antifreeze; sometimes monotonous, gray.

The house was left to the son after his parents died. But then (decades later; a decade ago) the son died; the house passed to the son's children. (Here the plot shifts from Midwestern immigrant to California native.) Such a burden the house had become in recent years—too big and too drafty, too leaky, too weathered, too expensive to maintain. (The daughters knew what very few know: life in a castle.) The daughters decided to sell. They located a buyer besotted by California, a Chicago businessman. The new owner has restored the house to its pristine austerity.

So there we were on a colorless Saturday, summer fog gathering as we gathered about a woodburning brazier in the courtyard. On trestle tables were the latest-fangled California salads. The correct Cabernets. With the other guests, I wandered through rooms that had already passed into someone else's privacy. I noticed the swift and silent appraisals of the new owner's paintings and books, some still bearing the auction-house tags.

All afternoon, I had the sense of the two Californias. On the one hand, glamorous Midwestern California. (Upon the mantels and atop the piano, the founding family's photographs and mementos had been returned for the occasion. We saw the parents' lives—they were theatricals—the beauty of their youths, their famous friendships; the books they had written, including the book for a Broadway musical about the Midwest.) On the other, the leisured puritanism of the native Californians. Jeans and faded shirts, no makeup, sun-bleached hair, sensible hors d'oeuvres.

There was something British about the afternoon—not American and certainly not Kansan. The native daughters were consigned by history the role of docents within their grandparents' house.

I am thinking now of those women, the first American generation of native-born Californians, born in the gold country. They came of age in the 1860s, naming themselves "Native Daughters of the Golden West"—California's first historical society. They organized their "parlor" in a foothill town and recruited others like themselves to the observances of memory.

The sole requirement for membership in the Native Daughters was California nativity. The pioneers the sorority honored, however, were people who were born elsewhere.

What the Daughters knew, a generation after their parents' ambition had spent itself in the gold fields, was that the audacity of their parents would be forgotten as soon as the cabins and schools and churches they built fell to ruin. The Daughters preserved things in order to remember lives. But the task of preserving the past is a thankless one, even comic, in a state given to futurism—like trying to preserve a fifties moderne bowling alley. The heedless vulgarity of the bowling alley is distorted the moment it becomes (from our postmodern vantage point) worthy of preservation.

Joan Didion discloses in her 1965 essay "Notes from a Native Daughter" that she comes "from a family, or a congeries of families, that has always been in the Sacramento Valley." Californians immediately note the ironic weight of "always" in her native syntax. Though some families may still have Spanish land grants tucked away (one notices occasionally in obituaries), one need not live very long in California to qualify as "old family." Didion describes Sacramento in the late fifties (the Valley town becoming the city I came to know) as "a place in which a boom mentality and a sense of Chekhovian loss meet in uneasy suspension."

As I recall, my own Russian summer ended each year with a blast of heat, the threat of school, the smell of unbroken denim. Summer's last stand was the California State Fair on Stockton Boulevard. I loved especially the domed Victorian-style pavilion, with booths of arranged fruits and vegetables from every county and climate. Inevitably, my Victorian fair was replaced by something ugly and new across town. "Cal Expo" was built on an amusement-park model and boasted third-rate lounge acts and destruction derbies. This was the first time I remember having to come to terms with my meaning in California.

I decided it was OK for them, but I didn't go. I was an old-timer at the age of twelve.

One needle-sharp morning in 1968, I was walking up Madison Avenue, where I happened upon the funeral of John Steinbeck. I paused at the edge of the crowd of celebrities. I saw Steinbeck's casket—an expensive affair covered with boughs of evergreen—carried down the steps of St. James Episcopal. This I approved—approved the approbation of the East Coast—as a native Californian would.

Hard for anyone not born at the destination to understand my preoccupation with originals, with provenance. I grew up in California dreaming of elsewhere—as did Saroyan, as did Didion, as did Steinbeck. I wondered about those places of which California had always seemed the mirage. Jalisco. Minnesota. Bombay. And New York, especially New York—which had concocted ideas of "the Coast" as its Hegelian opposite.

At my present age, I have forsaken the study of contributing strains, original forms, for a pleasure in the hybrid itself. Indeed, I impatiently listen when native Californians, far afield, tell me they have abandoned the crowds and cost of California for a simpler grid. The native daughter, for example, (still restless, I notice) sits beside a pool in Phoenix and deplores the traffic in Los Angeles. Having departed California, where she was forever bemoaning the loss of the department stores of her youth, she becomes a tiresome seer in Arizona. Nothing does she see more clearly than the coming of California. California coming to Austin and Portland. In Boulder, she is dismayed by tract houses along the front range that remind her of Anaheim a generation ago. She can't wait to say, "I told you so."

In our parents' generation, too, there had been talk of divorce—a legal separation of North from South. All to do with water rights and political incompatibilities. The North represented agriculture, abstemiousness; a liberal coast. The South was heedless, sprawling, splashy, wasteful; a conservative coast. In the fifties, I remember, too, an ethical resentment. The Central Valley resented the playful urbanity of the coast.

The boldness of the fifties, however, was that Californians came up with ideas of the state larger than their differences. By mid-century, when California became the most populous state in the union, our parents felt themselves resistant enough to tragedy to celebrate. California constructed eight-lane freeways to join city and country; built a sub-urban architecture with two-car garages and sliding glass walls to allow each Californian simultaneity—inside and outside at once.

California's most flamboyant reconciliation was the horizontal city, in distinction to the verticality of the East Coast. Separate freeway exits, even separate climates, distinct neighborhoods, faiths, languages—all were annexed to one another, stood united beneath a catholic abstraction called "San Jose" or "Sacramento" or—the greatest horizontal abstraction in the world—"L.A." The horizontal city not only tolerated incoherence and disharmony, it found its meaning in the juxtaposition of a chic restaurant, a Jesus Saves storefront, a taco stand. The horizontal city was crisscrossed by freeways that promised escape from complicity while also forcing complexity. The surfer, who grew up on the premises in loco parentis, grew up knowing (without having to learn exactly) nakedness, leisure, freedom, pacificism, also chopsticks and Spanish.

Didn't Walt Disney tantalize California with the idea of floating over street-level congestion on a monorail? In the fifties, Disney purchased some flower farms from Japanese families in Orange County and plowed them under. Then he plowed under someone else's citrus grove. Walt Disney's new crop was to be innocence. Disney had come from Chicago, so immediately he got the point of California. He constructed very different magic kingdoms, side by side. In that first summer after Disneyland opened, I happily made my way through the chambers of Walt Disney's rather interesting imagination.

Only in one respect did Disney seem at odds with his adopted state. Prudishly, he insisted upon a discretion among the several kingdoms analogous to the nonpermeable black lines that surround cartoon characters. Main Street must never betray a knowledge of Tomorrowland. Costumed employees were required to travel through underground tunnels, before and after their shifts, thus maintaining strict narrative borders, thus precluding surrealism. Cinderella will never meet Davy Crockett in the Magic Kingdom.

Whereas within the horizontal city, California's children grew up accustomed to disjunction. In the light of day, and at street level, all over California, Fantasyland is right next door to Frontierland. And the adolescents of alternate fantasies began to blend and marry one another. Which is why California is famous today for the tofu burrito and the highest rate of miscegenation in the mainland U.S.

Disneyland was so little rooted in California, it flourished here. Disneyland was so little rooted in California that the Disney corporation could pack it up and ship it entire to Florida and Tokyo and France, where it flourished as emblematic of California.

A few years ago, I spent a day with a friend who worked in the art department of the Warner Brothers studio in Burbank. My perception of Warner Brothers had always been of a purveyor of secular cartoons, as opposed to the Disney insistence upon a spiritual dimension to their product. Disney cartoons were not funny. Warner Brothers cartoons were not charming. The Warner Brothers lot was clearly an industrial park. We toured the studio in a golf cart. There was no discretion between miracles at Warner Brothers—between Batman's Gotham and the parting of the Red Sea. We had lunch at the commissary.

In late afternoon, my friend left me for a time, and I wandered alone through a wooden warehouse—the costume department— a temporary structure surviving from the forties. One side of the building was open to the spring air. A door, like the sliding door of a freight car, had been rolled aside. There was no one about.

I began to smell what I can only describe as California. I remember the moment most clearly as a scent—of optimism, or perhaps its residue—not some quail-colored, reedy smell of country but the smell of my family's kitchen, now long gone: An overheated electrical cord, scorched fabric, steam, starch, a spring day. The joined smells of imagination and making do; smells of dream and industry. Here was room after room of costumes and all the appliances of fantasy—scepters, masks, tiaras, gloves, window dressings from stricken sets. Yards and yards of every imaginable silk and tartan and shape and period dance. So many dreams, folded into boxes or hanging in rows; a confusion of narratives unaccountably readied for a return to the potent light of day. This gladdened me.

Out of sorts. I should think you would be, too, if you had been sweating blood on the Santa Monica Freeway for an hour—even though she waited till well after the rush, it took that long. Let them honk! Go on. Go on. Over an hour from Santa Monica and she found the lots filled. What? This lot is full, ma'am. You have to go around *that* way. *That* way. What? And so on.

And now the museum is crowded with schoolchildren— rolling thunder, static electricity, indecipherable bird calls—her hearing aid takes its adjectives from vast storm-laden canvases surrounding her in the atrium. She decides to do the exhibition in reverse—"flee the children's hour." Work back to the beginning in peace and quiet. And see without precedent, as if such a thing were possible.

But in no gallery is she free of racket, the crude translations of the serpentlike coil in her ear, which is the knowledge that she is getting too old for this. This being everything. The supermarket. The drugstore. What? Christmas. An atrium full of schoolchildren.

She is not one of those old women who is afraid of children. She had been a grammar-school teacher before the war, and just after. She cannot imagine being afraid of a child. She reads in the paper of fearful teachers and she cannot imagine it. The business of the child is to push at the perimeters. The business of the teacher is to push back. Her own grandchildren don't interest her very much, in truth. They don't push at all. Since they turned fourteen, they know everything there is to know. They smile, and school's fine, thank you, and may I be excused as soon as possible? *There, there, mother.* Well, they're so jaded. They don't take delight in anything. Nothing is wonderful to them, is it? Except loud. They seem to like loud.

She deposits her gloves in her purse. Fishes for her glasses case. What would she tell them, the children in the atrium, about California? About anything? Don't get old in the first place. *gnszzzz,* sneers the hearing aid. Oh, do shut up! She fiddles with the little wheel behind her ear, turns it the wrong way till it shrieks with pain. She reverses the wheel. *shhhhhh.*

Imported to California, in the second place, she silently corrects the banner over the exit sign: MADE IN CALIFORNIA. She is reminded of how many versions of California…

You will notice, boys and girls, how many artists in this exhibit came from elsewhere…

A lucky place. They were lucky to live here. Felt themselves lucky. She had known one or two of these painters, before the war. *He* was a bit of an old goat, as she recalls. But that's just it, she can't recall. The half-life of emotions! The impression more lasting than the incident; color more lasting than fugitive form.

You should memorize the things that please you; then when you're old and sitting by yourself, you'll have something…

Silently instructing the children, as if they were her boys and girls of yore, even though she had left the children behind in the first room, left all consideration of children behind in a life she couldn't completely recollect. But were they lucky to live here? She didn't know anymore.

Her own parents from Wisconsin: Her father a gentle architect of bungalows. Of the hundreds of bungalows her father built—well, she doesn't know; they were all over the place—but of the ones in Santa Monica only seven remain, mainly in the blocks off Montana. They weren't brilliant houses, no. They were meant to be comfortable and solid, to withstand the wear and tear of ordinary lives. Solid floors. Solid cupboards. *Knock-knock*. Good plumbing. Good light. The light was the thing. Good porches, rooms of good size, and good light.

The light remains. You have to go away to see it again. Then come back, and there it is. Different from anyplace else. California light.

She raised her own three children—she tried to raise her children with a sense of place and history. All have moved away; seem to feel nothing for California. Well, maybe they do. They wanted the paintings. *(Knock-knock.)* But they always expect her to visit them. Boston. Phoenix. Denver. Whereas she was always haunted by the California that had been bequeathed to her…Now why is it, she irritably addresses the hearing aid, why is it someone is always stacking cartons in my left ear? *Knock-knock*, says the hearing aid. What? Oh, very well, who's there? *It's your own footsteps, stupid old woman.* She looks down. Takes a step. So it is—it's this parquet.

After the children went away to school, she had formed many a committee in Santa Monica. To save things. But not for the sake of her children, as she would once have said. Or for any children. Just for the sake of the things themselves. Like a scholar's lonely knowledge. Intrinsic value. A few old places out on the pier. Houses in Venice. An old hotel on Ocean Avenue. "Madame Full Charge," Jack used to call her. "Scourge of City

Hall." Well, and they did groan when they saw me coming with my straw basket full of mimeographs.

She is becalmed now by a roomful of pastoral paintings from the twenties. Her hearing aid, dozing off, broadcasts only a neutral plane of sound, like the air in jet cabins.

I know which one I should buy...

She is inevitably reminded of her mother's voice whenever she enters a gallery. Her mother was "artistic," a sobriquet ready at hand for a woman who kept a kiln in her back shed; a leit motif, no more—as others in her mother's circle might be "musical" or "well read" or "devout Catholics" or "sharp as tacks." Native sarcasm waited to harvest any ambition that grew higher than a hollyhock. But Mother was a painter, truly, quite a good painter. Mother's "masterpiece," as the family always referred to the oil above the mantel (in that same vein of California sarcasm)—*Capitola, 1911*—would not suffer in comparison with this one. She puts on her glasses to read the legend; removes them to regard Prussian blue and blue violet, zinc...

Her reverie is interrupted by a clap of thunder, several claps, then a deluge—the arrival of the schoolchildren at the 1920s. Look at them all! Those tennis shoes. Like puppies not yet grown into their feet. Lately California had become such a mystery to her. Everything starting to melt. To slide. To quicken and to rust. What is the point? Boys and girls, indeed! Look at them, only interested in that earphone tour thing.

Click. Click.

Still, the faces interest her; those boys over there with their pants falling down interest her. Black parents, obviously. But something else, too. Mexican, I suppose. How do they keep their pants on? A question for her grandchildren.

Then, beyond the nervous boys, she notices the girl in a pale green dress. Not much of a dress, but it is properly ironed. Vietnamese? Homely, solitary—as she was, too, at that age. Probably bright, and their parents make them work. There is a serenity about the child for which the hearing aid can gather no simile. The girl's lips part slightly. Then the girl moves one hand to shade her eyes, as if she is searching the distance of the landscape before her. Good girl. Good girl. She has clearly entered the landscape. And welcome: Granville Redmond, *California Poppy Field*, c. 1926.

The girl's classmates have tumbled off together, clicking their gizmos, rubber soles screeching like violins into the next gallery.

The girl stays.

Granville Redmond. The Vietnamese teenager. The Native Daughter of the Golden West. Each is united to the others in thinking he sees the same thing.

A field of flowers, a painting of a field of flowers, a Vietnamese girl considering a painting of a field of flowers.

California, c. 2000.

Robinson Jeffers

"Hands"

Robinson Jeffers was born in 1887 in Pittsburgh, Pennsylvania, and was educated in Pennsylvania, Washington, southern California, and Europe. He eventually settled near Big Sur, California, where he composed the majority of his poetry, a large body of influential work that celebrated the rugged California landscape in that region. Jeffers published upwards of twenty-five volumes of poetry in his lifetime and, after his death in 1962, a dozen or more collections were gathered.

> Inside a cave in a narrow canyon near Tassajara
> The vault of rock is painted with hands,
> A multitude of hands in the twilight, a cloud of men's palms,
>   no more,
> No other picture. There's no one to say
> Whether the brown shy quiet people who are dead intended
> Religion or magic, or made their tracings
> In the idleness of art; but over the division of years these careful

Signs-manual are now like a sealed message
Saying: "Look: we also were human; we had hands, not paws.
    All hail
You people with the cleverer hands, our supplanters
In the beautiful country; enjoy her a season, her beauty,
    and come down
And be supplanted; for you also are human."

Appendices

Discussion Guide

In April 2005, the California Council for the Humanities will launch a statewide campaign under its California Stories initiative, which seeks to uncover and reveal today's California by engaging thousands of people throughout the state in sharing their own stories, reading and discussing contemporary and classic works by California writers, and examining what these stories tell us about who we are as individuals and as a state. It is the Council's hope that this anthology will stimulate reading and discussion groups in libraries and other settings, both formally and informally. Here are some questions to help you think about and discuss the selections in this anthology as you read it alone or with a group.

1: The Pleasures of Reading

"I love to read—Buddha, the Bible, Marx, Jung, Black Elk, Stephen King. I mean if you're going to put everything behind anything, you might as well know as much as you can about everything." From "My Ride, My Revolution" by Luis J. Rodriguez

Questions to consider:

1. In her introduction, Chitra Banerjee Divakaruni writes that this anthology hopes to "capture the multiplicity of voices that tell the California story." Is the combination of voices in this anthology satisfying to you? Do you prefer stories that reflect your own experiences or those that portray experiences different from your own? Why do you think that is? Which selection did you find the most surprising or unusual? Why?

2. Which selections in the anthology did you enjoy most? Least? What elements or features of the selections affected your preferences?

3. Regarding the multiplicity of voices mentioned above, what do you think about the reading list quoted at the beginning of this section by the self-styled revolutionary in Luis J. Rodriguez's story "My Ride, My Revolution"? What do you think about his idea that "you might as well know as much as you can about everything"?

4. Sara, the book restorer in Yxta Maya Murray's novel *The Conquest*, says, "The book is a body and your mind will mold to its individual curves much in the way it will to any other lover." Sara's mentor, however, comes to a different conclusion: "I have discovered that I've made the terrible error of substituting *objects* for people in my life." What is your response to these statements? How did you become a reader? And how much a part of your life is reading now?

5. If you're reading and discussing this book in a group, how does the experience compare to reading on your own? What brought you to this particular reading group? To other groups you've participated in?

II: Arrivals and Departures

"Each arriving traveler had been, by definition, reborn in the wilderness, a new creature in no way the same as the man or woman or even child who had left Independence or St. Joseph however many months before: the very decision to set forth on the journey had been a kind of death, involving the total abandonment of all previous life,

mothers and fathers and brothers and sisters who would never again be seen, all sentiment banished, the most elementary comforts necessarily relinquished." From *Where I Was From* by Joan Didion

Questions to consider:

1. What do you think of Joan Didion's idea that coming to California involves a kind of death and rebirth? What do the other stories in the anthology lead you to think about Didion's view? Do stories from your own family and community tend to support or contradict Didion's idea?

2. In stories like Khaled Hosseini's *The Kite Runner*, Brian Ascalon Roley's *American Son*, and Chitra Banerjee Divakaruni's "Mrs. Dutta Writes a Letter," newly arrived parents react to California quite differently than their children and grandchildren do. To what do you attribute these differences? How do these families deal with the differences? Has your family had similar experiences? How have you dealt with them?

3. Based on the selections in this anthology and your own experiences, who is coming to California and why? Who is staying in the state and why? How well—and how fully—do the stories in this anthology represent the range of immigrant experiences?

4. In "Where the Poppies Grow," Richard Rodriguez writes, "Without the cues of newcomers, I would not have noticed the austerity, the beauty of California." Do you agree with Rodriguez that newcomers give us new perspectives on our own lives and surroundings?

III: Encounters

"I have never resisted change, even when it has been called progress, and yet I felt resentment toward the strangers swamping what I thought of as my country with noise and clutter and the inevitable rings of junk. And of course these new people will resent the newer people. I remember how when I was a child we responded to the natural dislike of the stranger. We who were born here and our parents also felt a strange superiority over newcomers, barbarians, forestieri, and they, the foreigners, resented us and even made a rude poem about us." From *Travels with Charley* by John Steinbeck

Questions to consider:

1. John Steinbeck portrays a seemingly unbroken chain of resentment for successive waves of newcomers to California. Do you agree with his assessment? Why or why not? Is there any room in his description for accommodating newcomers? How do other selections in the anthology support your views?

2. In Dana Johnson's shrewdly comic story "Melvin in the Sixth Grade," Avery, a city girl new to a suburban school, forms an alliance with Melvin, another recent arrival and outsider. Why does Avery eventually betray Melvin and how does she feel about her actions? How might what Avery learns—or fails to learn—be applied to the circumstances of other characters in the anthology or to current newcomers to California?

3. Central to the selection from Dao Strom's *Grass Roof, Tin Roof* is the confrontation between Hus Madsen and William Bentley over the death of Bentley's dog. What other tensions

feed this confrontation? What is the impact of this confrontation on those around it? Who, if anyone, do you think is right?

4. What other kinds of encounters do you find in these selections? Which ones disturbed you? Which encouraged you?

5. What memorable encounters have you had, either as a native Californian or as an immigrant? What did you learn from these experiences and how have they shaped your life in the state?

IV: Becoming Californian?

"The family called him Fleaman. They did not understand his accomplishments as an American ancestor, a holding, homing ancestor of this place. He'd gotten the legal or illegal papers burned in the San Francisco Earthquake and Fire; he appeared in America in time to be a citizen and to father citizens. He had also been seen carrying a child out of the fire, a child of his own in spite of the laws against marrying. He had built a railroad out of sweat, why not have an American child out of longing?" From China Men by Maxine Hong Kingston

Questions to consider:
1. In his essay "Where the Poppies Grow," Richard Rodriguez writes that California has served as "America's America." What does he mean by that? Do you agree with him?

2. Both David Mas Masamoto and D. J. Waldie locate themselves as Californians in very particular places. How important is a sense of place to the stories in this anthology? How important is place in your own idea of California?

3. What do you think of the life and exploits of Ah Goong, the hero of Maxine Hong Kingston's story? What are "his accomplishments as an American ancestor"? How do you feel about his family's inability to understand those accomplishments?

4. In Chitra Banerjee Divakaruni's story "Mrs. Dutta Writes a Letter," Mrs. Dutta decides in the end to return to her home in India. To do that she must free herself from her own culture's expectation that a widow is the responsibility of a son. What, if anything, does Mrs. Dutta's newfound independence have to do with California?

5. During his interviews with a diverse set of Californians, James Quay reports that hope was a common characteristic associated with California. Do you associate hope with California? Do you see it in the stories collected here?

6. Taken as a whole, what does this collection say to you about California and being or becoming a Californian?

7. Has reading this book caused you to think differently about yourself, you family, your community, the state of California? If so, in what ways?

Alternate Table of Contents

This alternate table of contents is intended to aid readers who would like to experience these stories in a more thematic way, paying special attention to how specific issues and ideas are experienced by people from different backgrounds and in different contexts.

Becoming Californian

Permissions

Paul Beatty. "Chapter Two" from *The White Boy Shuffle* by Paul Beatty. Copyright © 1996 by Paul Beatty. Reprinted by permission of Houghton Mifflin Company. All rights reserved.

Joan Didion. From *Where I Was From* by Joan Didion. Copyright © 2003 by Joan Didion. Used by permission of Alfred A. Knopf, a division of Random House, Inc.

Chitra Banerjee Divakaruni. "Mrs. Dutta Writes a Letter" from *The Unknown Errors of Our Lives*. Copyright © 2002 by Chitra Banerjee Divakaruni. Reprinted by permission of the author.

Laila Halaby. "The American Dream" from *West of the Jordan*. Copyright © 2003 by Laila Halaby. Used by permission of Beacon Press.

Robert Hass. "Palo Alto: The Marshes" from *Field Guide*. Copyright © 1973 by Robert Hass. Used by permission of Yale University Press.

Khaled Hosseini. From *The Kite Runner* by Khaled Hosseini. Copyright © 2003 by Khaled Hosseini. Used by permission of Riverhead, a division of Penguin Group USA, Inc.

James D. Houston. "The Light Takes Its Color from the Sea" from *One Can Think About Life After the Fish Is in the Canoe*. Copyright © 1985 by James D. Houston. Reprinted by permission of the author.

Robinson Jeffers. "Hands" by Robinson Jeffers from *The Collected Poetry of Robinson Jeffers, Volume 2: 1928–1938*, edited by Tim Hunt. Copyright © 1938 and renewed 1966 by Donnan Jeffers and Garth Jeffers; editorial matter © 1989 by the Board of Trustees of Leland Stanford Jr. University. Reprinted by permission of Stanford University Press.

Photo Credits

Joan Didion photo © Christopher Felver/CORBIS.

Chitra Banerjee Divakaruni photo courtesy of the author.

Laila Halaby photo courtesy of Lance Fairchild Photography.

Robert Hass photo © Rachel C. Zucker. Courtesy of the author.

Khaled Hosseini photo courtesy of the author.

James D. Houston photo by Greg Pio. Courtesy of the author.

Robinson Jeffers photo courtesy of the Bancroft Library, University of California, Berkeley.

Francisco Jiménez photo courtesy of the University of New Mexico Press.

Dana Johnson photo courtesy of the author.

Maxine Hong Kingston photo by Gail K. Evenari. Courtesy of Vintage/Anchor Publicity.

Shirley Geok-Lin Lim photo © Shirley Geok-Lin Lim.

Rubén Martínez photo courtesy of the author.

David Mas Masumoto photo courtesy of the author.

James Quay photo courtesy of the California Council for the Humanities.

Luis J. Rodriguez photo © Donna DeCesare, 1997. Courtesy of the author.

Richard Rodriguez photo by Christine Alicino. Courtesy of the photographer.

Brian Ascalon Roley photo by Carla Roley. Courtesy of the author.

Greg Sarris photo by Jerry Bauer. Courtesy of the author.

Gary Soto photo courtesy of the author.

John Steinbeck photo © Bettmann/CORBIS.

lê thi diem thúy photo courtesy of Vintage/Anchor Books.

D. J. Waldie photo courtesy of the author.

Index

About the Editors

Chitra Banerjee Divakaruni is the award-winning author of *The Mistress of Spices, Sister of My Heart, Queen of Dreams,* and many other books.

William E. Justice studied Russian literature at the University of Kansas and is currently special projects manager at Heyday Books.

James Quay has served as the executive director of the California Council for the Humanities since 1983.